THE ROAD TO ELSEWHERE

Jim McJunkin

Published by:
2nd Tier Publishing
13501 Ranch Road 12, Ste 103
Wimberley, TX 78676

ISBN 978-0-9862290-6-0

Edited by Nancy Scalise
Cover design by Shiila Safer
Book design by Dan Gauthier

Thanks to Beth McJunkin, Pat and June Macarelli, David and Phyllis Snell, Dick and Pam, Jim and Nancy Scalise, Jason and Justin. To Dan Gauthier and Shiila Safer, David Delph, Sami, Becca, and Karen. To Rick Klugman, Charley, Rick Nelson, Miles and the East Ethiopia Hunting Club guys. To Igor Mitoraj, Allen and Patty, Mike, Randy, Rusty, and Lil Darlin, Suzanne, Lindsay, and Peter. To Greg, Gregorio of La Vista, and Roy Flukinger, Bill Witliff, and Troy Penney. To Max Crace for encouraging me to go digital, and Holland Photo for putting up with me after I did. To John and Marjory for their Canadian hospitality. To Tabu, Chula, Marley and Maddie Mc, and to all the artists from Frederic Remington to the graffiti taggers whose creations I have pilfered.

Although some names have been altered or omitted, and conversations have been fabricated, most of this story is true. It begins almost fifty years before the publication date, so some of the facts could be incorrect. For those reasons it is a work of fiction.

On Memorial Day 2015, the Blanco River rose out of its banks and washed people, houses, possessions and five-hundred-year-old cypress trees downstream. Everything in 2nd Tier Publishing went underwater, including almost all of Dan Gauthier and Shiila Safer's possessions. The template for *THE ROAD TO ELSEWHERE* resurfaced and dried out, as did many artifacts along the Blanco River. This book is dedicated to the lives lost, and the lives that will never be the same because of that flood.

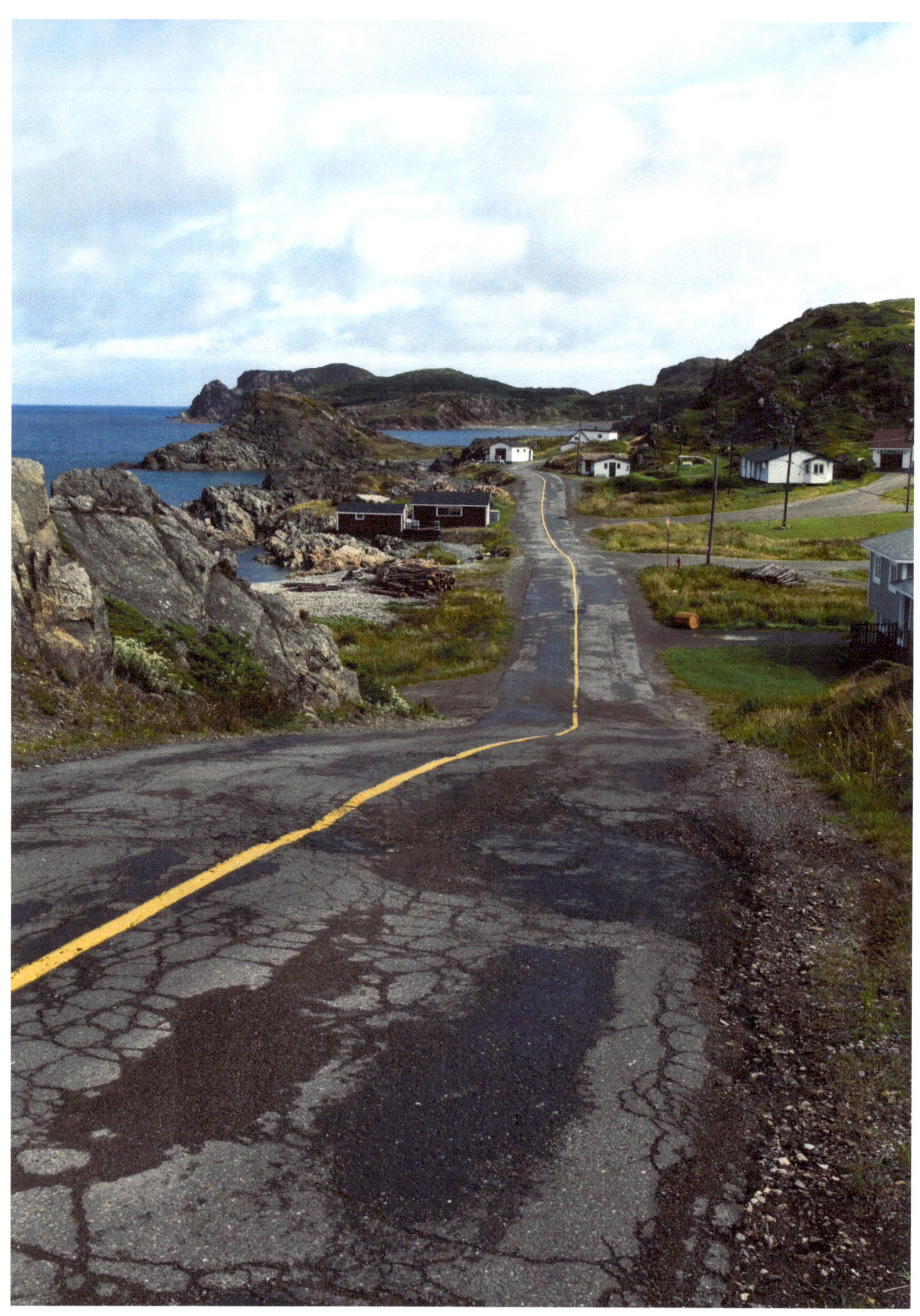

Table of Contents

People travel to faraway places to watch, in fascination,
the kind of people they ignore at home.

—Dagobert D. Runes

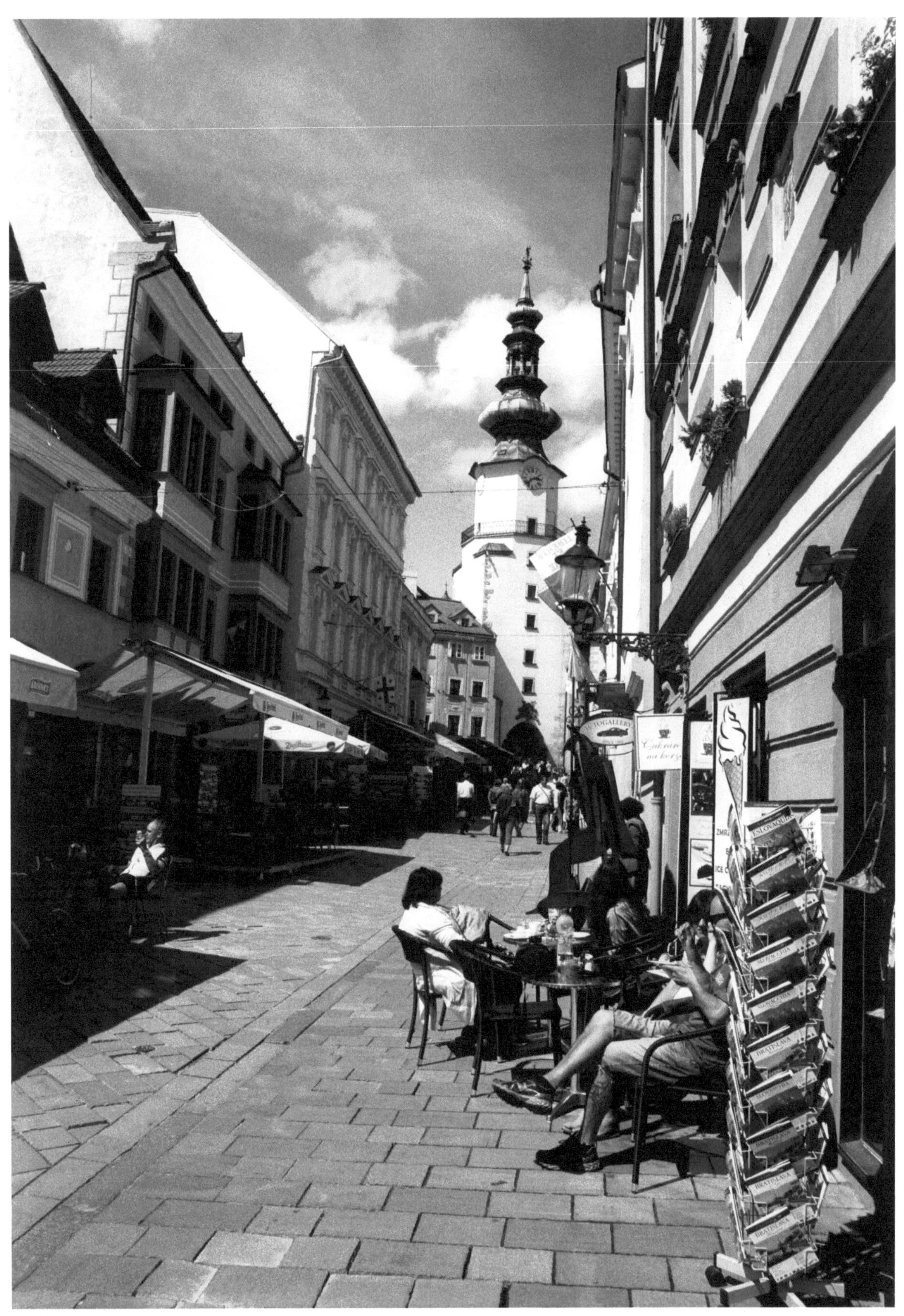
ESLOVAQUIA
BRATISLAVA
BRATISLAVA
BRATISLAVA

THE ITCH

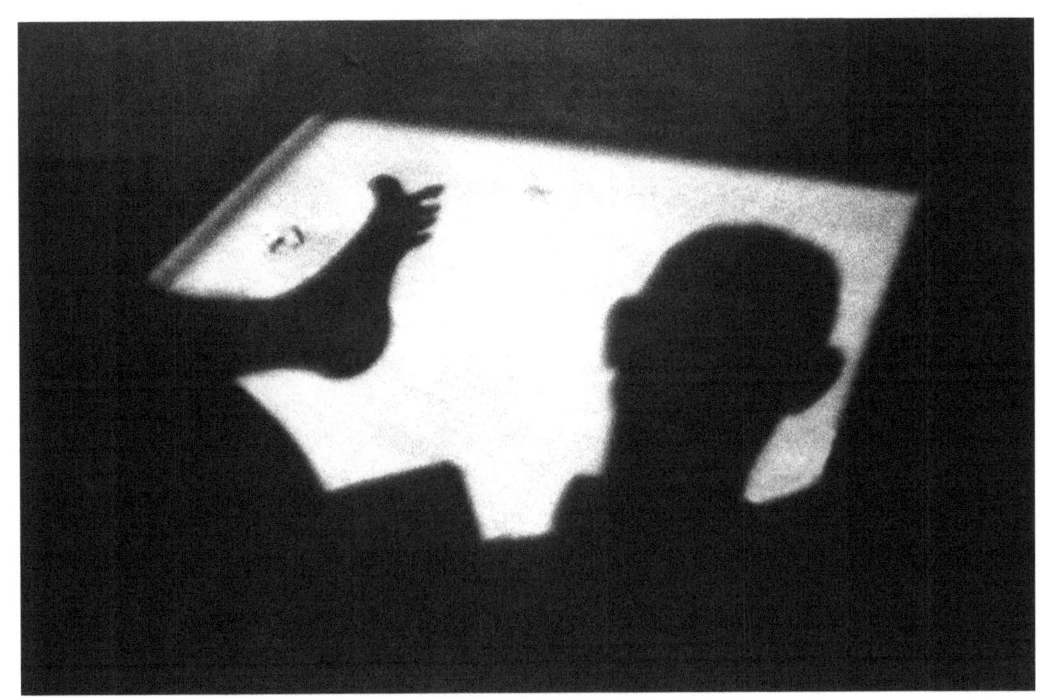

Wanderlust is a term that describes an impulse to travel. I used to think of it as the precursor of some great adventure, but now I can see it as the illness that it is. It is a “home” disease, whose symptoms emerge as an antidote to contentment. Those feelings of discontent usually hit hardest when life is at its easiest.

That is what happened several years ago after my wife and I retired, and moved to the country. I wanted to visit the rest of the world. Beth wanted to kick back and relax.

“We aren’t getting any younger”, I said. “We should travel while we can.”

“We just moved into our dream home. Let’s enjoy it.”

“This is our big chance to see the world. It’s what we worked for all those years.”

“I thought we were working for comfort and security.”

I have had that same argument all by myself, although my temperamental position changes according to location. When at home, I want to travel. When traveling, I can not stop reminding myself how good life is at home, where I speak the language, and know the territory, and get to sleep in my own bed at night. In both cases those thoughts only occur when the action ebbs, and there is nothing physical or visual to occupy my mind. Aside from the occasional mishap, situational discontent happens during the course of reflection.

There is nothing wrong with sitting on the back porch and staring into space while thinking about how you would like to visit a part of the world you have never seen. Trying to decipher the transportation schedule in the train station of some foreign country does have a down side, but for some reason the negative aspects of travel are absent during the planning stage. Sometimes you just have to take the bad with the good. The only real cure for wanderlust is the anxiety of travel.

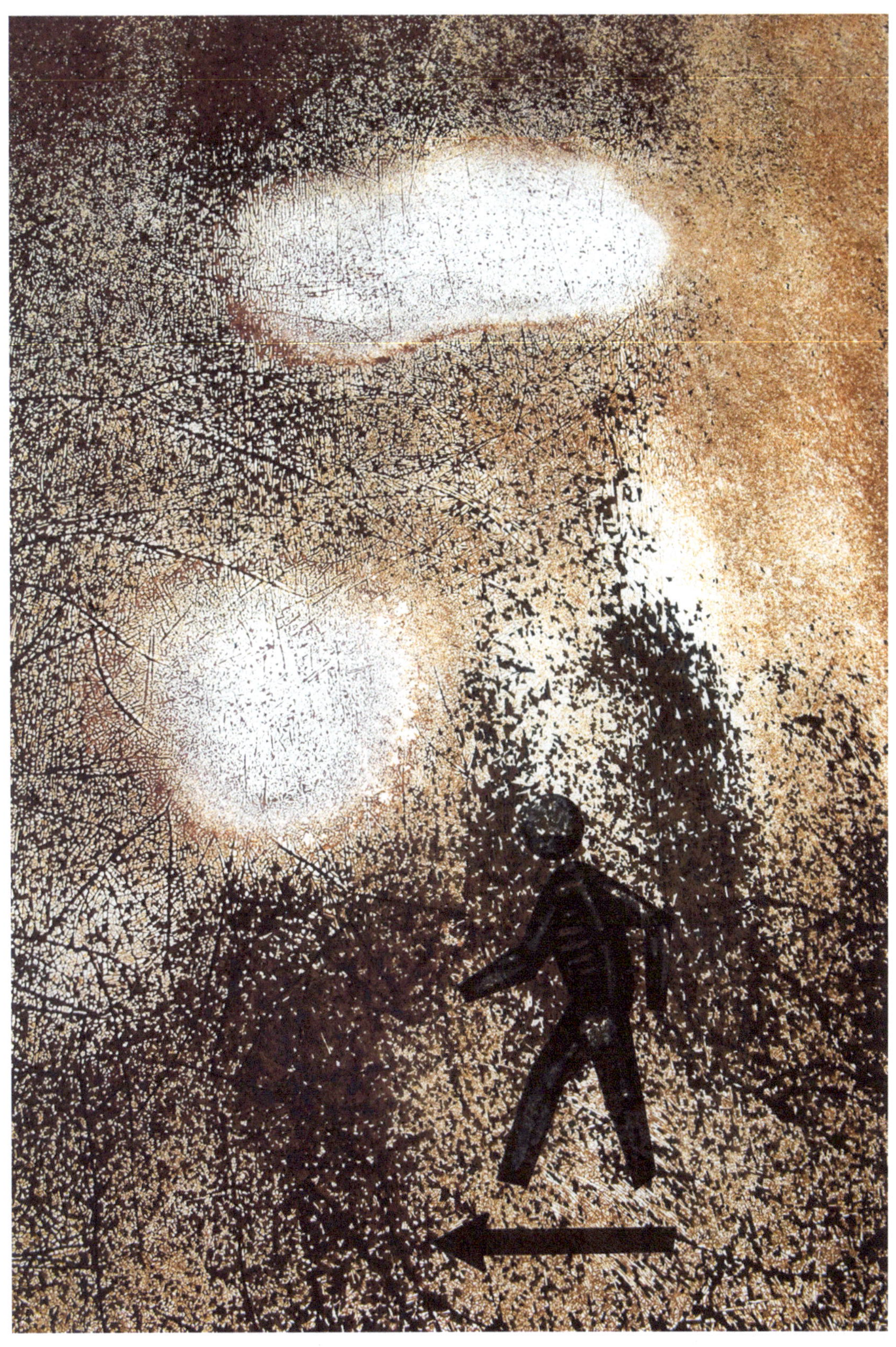

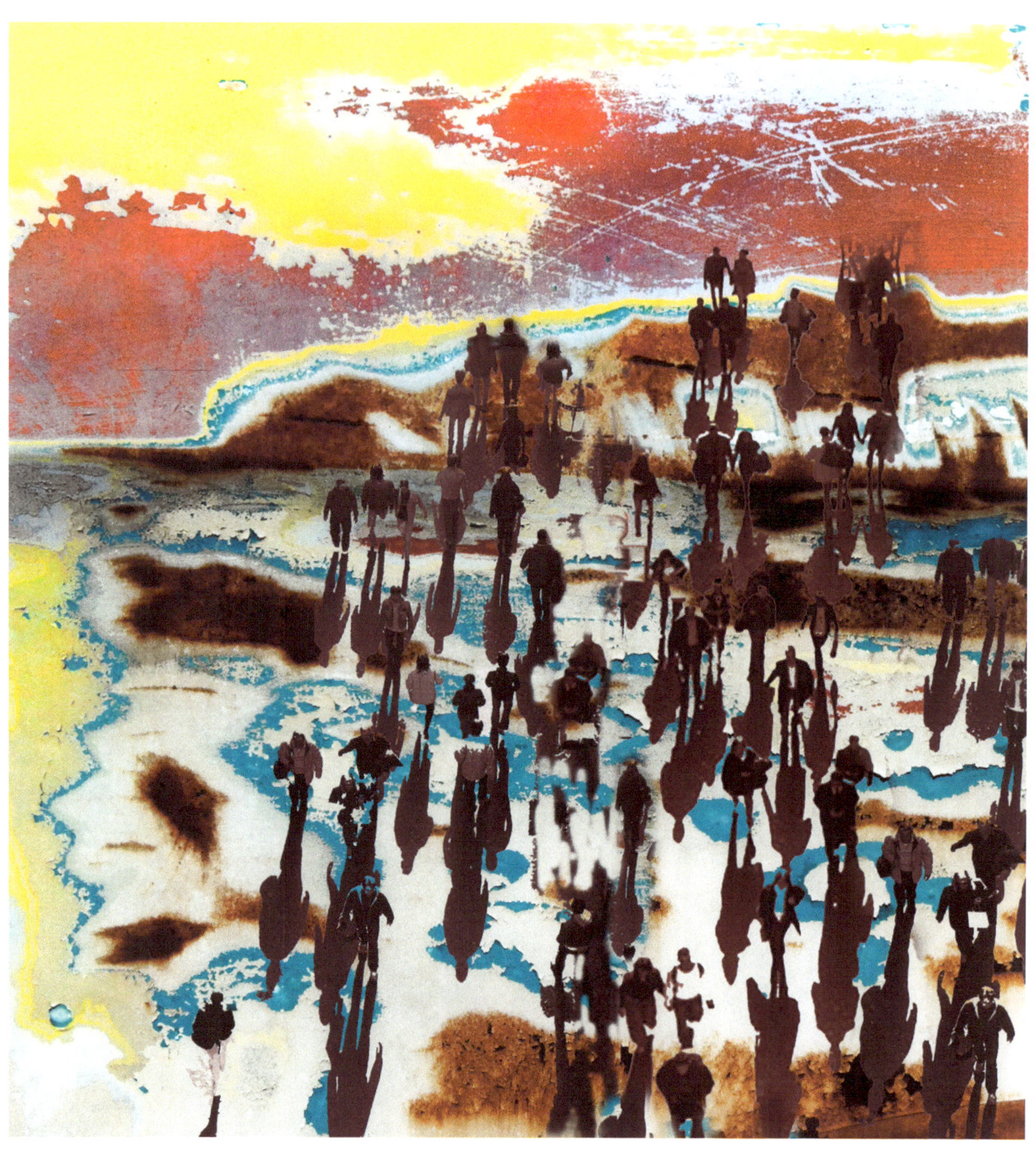

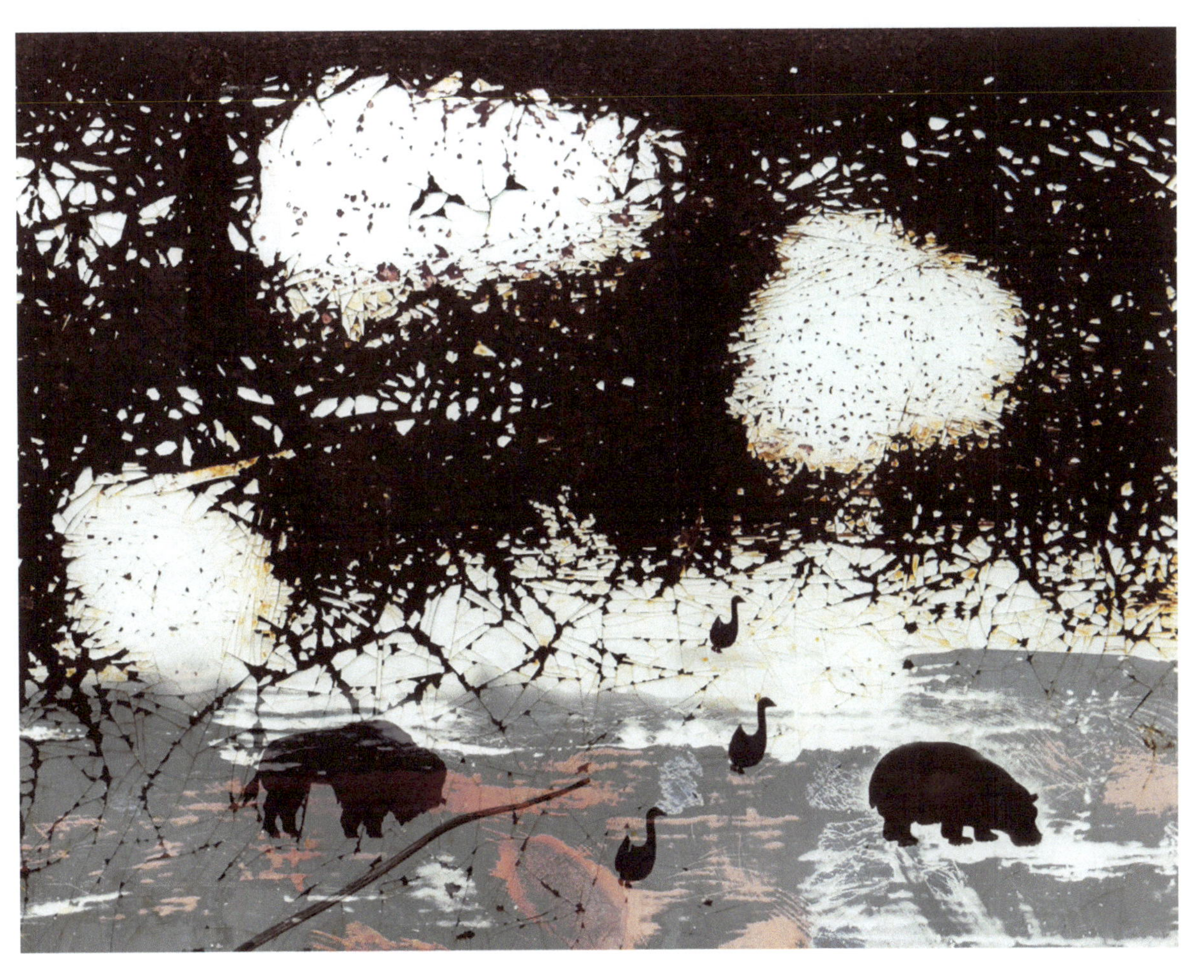

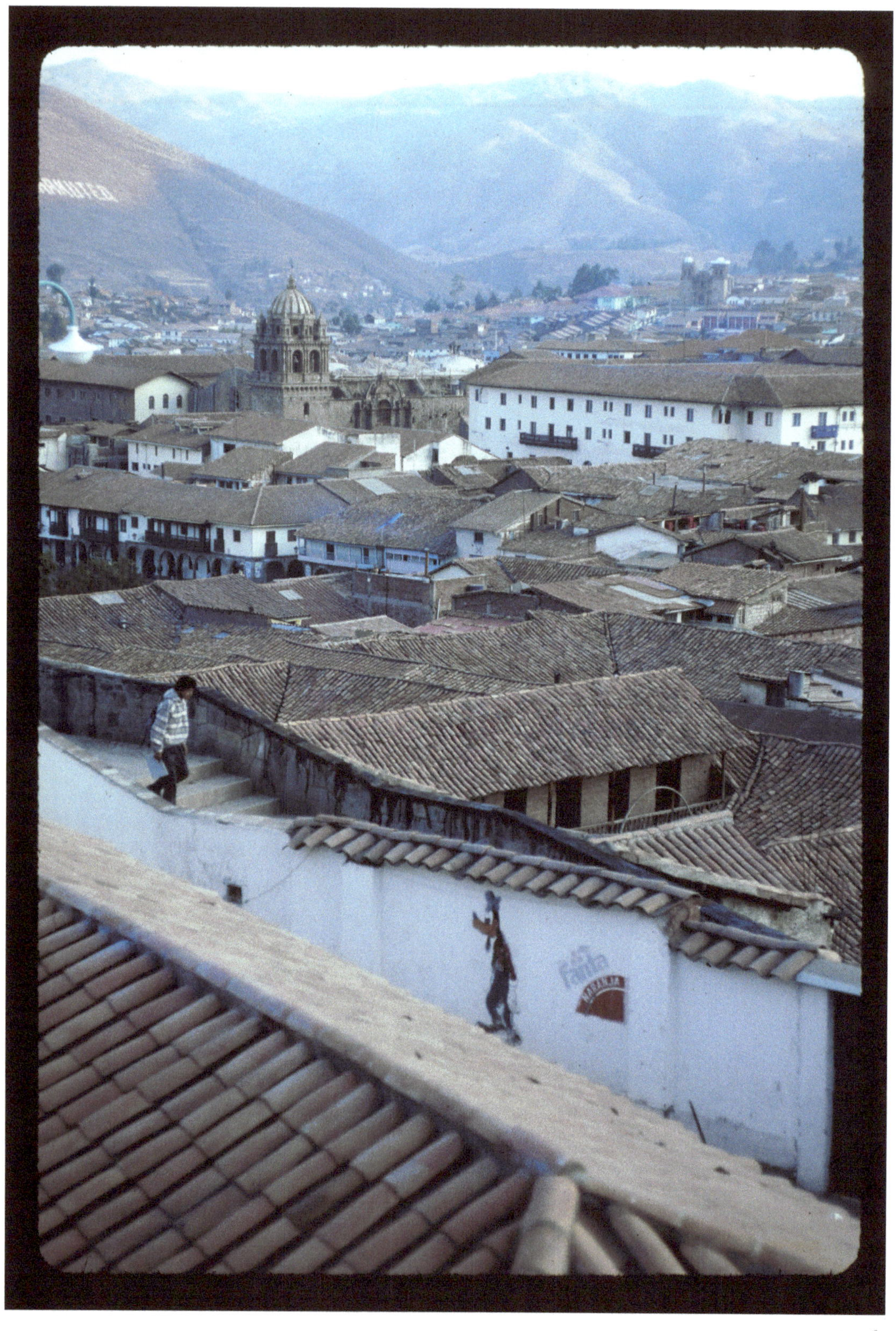

Fanta

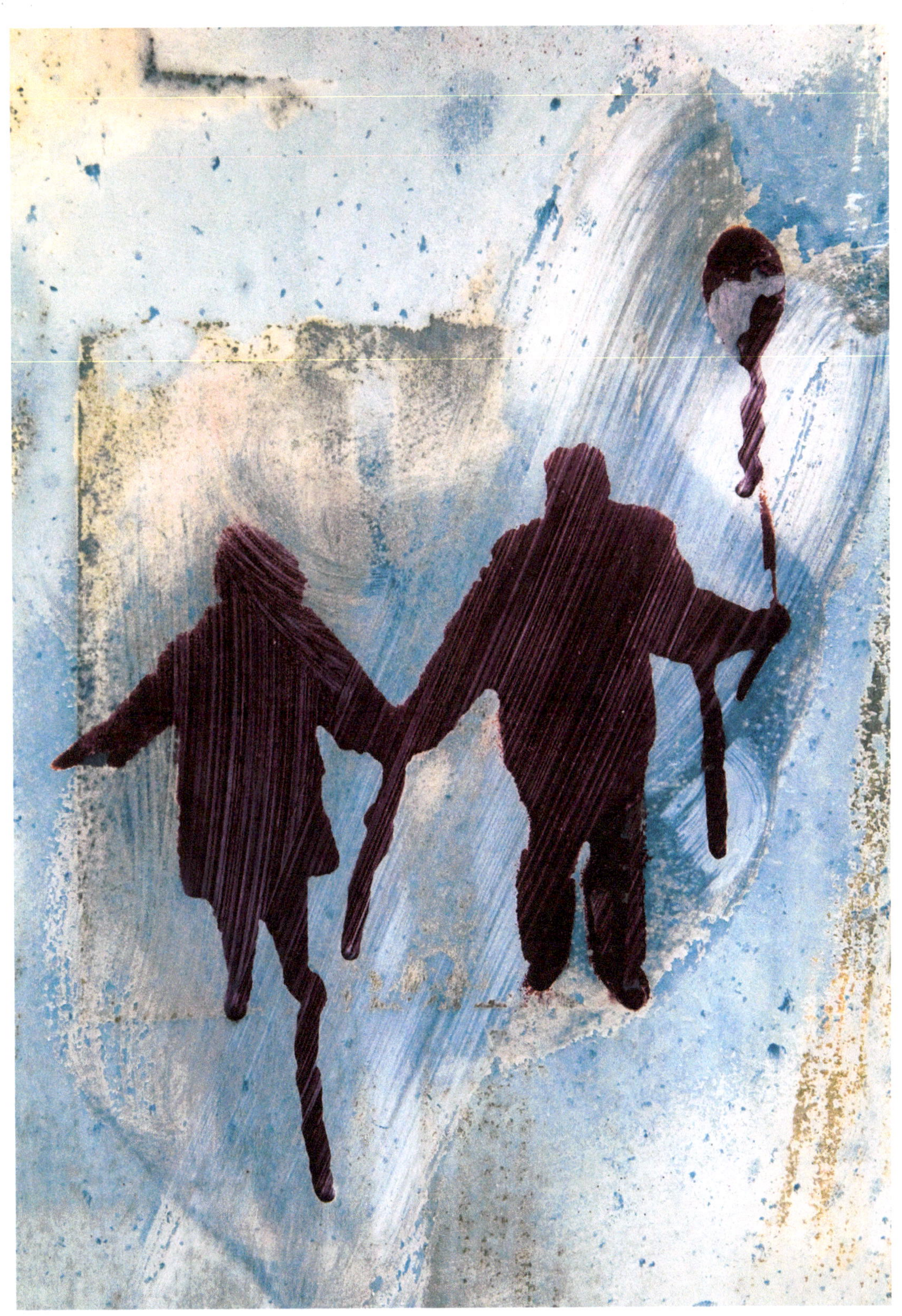

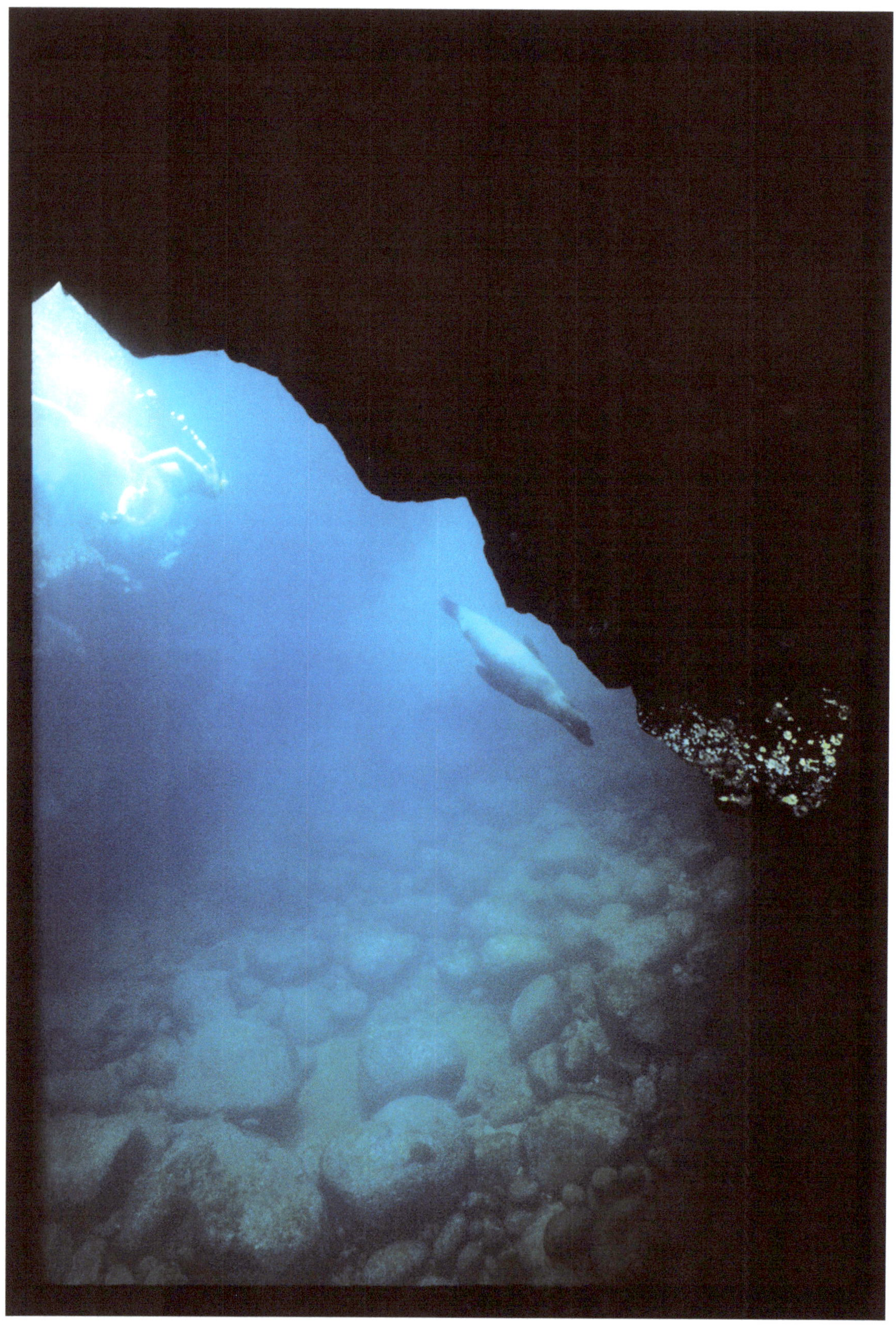

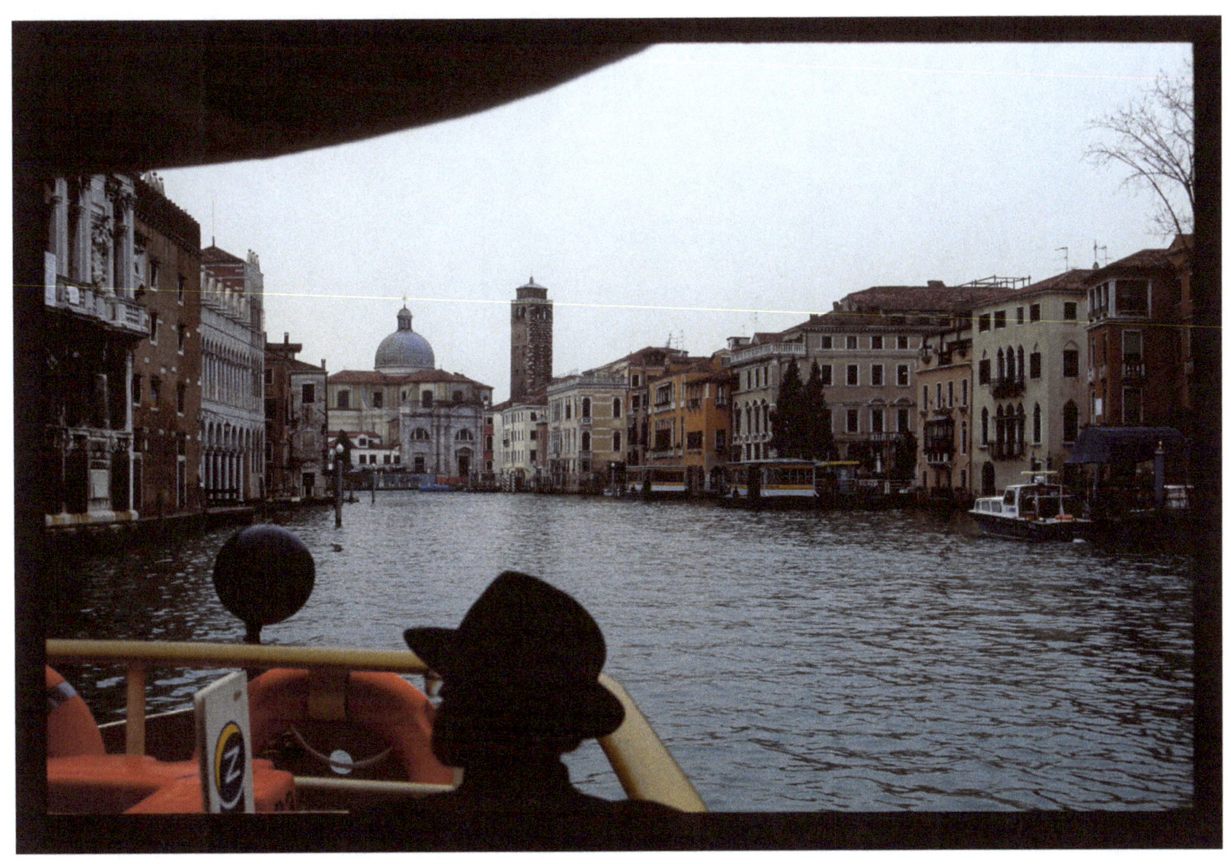

Tourists don't know where they've been. Travelers don't know where they're going.

—Paul Theroux

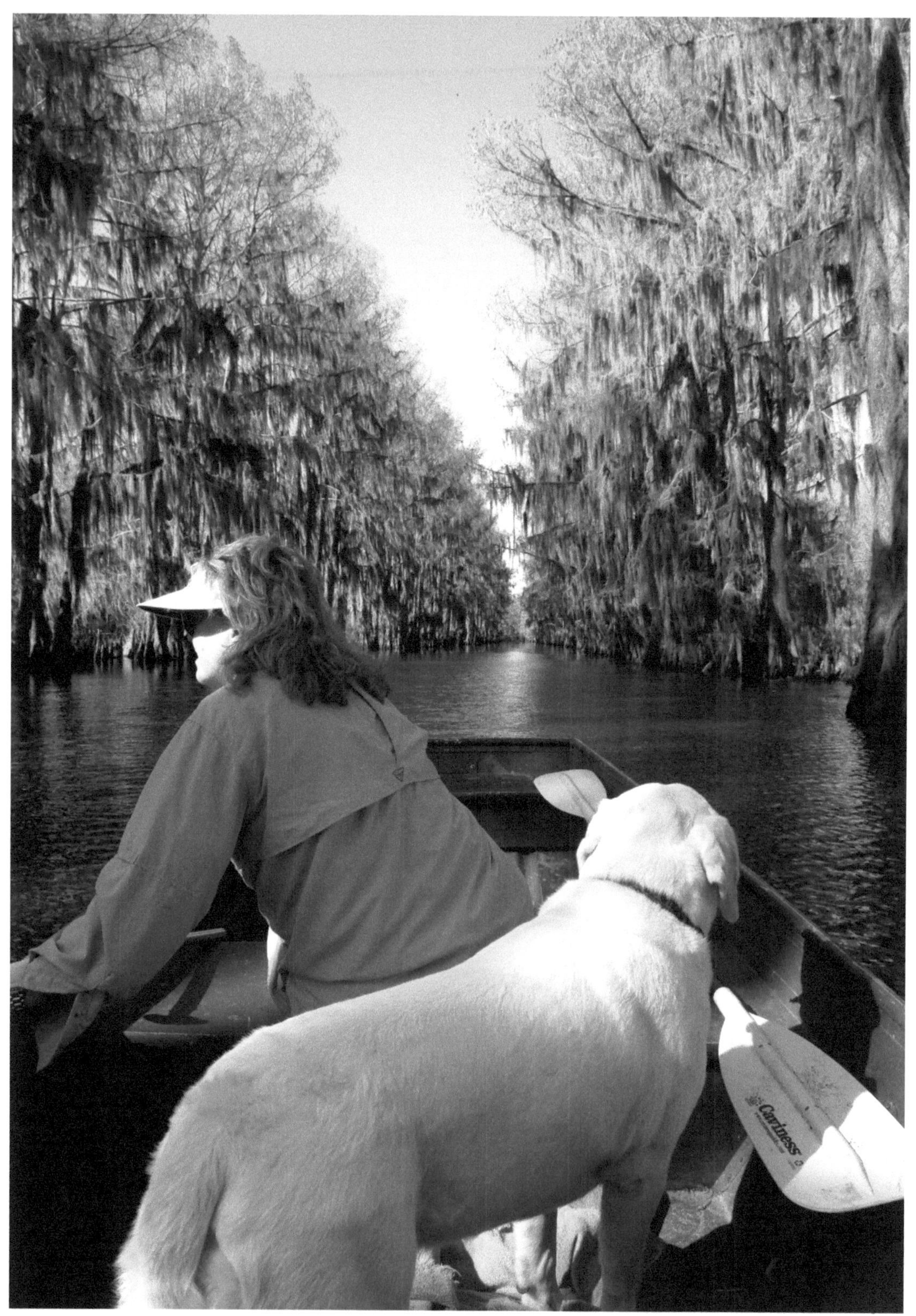

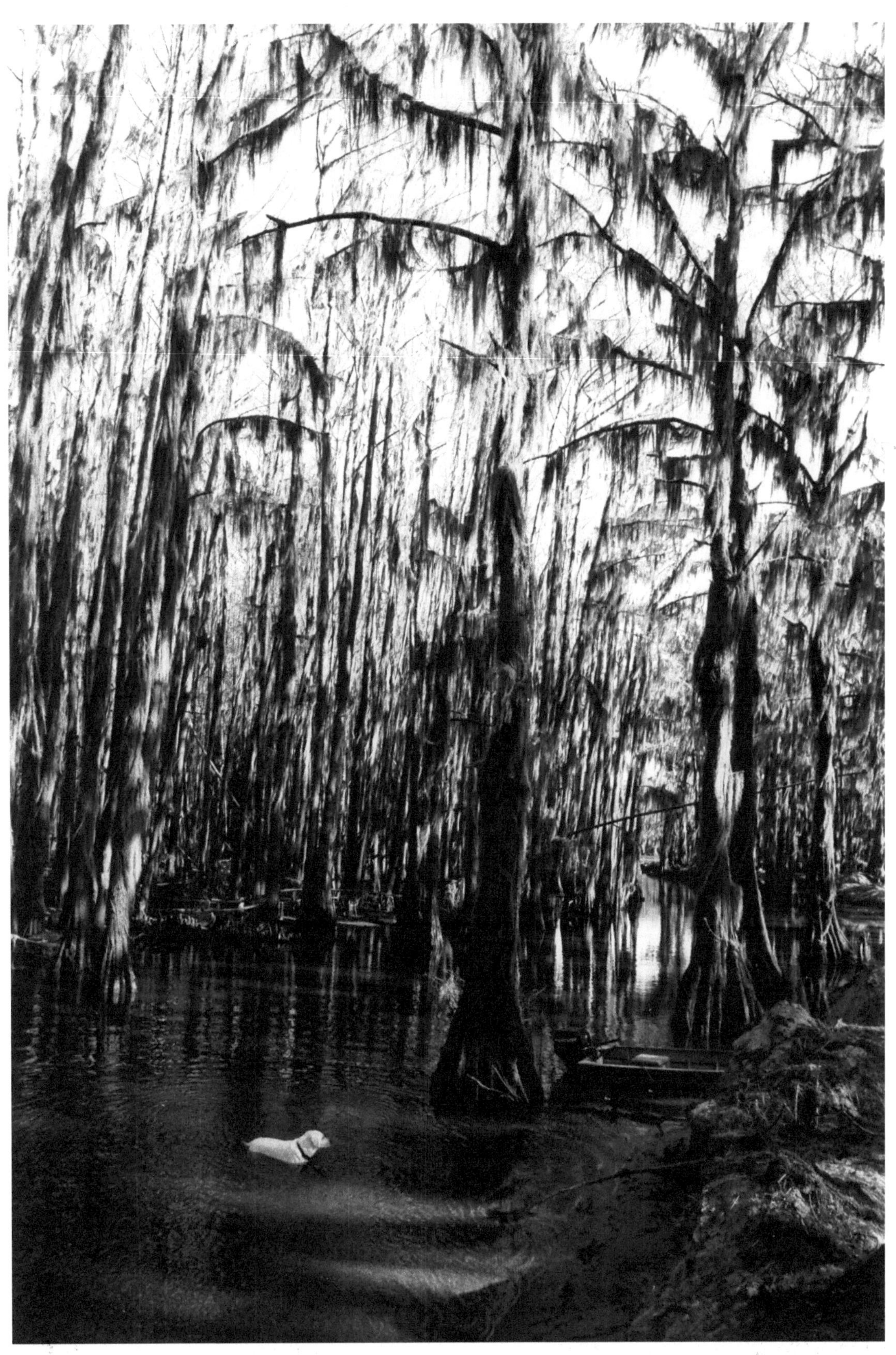

THE SCRATCH

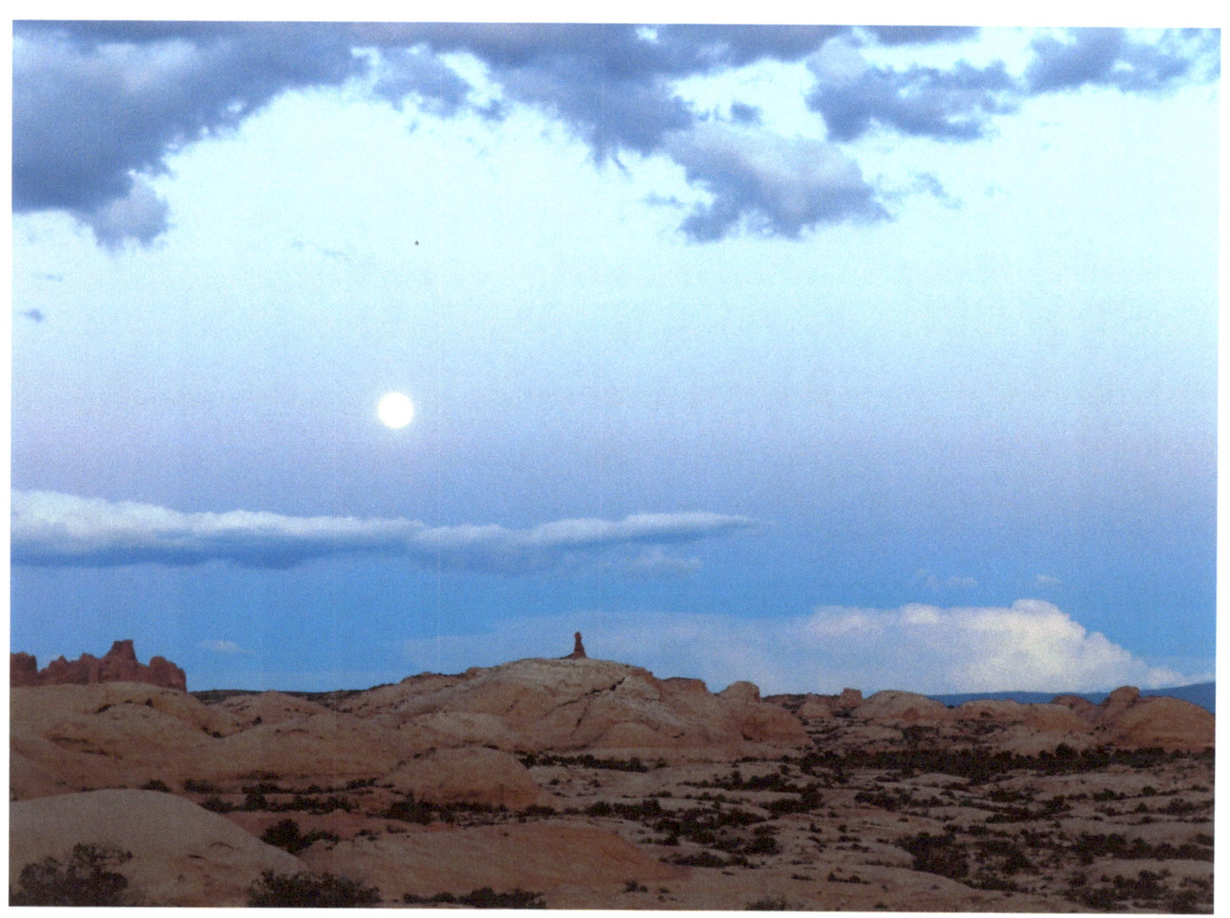

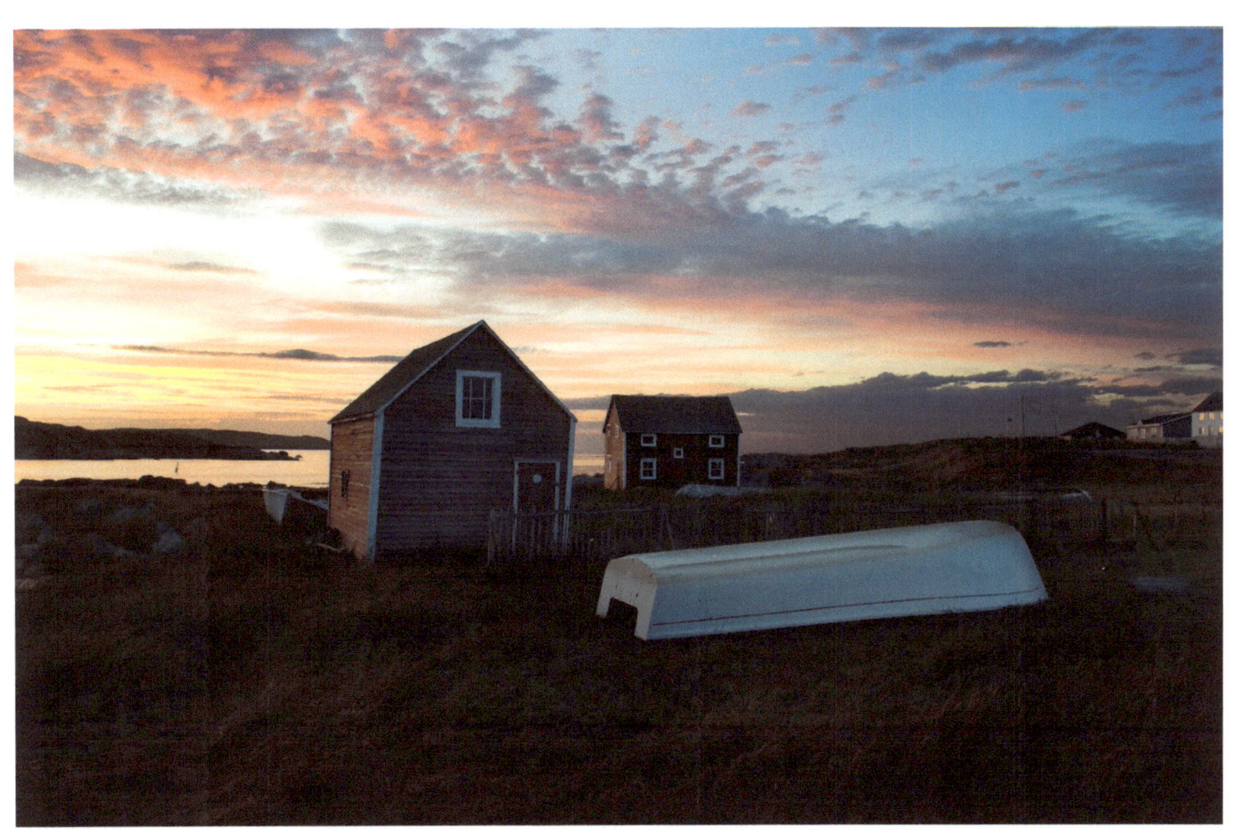

March, 1971

Discharge from US Army, (early out). Must finish at least one semester at Metropolitan University, Denver, Colorado to complete military obligation.

July, 1971

Obligation complete. Left Denver with a couple of buddies, (Pat and Rick). Original intention—Zigzag towards Florida in my 1961 Volkswagen bug. Camp out, stay with friends and family along the way. Second half of the plan—sell the car in Florida, and fly to Puerto Rico where we will become beach bums, or fishermen.

Stopped in Austin, Texas for a few days to visit my parents, who had moved while I was in the Army. We all agreed Austin was a cool place, but did not fit our travel plans. Moved on to New Orleans, and spent a few days with my sister.

August, 1971

There was bickering along the way. By the time we arrived in Florida, it had escalated into a series of hurt feelings, and one full-blown argument. Rick decided he was on the wrong coast, so we dropped him off at Miami International Airport where he flew to California.

My other partner was Pat Macarelli. More to say about him later. Pat had such a sunburn that he decided not to become a beach bum. We scrapped our plans for Puerto Rico, and headed up the east coast in search of cloudy weather.

August, 1971 – Charleston, South Carolina

Spent the night in a Salvation Army Shelter. We checked in and picked a couple of cots out of maybe two dozen beds that filled the room. Not much other furniture in that area, but there was a smaller room with magazines, and checkerboards. Also, a dining area. We had planned to go out for a few beers before retiring for the night, but that turned out to be against the rules. Once in, you are in for the day, or you are out for the night. Played a game of checkers, and went to bed early.

That night I caught somebody trying to crawl under my cot, where I had stashed my clothes. Chased him away, loud enough to let everybody else in the room know there was a thief among us. He came back a couple of hours later, yelled at him again. Slept fitfully with my small bundle of belongings under the sheet with me.

August, or September, 1971 – Virginia

Pat became ill, so we checked into the Billy Bud Motel. Pat wants the curtains drawn, so he can sleep. Too dark and depressing for me. Went for a hike on the Appalachian Trail and did not return until the next morning. Pat looked about half dead, so I rushed him to an infirmary where he was diagnosed with hepatitis. Drove Pat to an airport, and put him on a flight back to Denver, where his parents checked him into a hospital.

September, 1971

Took the long way back to Denver, and much of that part of the trip is a blur. We had left with a half-ounce of hashish, courtesy of Pat and Rick, since I provided the car. Still a sizable chunk left. Must diminish the evidence. One day I ate nothing but hash, just to see what would happen. No nutritional value. Got stoned and hungry.

September, 1971 – North or South Dakota

Pulled off the highway, and parked on a dirt road. Hopped a fence, and set up my mosquito net. Laid my sleeping bag out, and fell asleep. Awakened by muffled snuffling. Opened my eyes, to the realization that I was surrounded by cows. Sat up, and caused a small stampede, but when I lay back down, I could hear them moving in again. That happened several times, until I fell back asleep. Don't remember if they were still there when the sun came up, but I do remember thinking I would probably move to Texas.

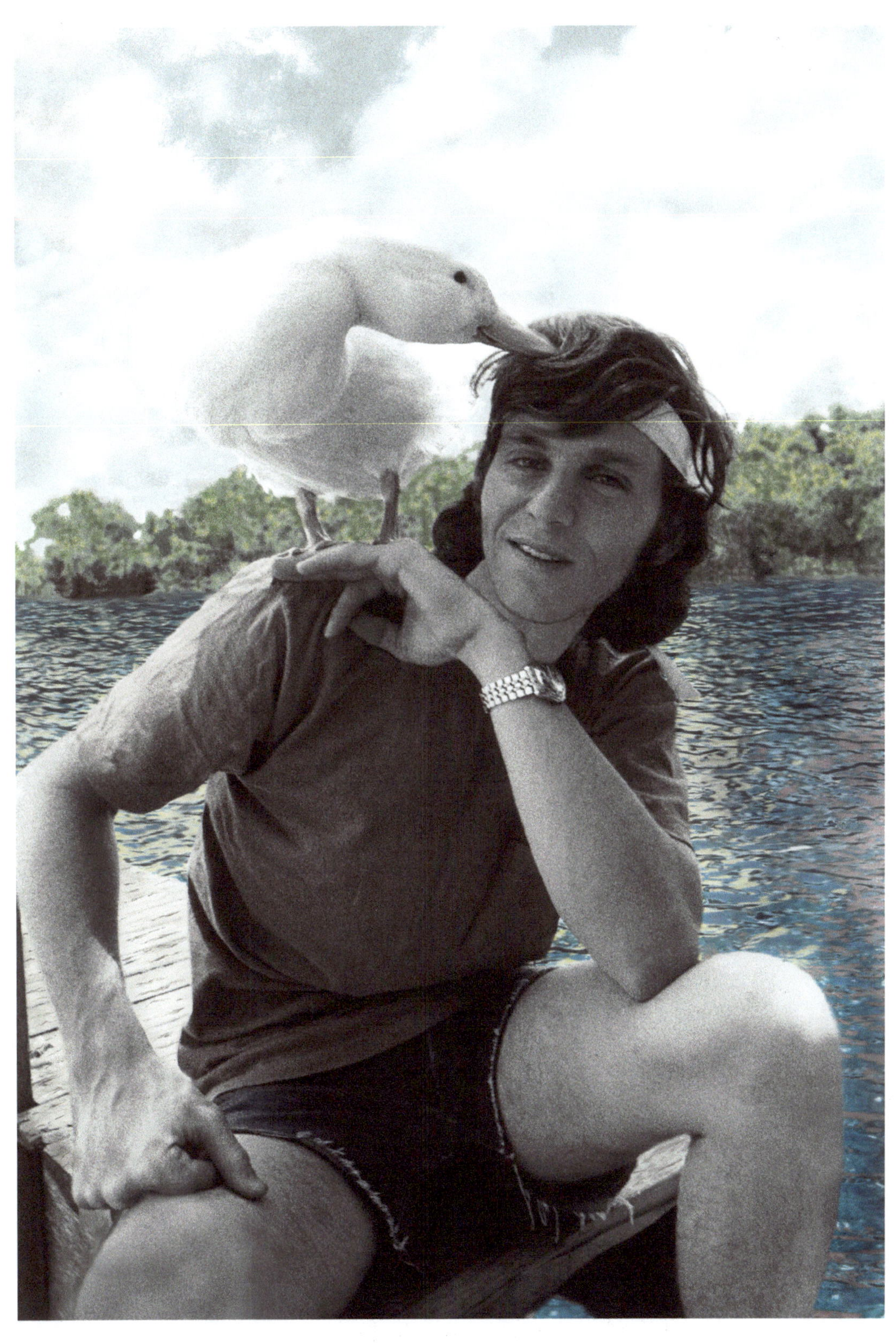

ONWARD: THRU THE FOG!

—Oat Willie

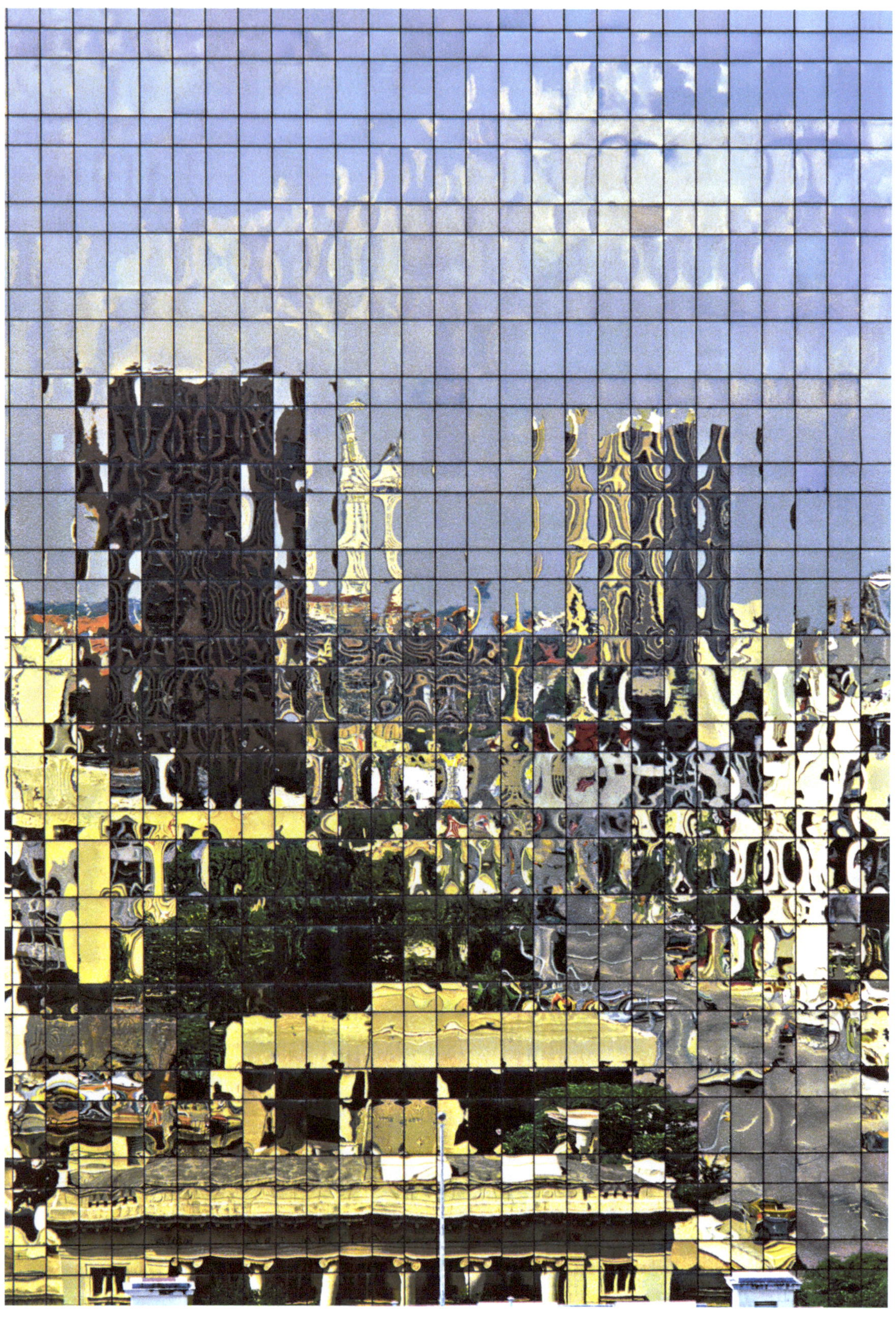

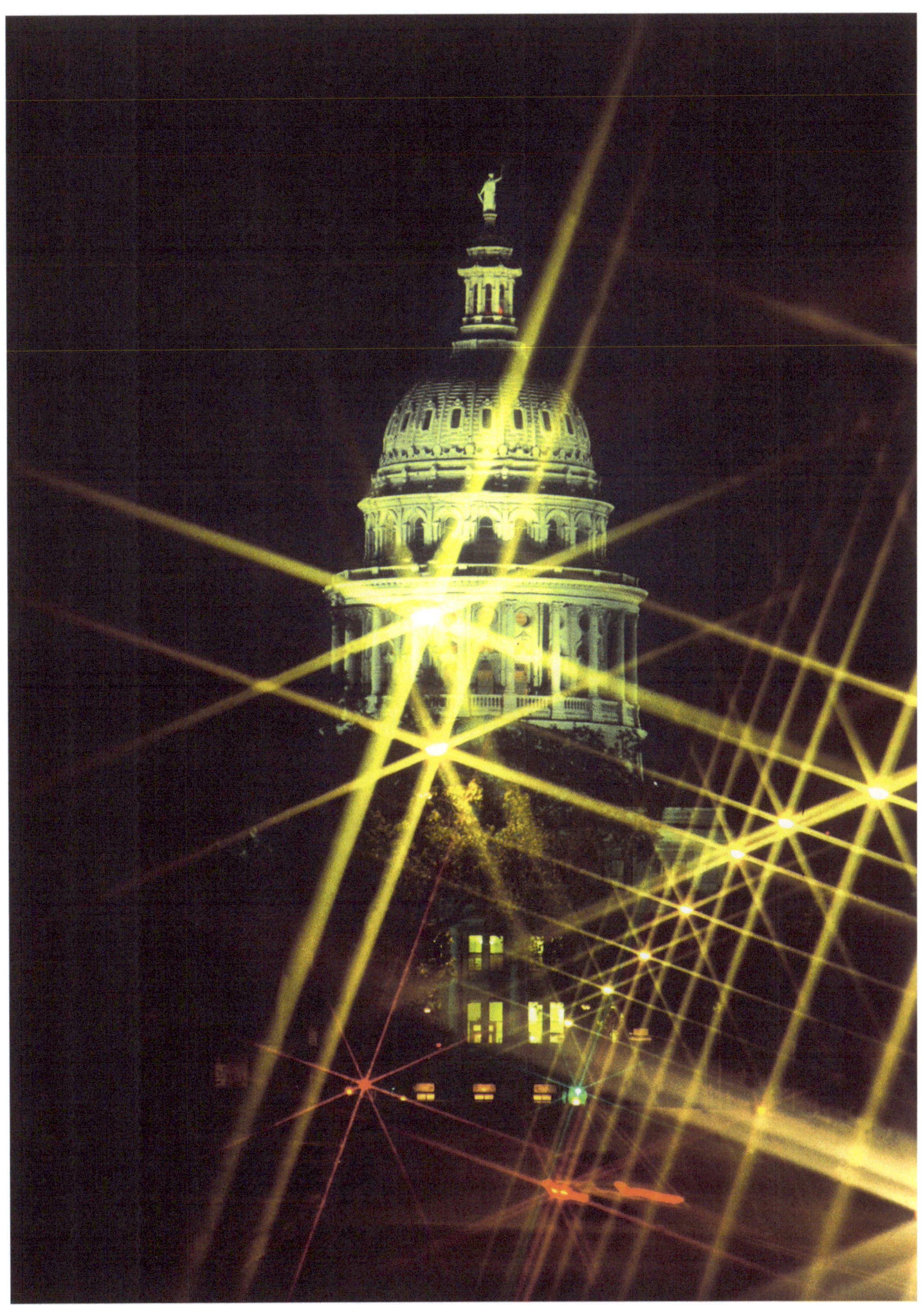

Austin, Texas, in the early 1970s had everything someone without much ambition could want. It was slacker's paradise, a community looking for something to celebrate. Eyore had his first real birthday party in that era, and so did Willie Nelsons annual event, in the form of the Hill on the Moon Concert. The Armadillo World Headquarters was the nucleus that a galaxy of clubs, bars, and happenings orbited at night. Barton Springs, Hippie Hollow, and an ocean of other swimming holes were places to laze away the day. An occasional construction job provided enough to scrape by.

Then I met Beth and life got even better. She enjoyed all the things I did, if not quite to the same excess. Best of all, she enjoyed travel.

Some changes are so subtle that they creep into daily life. Those alterations of thought and personal routine can become entrenched before any form of realization occurs. That is not what happened to me. I saw it coming.

Beth and I rented a place where other people were not allowed to crash for extended periods. We began accumulating items that had nothing to do with a record collection; chairs, a washing machine, frequent work routines. Every item we collected for the house was another tether to a distinct location. Every nick knack in the curio cabinet made it more difficult to leave, to travel the world, and live somewhere else until it came time to leave again. Without much discussion, she altered my ambitions, and we began to grow roots.

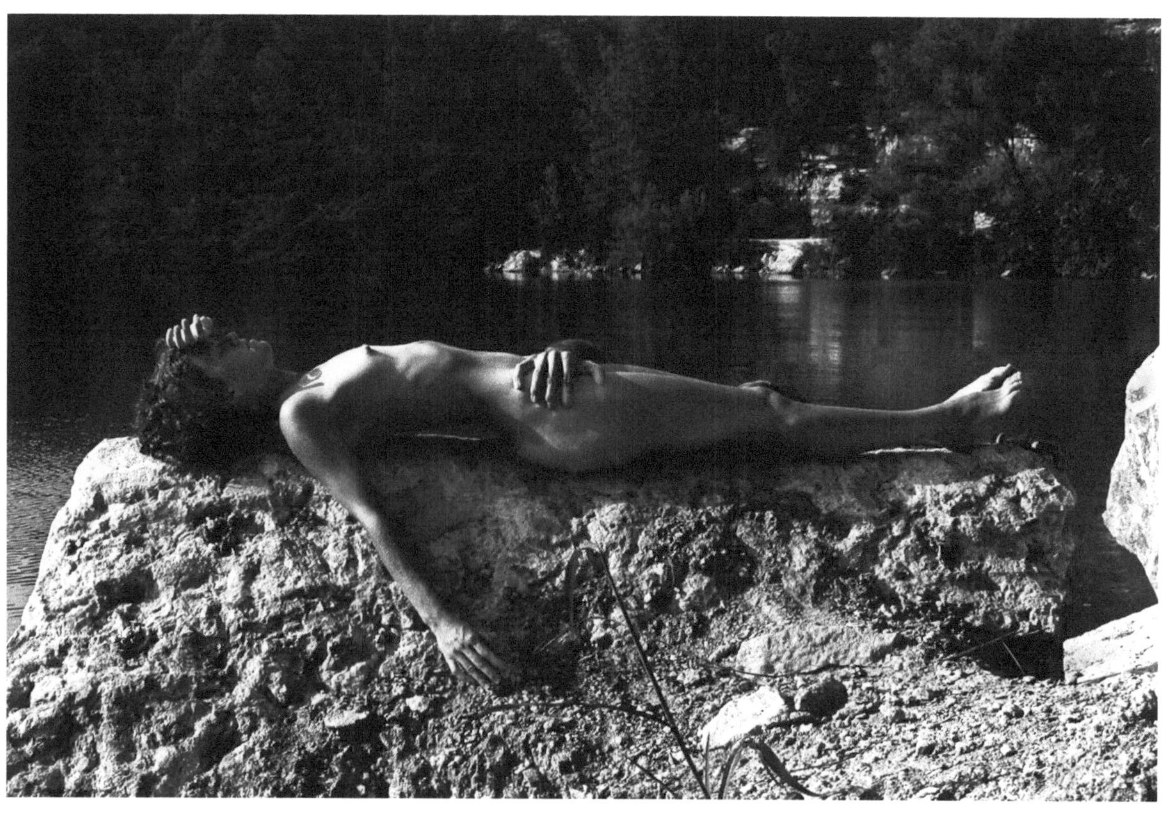

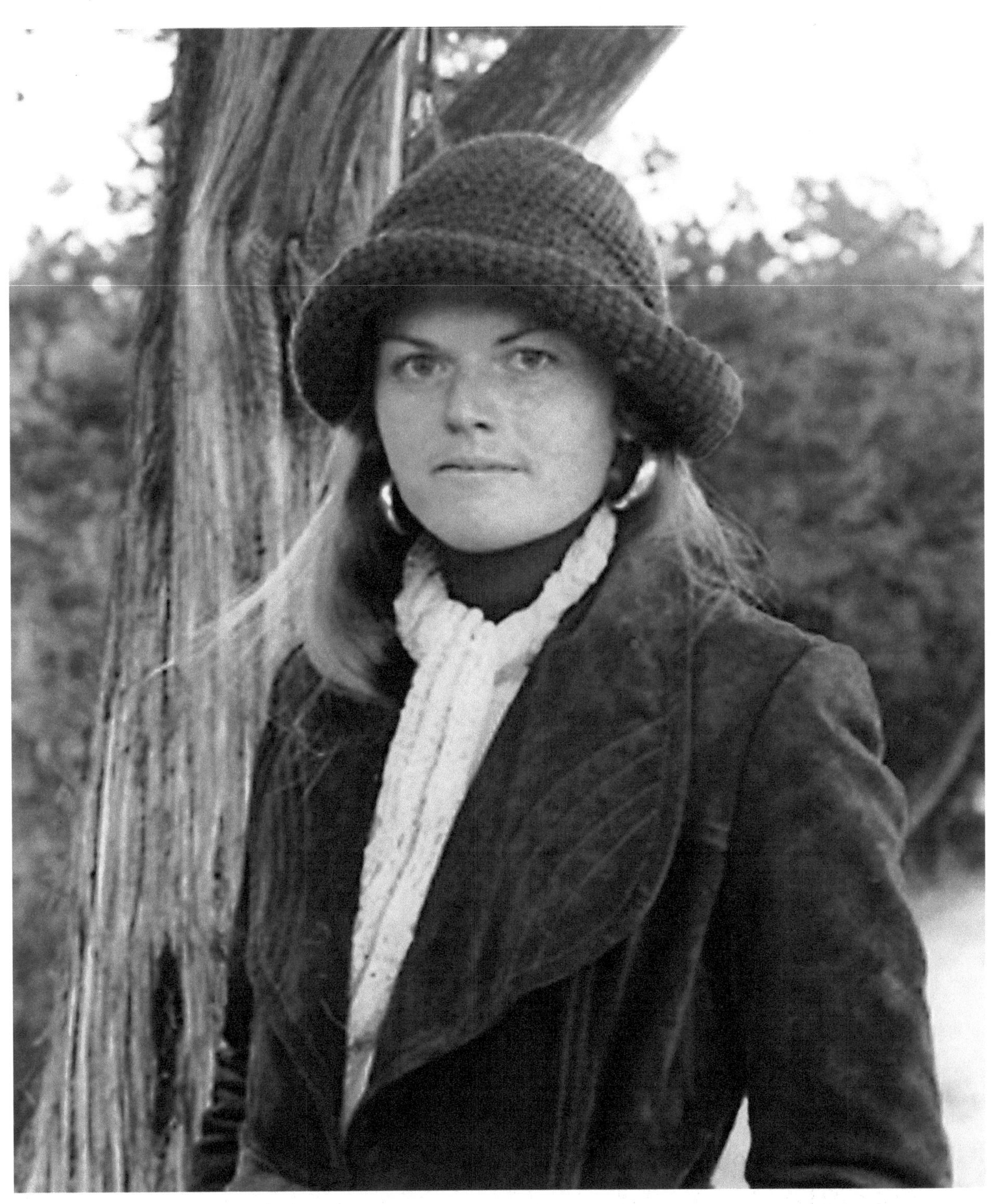

Life is a river, moving too fast.
It flows to the future from out of the past.
Let's see what the current can deliver.
Hold my hand and we'll jump in the river.

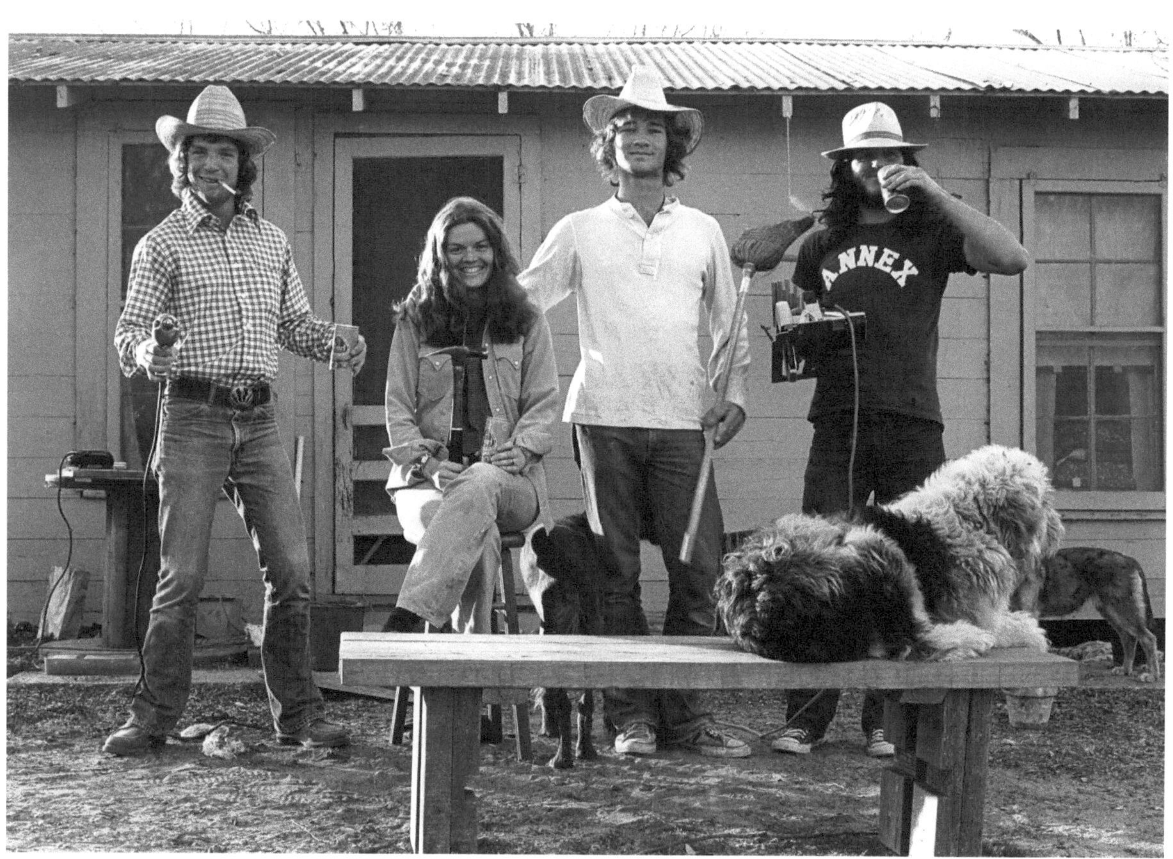

Beth and I married in 1974 and acquired a Sears and Roebuck charge card. We bought a house, and landed jobs at Southwestern Bell where we worked until retirement. Then we moved out of the city, away from traffic, to the comparatively small town of Wimberley.

More than forty years have elapsed since our wedding, and during that time the quality of travel has improved along with our lifestyle. This is how it happened.

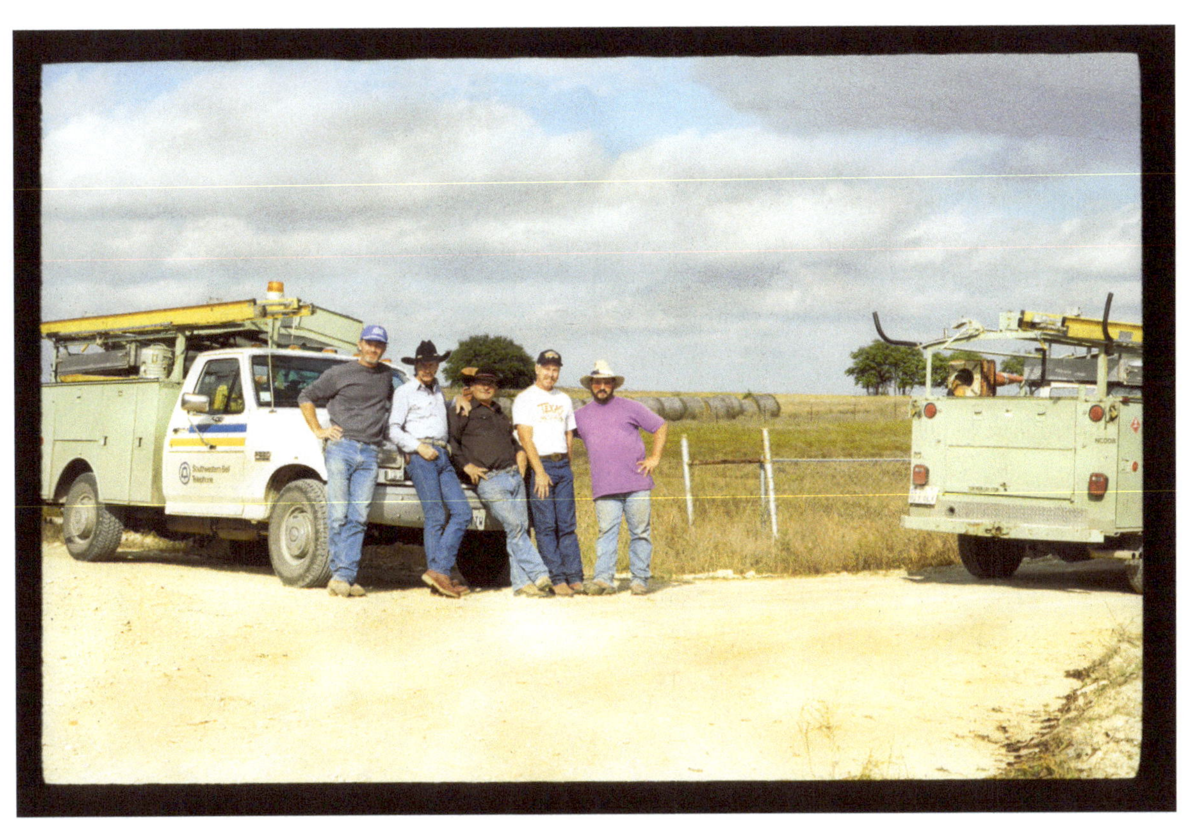

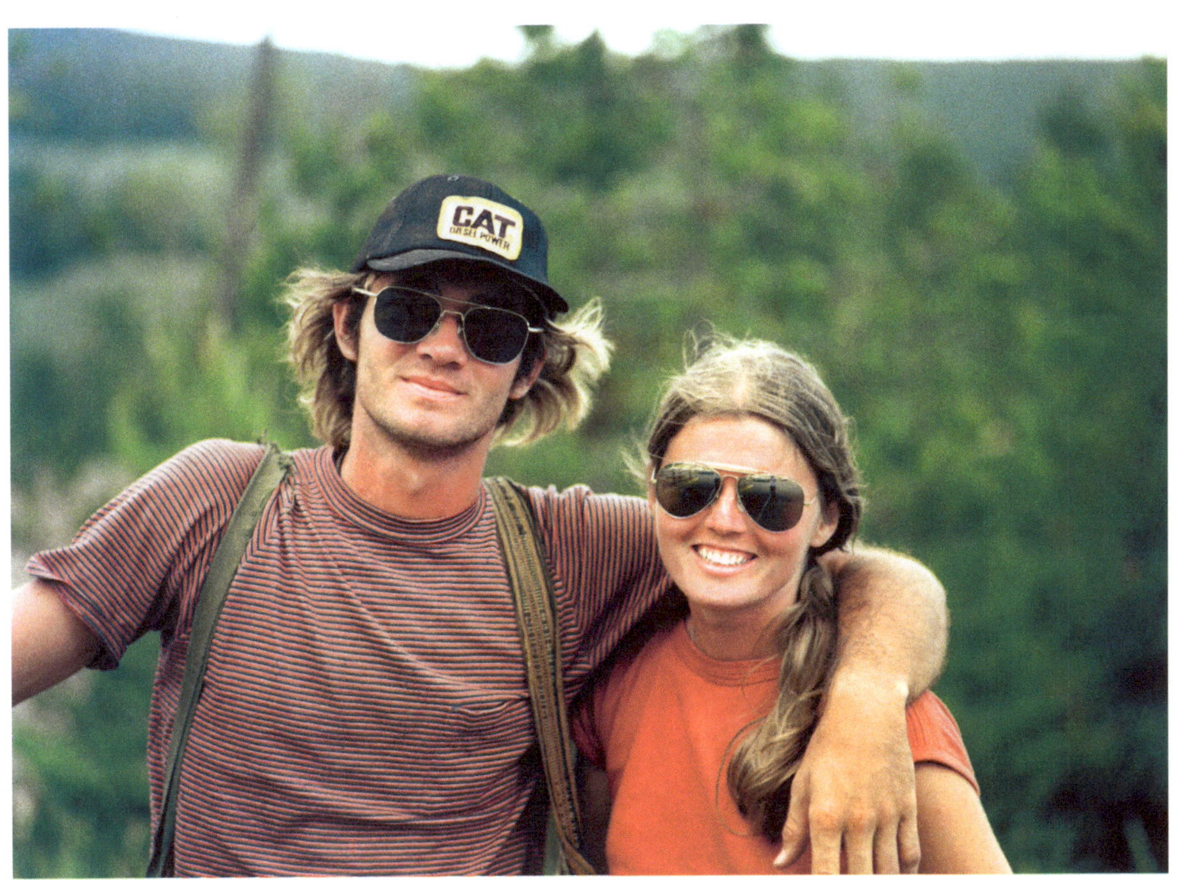
CAT
DIESEL POWER

Beth and I began taking day trips long before we moved to the country. We found Hamilton Pool, one of the finest spring fed swimming holes in Texas, not long after we married. That was almost forty years ago. Most of our day trips happened on the weekends, and the summertime excursions usually involved swimming. We found Wimberley's Blue Hole and the River Road section of the Guadalupe River as well as a number of less popular pools within easy reach of Austin, Texas.

Cool weather trips were joy rides, excuses to get out of town, and many of them involved camping. Those overnighters occasionally included two or three nights away from home, long enough to get us to the state border and still have enough time to explore the area. Port Aransas was the place to go when we were with other people. Big Bend and Caddo Lake were personal excursions. Each of those locations are visual and logistical extremes, and about as far as you can go in Texas without crossing the border. They are memories I would not want to forget, but I never considered any of them as a true journey, probably because we never had to cross the state line to get there.

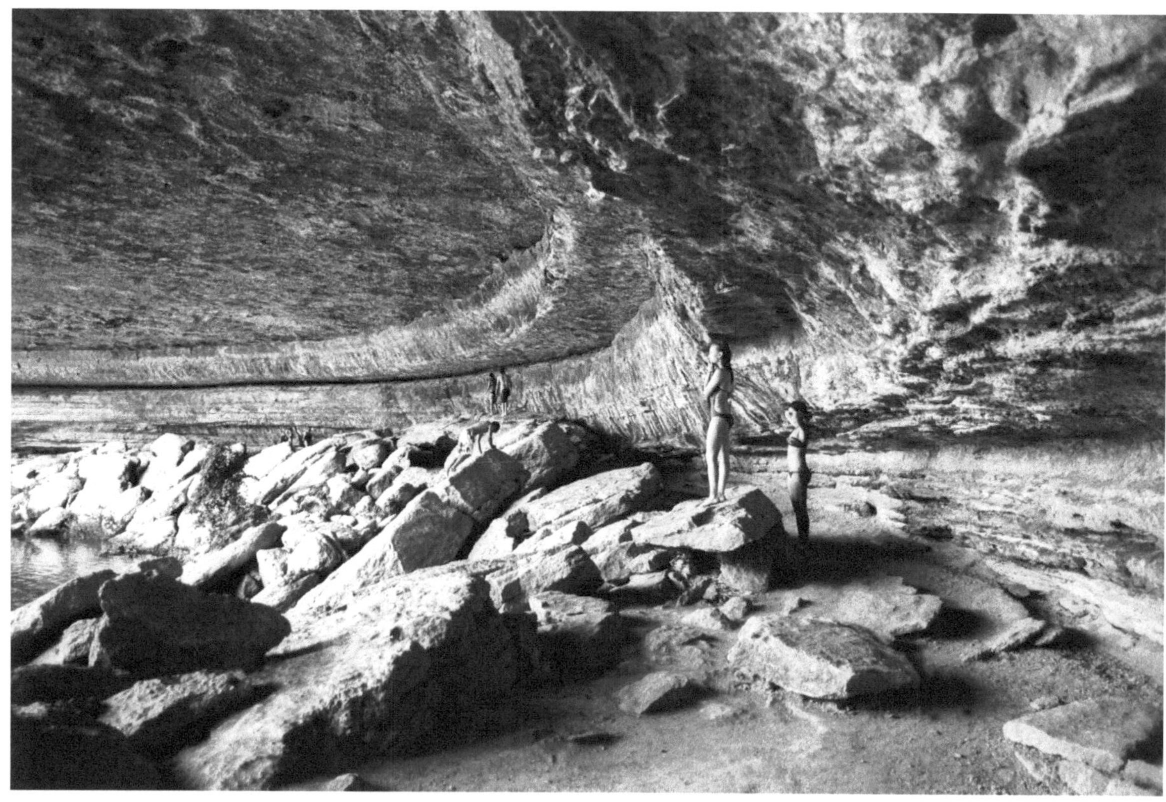

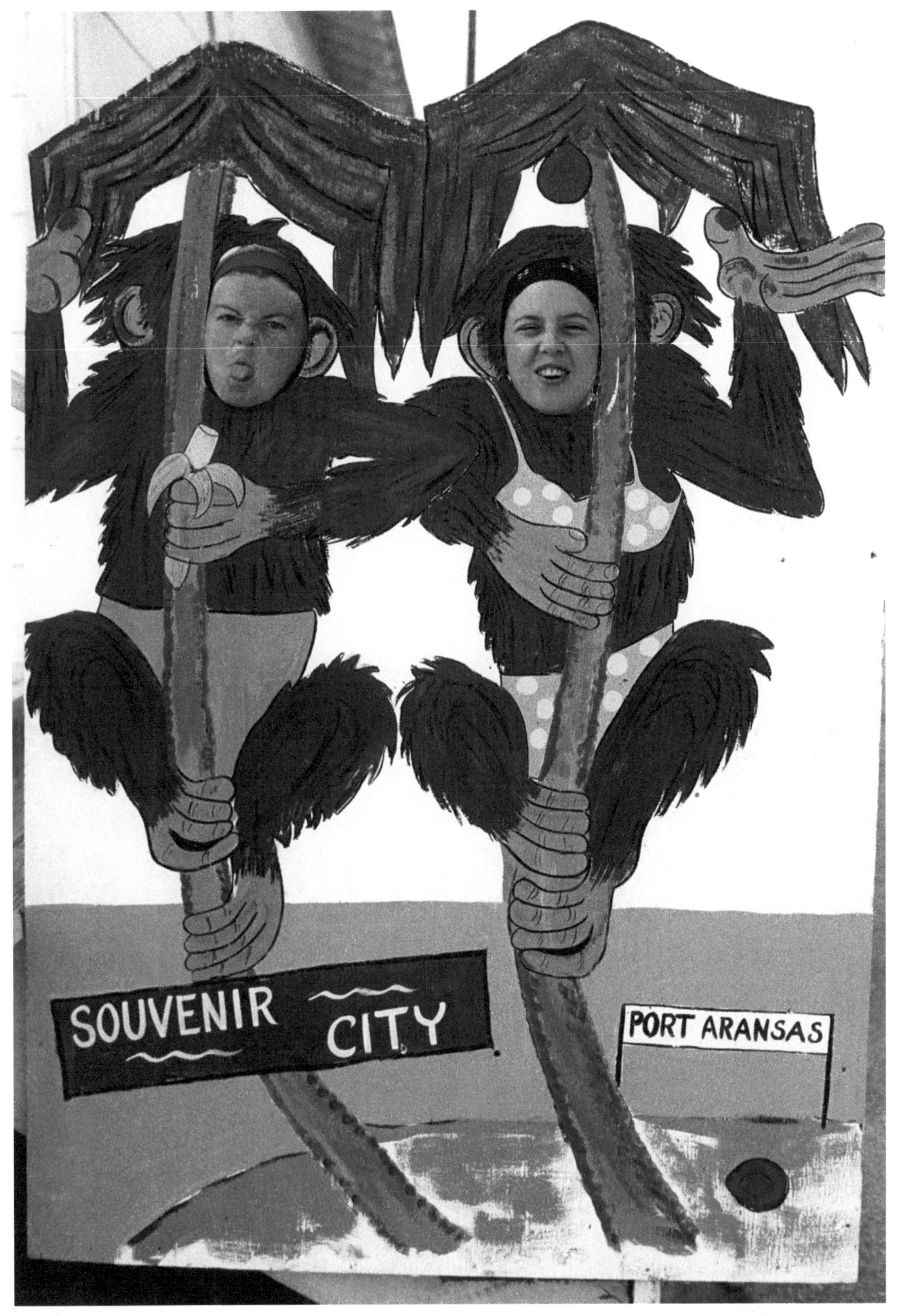
SOUVENIR CITY
PORT ARANSAS

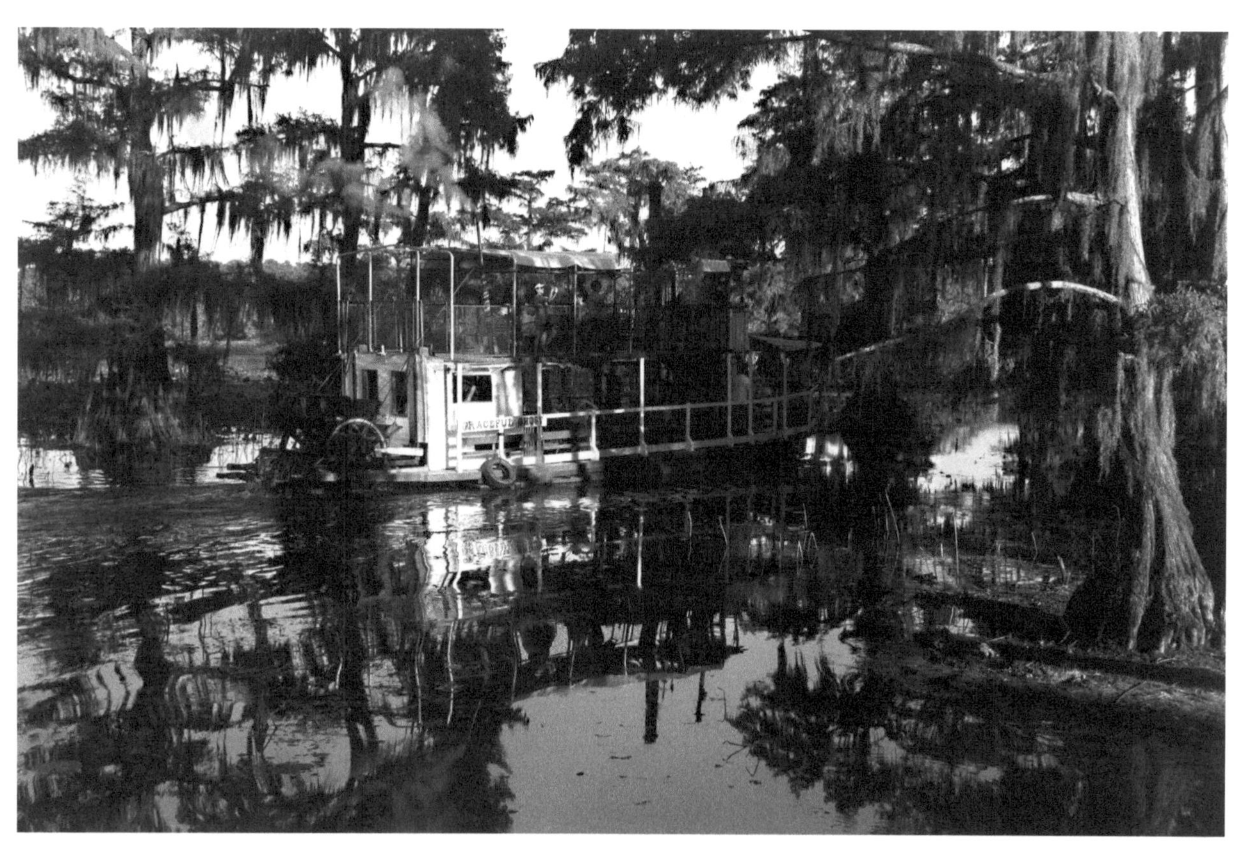

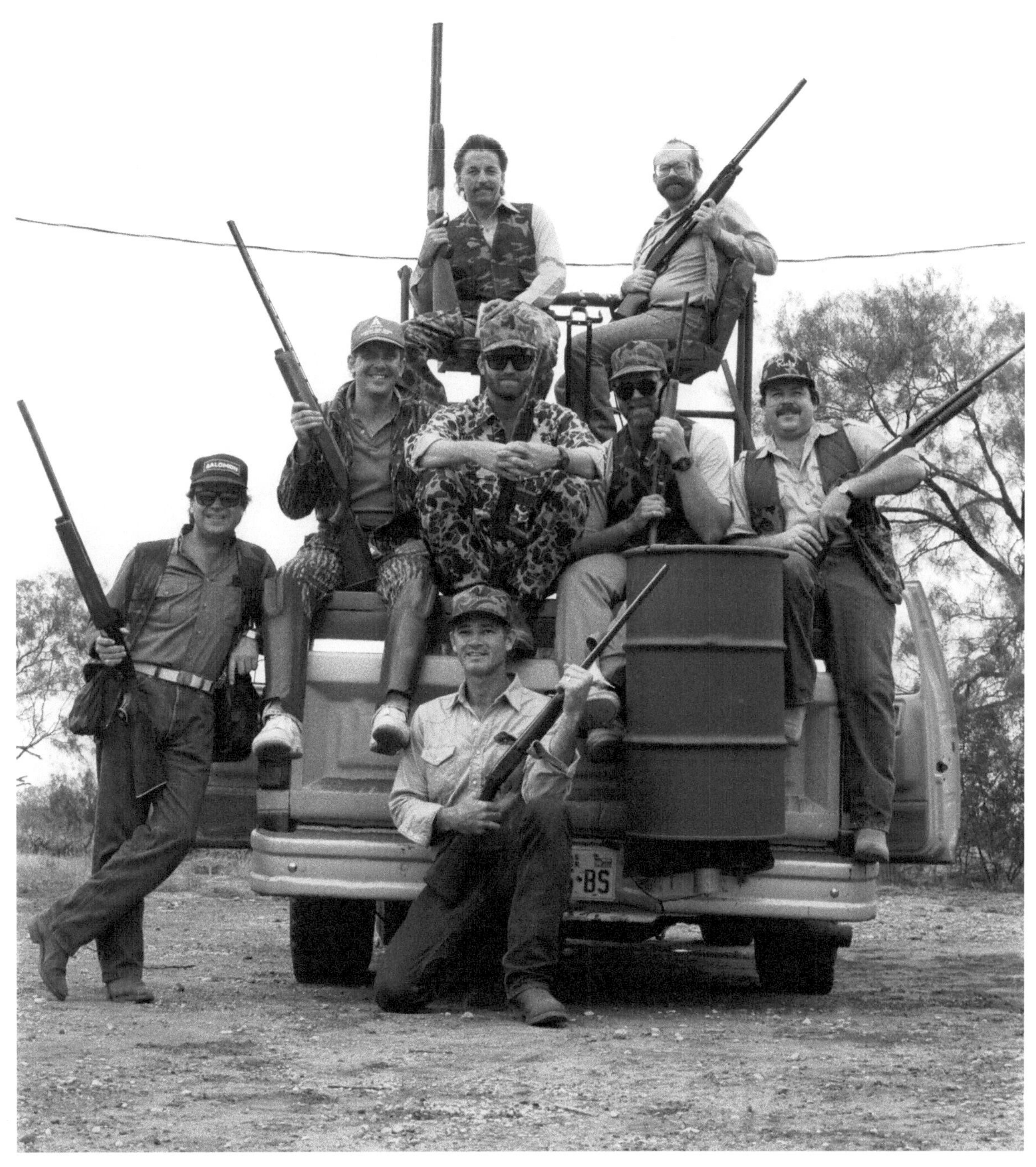
SALOMON

THE BORDER

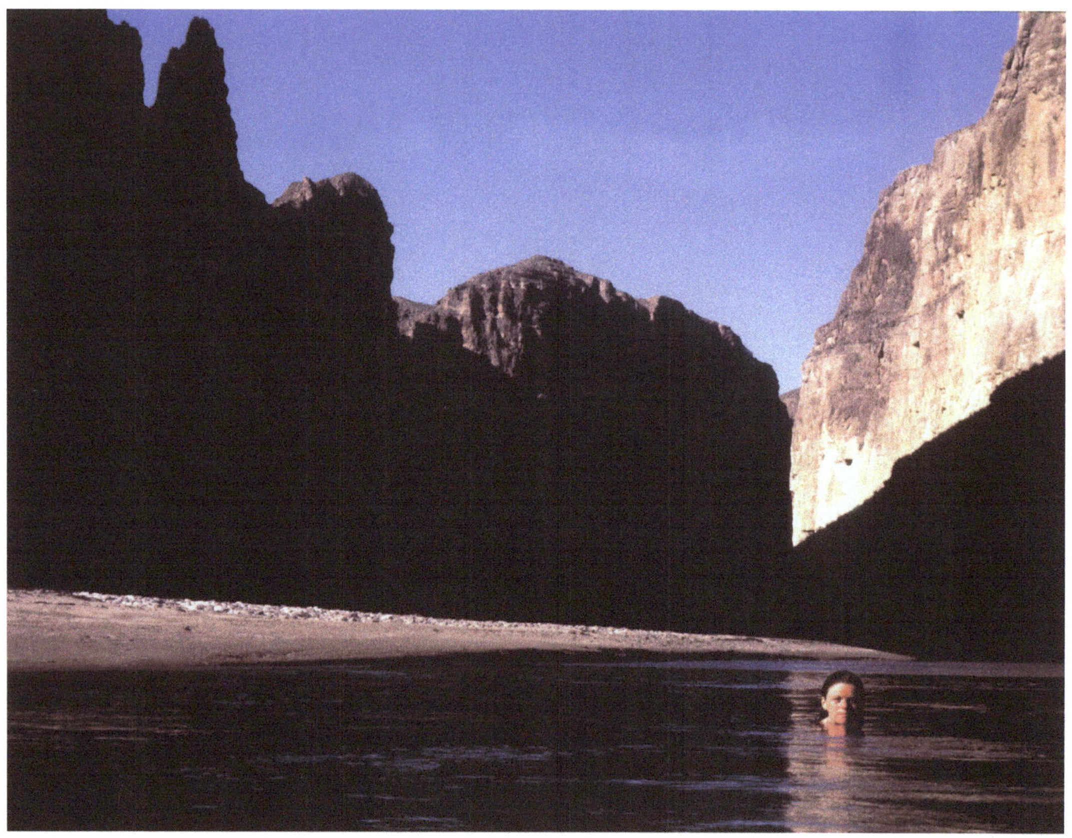

We left Texas in every direction and my favorite was always Southwest. From the U.S. side of Boquillas Canyon in the Big Bend National park you could immerse yourself in the border as you crossed it. When the Rio Grande was low enough, it was an easy thing to wade across. When the river was running, a few coins would buy space on a boat, and it was usually possible to purchase a donkey ride for the short trip to Boquillas, Mexico. That was pre-9-11, when parts of the Rio Grande seemed more like an obstacle than a national border.

Big Bend is one of the largest and most remote national parks in the lower 48 United States. Over one hundred miles of international border flows within the park boundaries, through canyons and desert, and winds its way past the ghost town of Terlingua. Cinnabar, a mineral from which metal mercury is extracted, was discovered in the area in the mid-1880s, and by 1900 there were a couple thousand people in town. The mines closed, and the people left, but by 2010 the population had increased to about sixty, and seems to be holding steady. Terlingua is still a place of desolate beauty and solitude, except for the first Saturday of November, when the population swells to about 10,000 for the World Chili Championship.

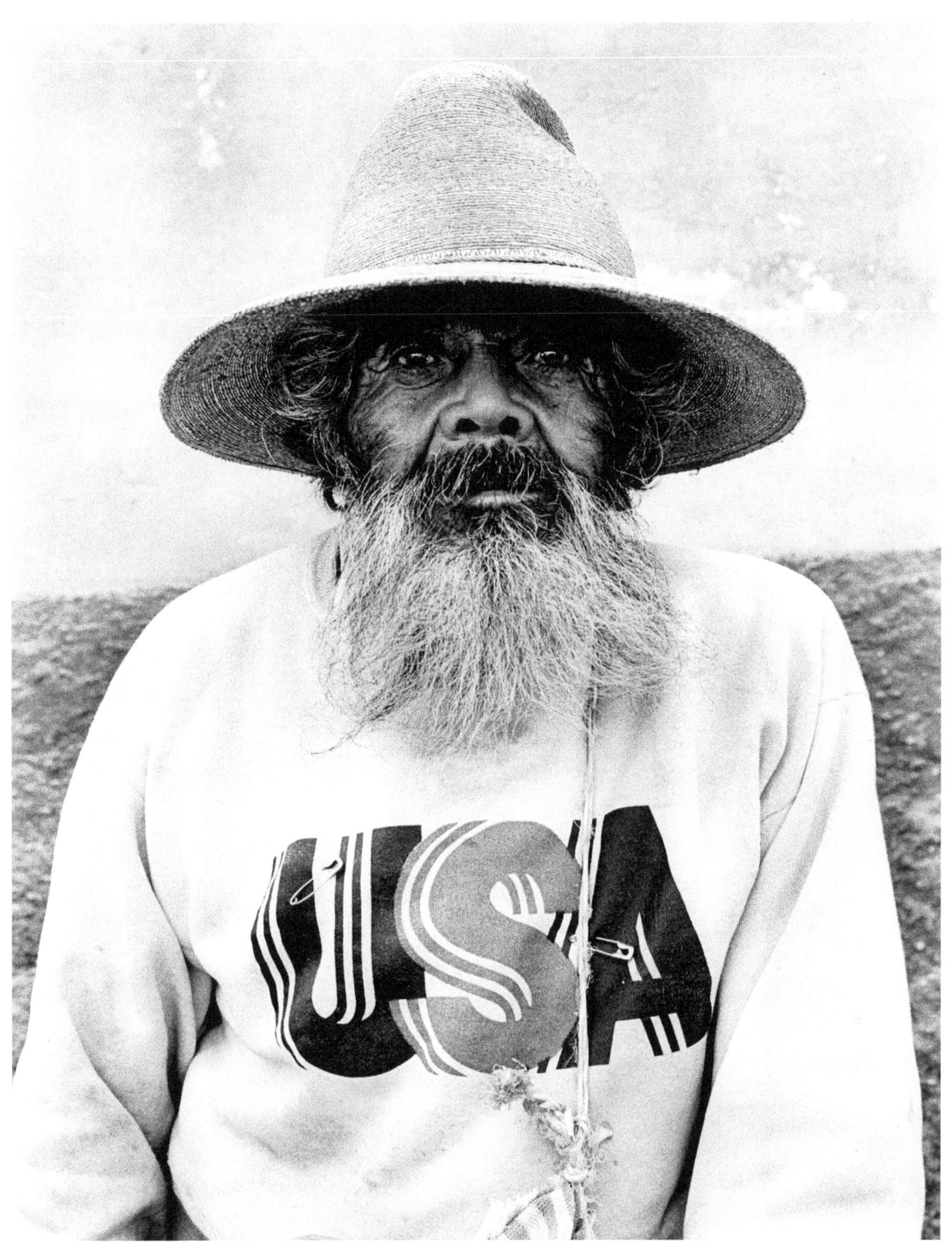
USA

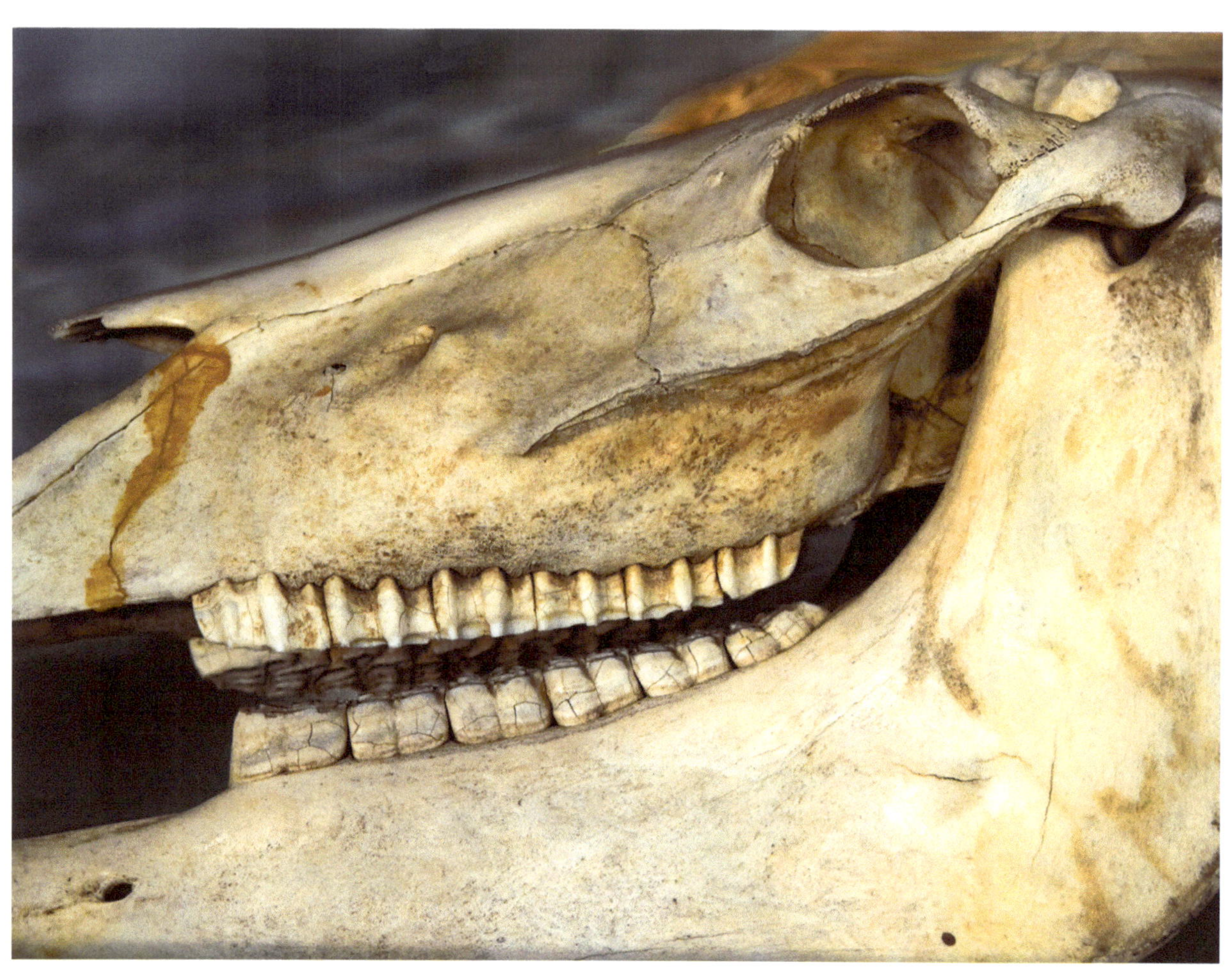

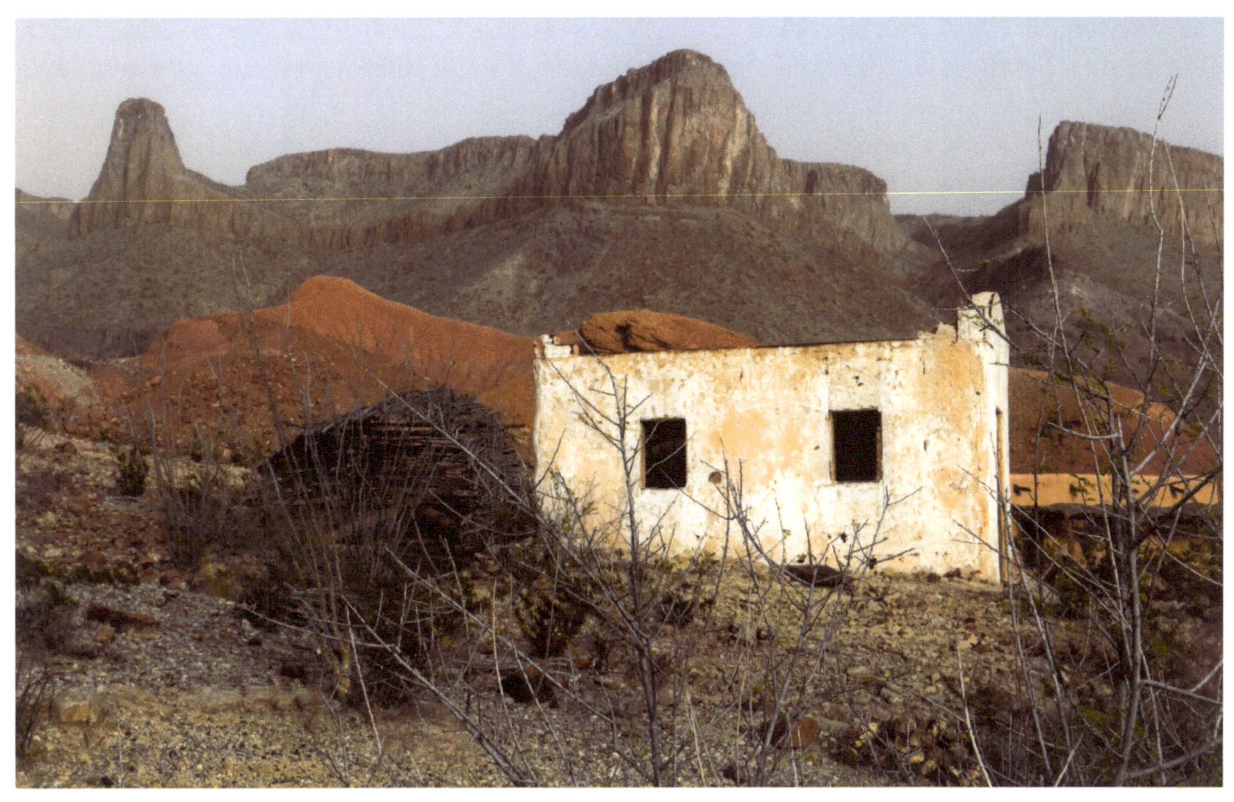

A journey of a thousand miles must begin with a single step.
—Lao Tzu

As years passed, we became more adventurous, and ventured into the Mexican interior. We crossed the border in cars, trains, and planes. In 1990 Beth and I rode a train from Juarez to Chihuahua, where we boarded the Ferrocarril Chihuahua al Pacifico for the rest of the ride to the Sea of Cortez. The rails skirt the edge of Barranca del Cobre, (Copper Canyon), which is a series of connected canyons, some of which are deeper than Arizona's Grand Canyon. The first tracks were laid in the late 19th century, but the Mexican revolution, lack of funding, and the difficulty of building a railroad in such rugged terrain stalled its completion until 1961. The railroad is an engineering wonder, with 86 tunnels and 39 bridges, and some of the most dramatic scenery in the Sierra del Madres.

Copper Canyon is Tarahuamara country. The tribe used to be known as Raramuri until their name and much of the culture was corrupted. They are known as endurance runners, and binge drinkers. The rugged Sierra Madre terrain is perfect for the reclusive tribe of Indians who would prefer not to be bothered by tourists, religious converts, and for the most part, non Indian Mexicans. We have all added and subtracted from the Tara culture.

The first time Beth and I made that journey we encountered Indians in traditional Tarahumara attire. Two years later the dress code had a more cowboy look, and there were hotels and KOA campgrounds overlooking the rugged landscape. There was also electricity and running water and an easier way of life for the locals. I remember complaining about the dilution of culture, while avoiding to mention that in a couple of weeks we would be back home with conveniences the Tara's could not imagine.

That train ride was such an exciting journey we returned a year later and caught a ride from the pine covered high country around Creel, to the sub tropical town of Batopilas. The road down was dirt and loose rocks, and so steep it felt like our 4-wheel drive would tip over. About 90% of the trip was accomplished at less than five miles per hour.

The Batopilas River runs between the town and the crumbling walls of an old silver mining facility. A couple of miles downstream is a Jesuit mission that is still in use. Inside is a mixture of Christian and pagan symbols.

Thanks to the silver mine, Batopilas was one of the first towns in Mexico to have electricity. Beth and I stayed in a hacienda that was owned by the silver baron, and there was a painting in his parlor of about a dozen Indians lugging a grand piano into the canyon for his wife.

When the silver played out, Batopilas once again became a nearly deserted town. The mine walls crumbled along with many of the buildings. A sporadic amount of tourism kept the place from returning to nature, but it was the narco industry that rejuvenated the economy.

The Batopilas canyon is studded with marijuana and poppy fields, and Beth and I were warned not to stray too far off the main roads without a guide. We never saw more than a few vehicles in the valley that were not up on blocks, and one was a fancy black truck that looked out of place.

One night I woke up to the sound of trucks rumbling over the short stretch of cobblestones in front of our hacienda. I stepped out onto the balcony and saw four tarpaulin-covered deuce and a half's passing below, led by the shiny black truck.

"Come back inside", Beth whispered, "Before somebody sees you".

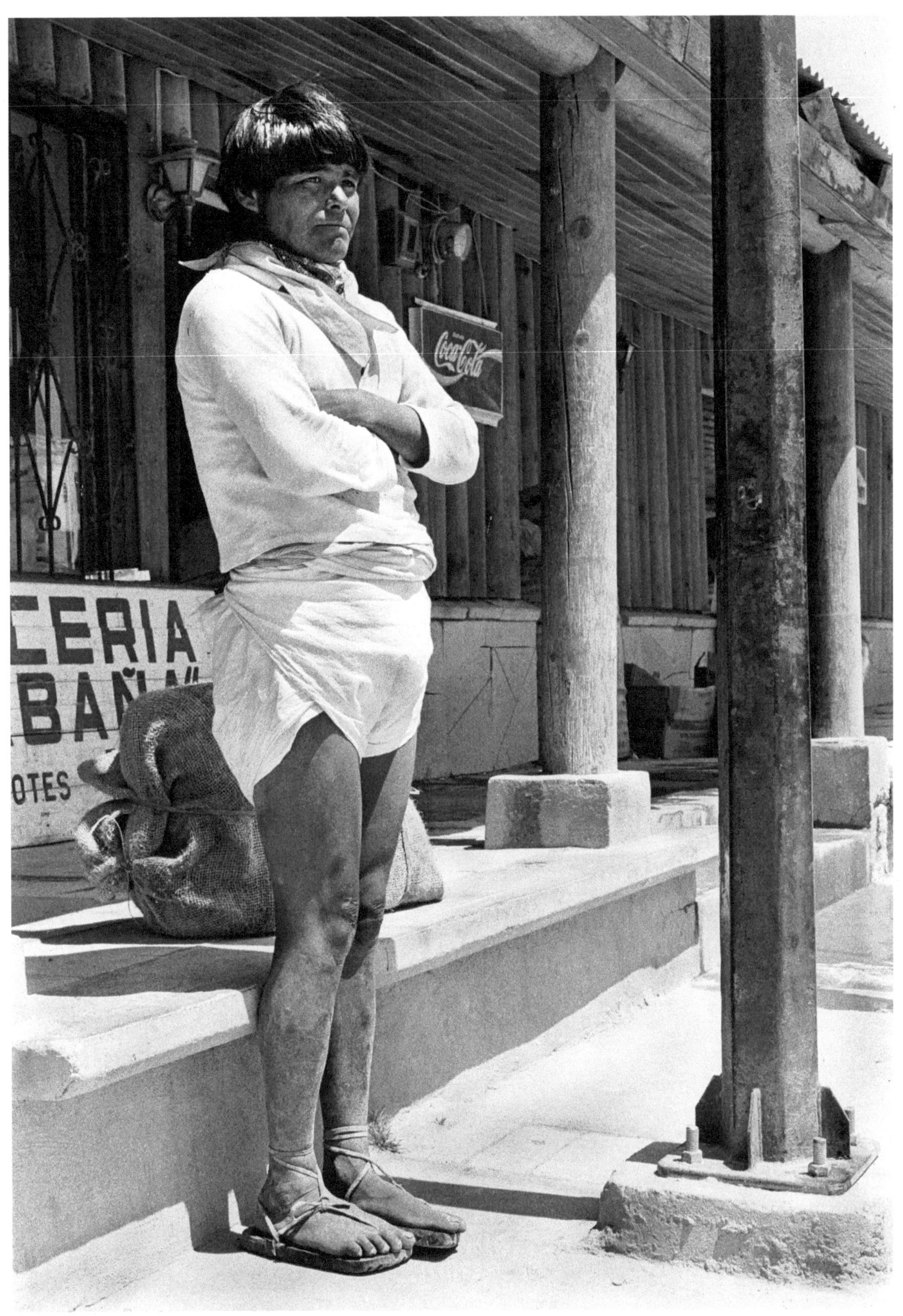
Coca-Cola
CERIA
OTES

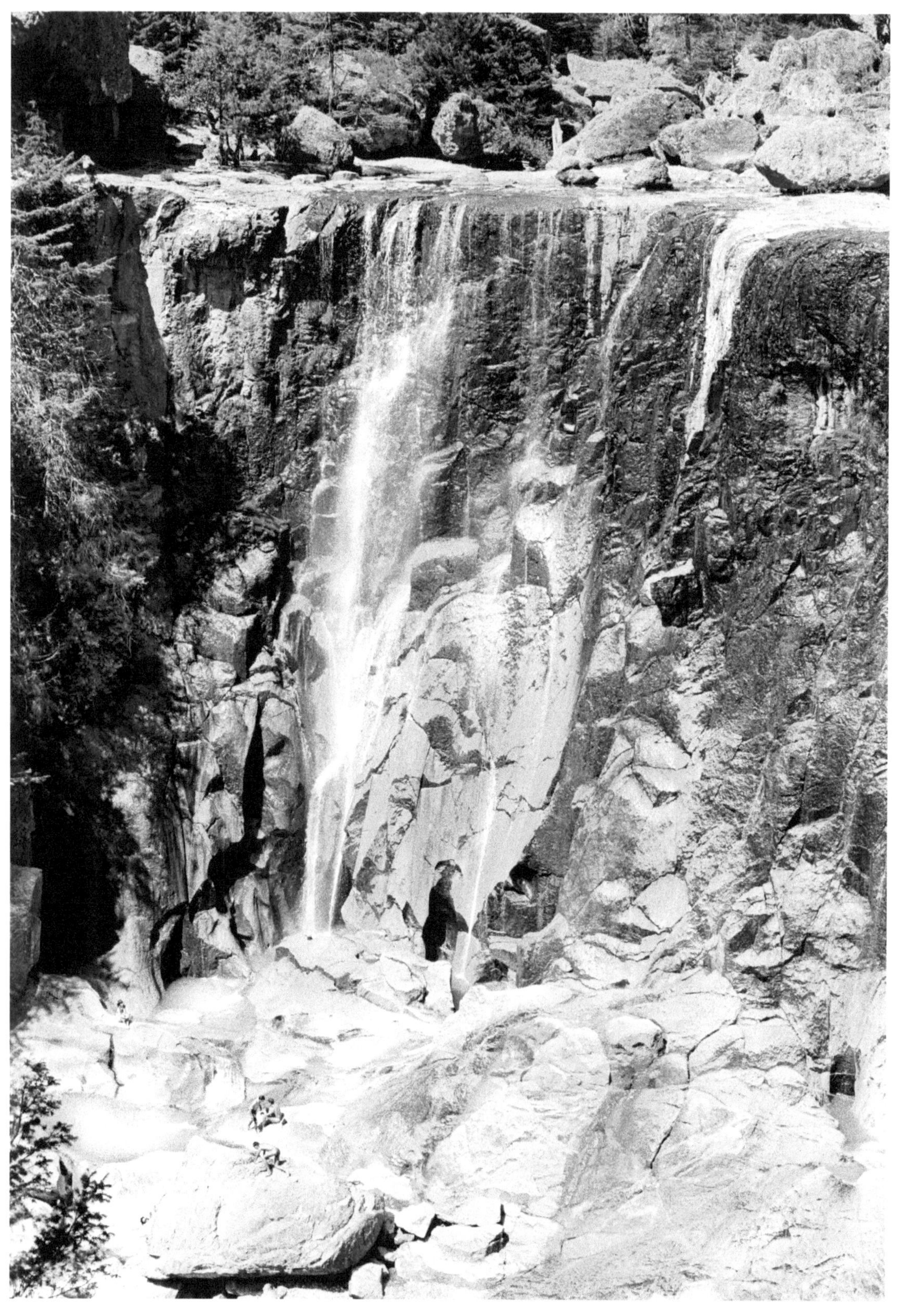

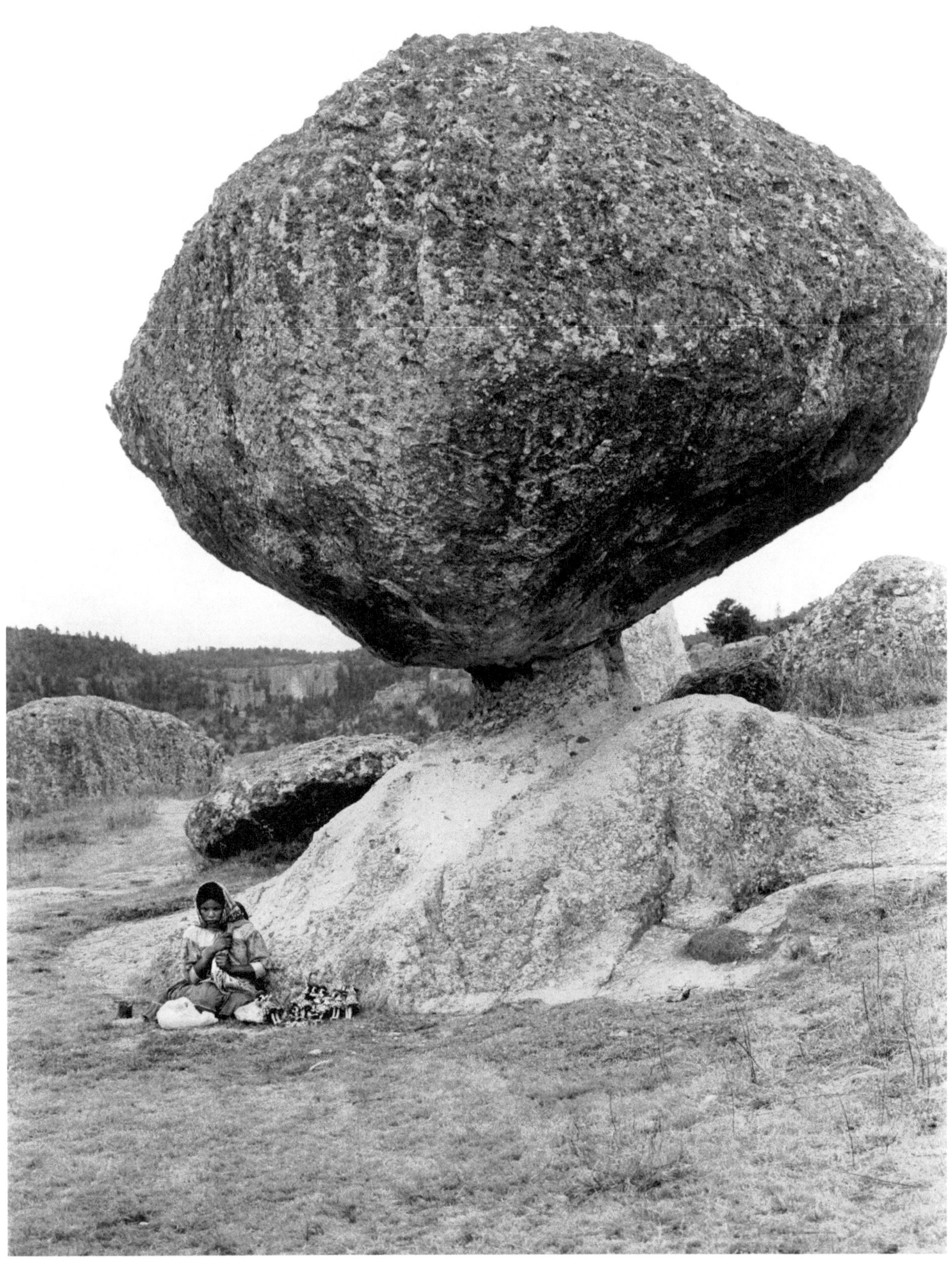

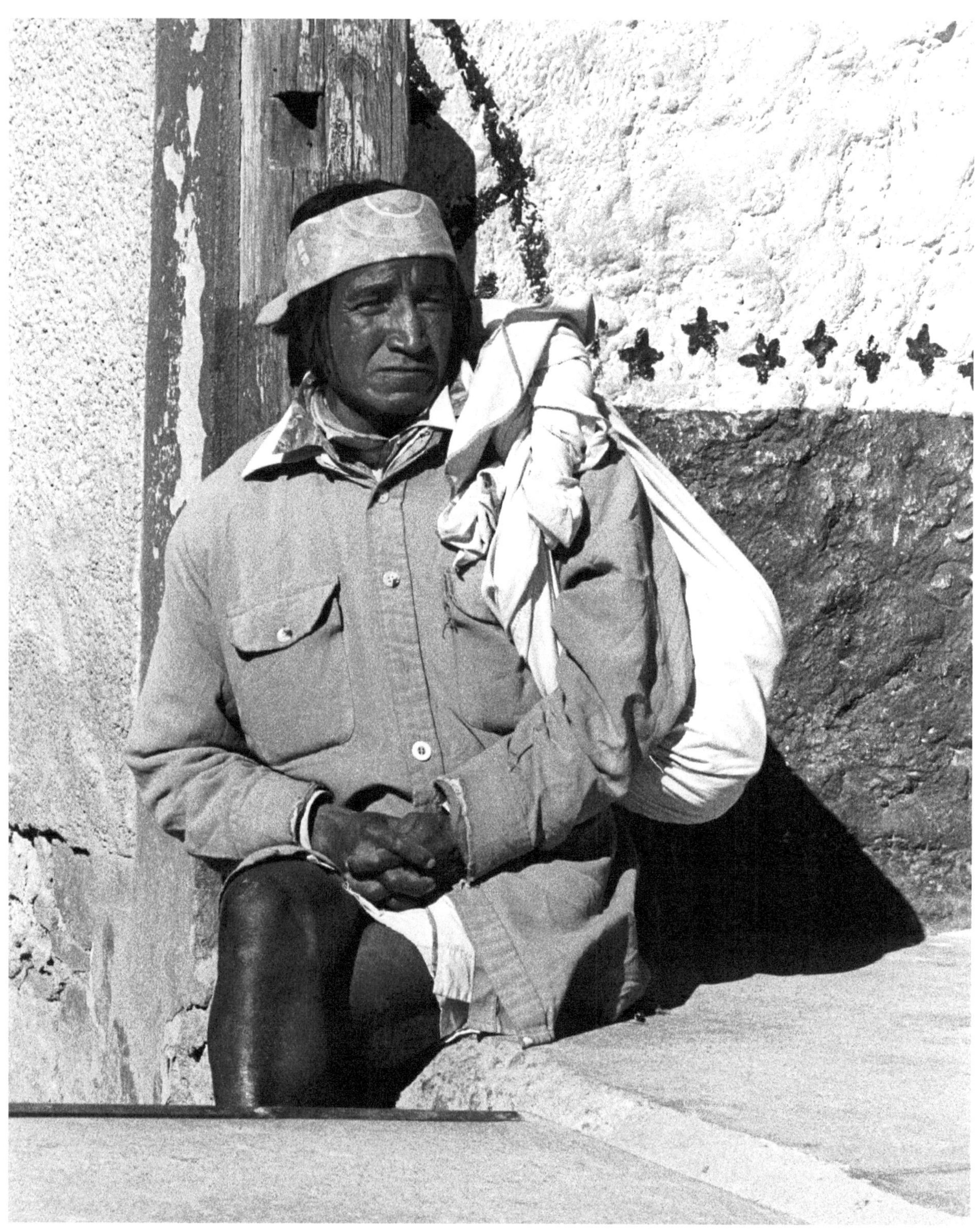

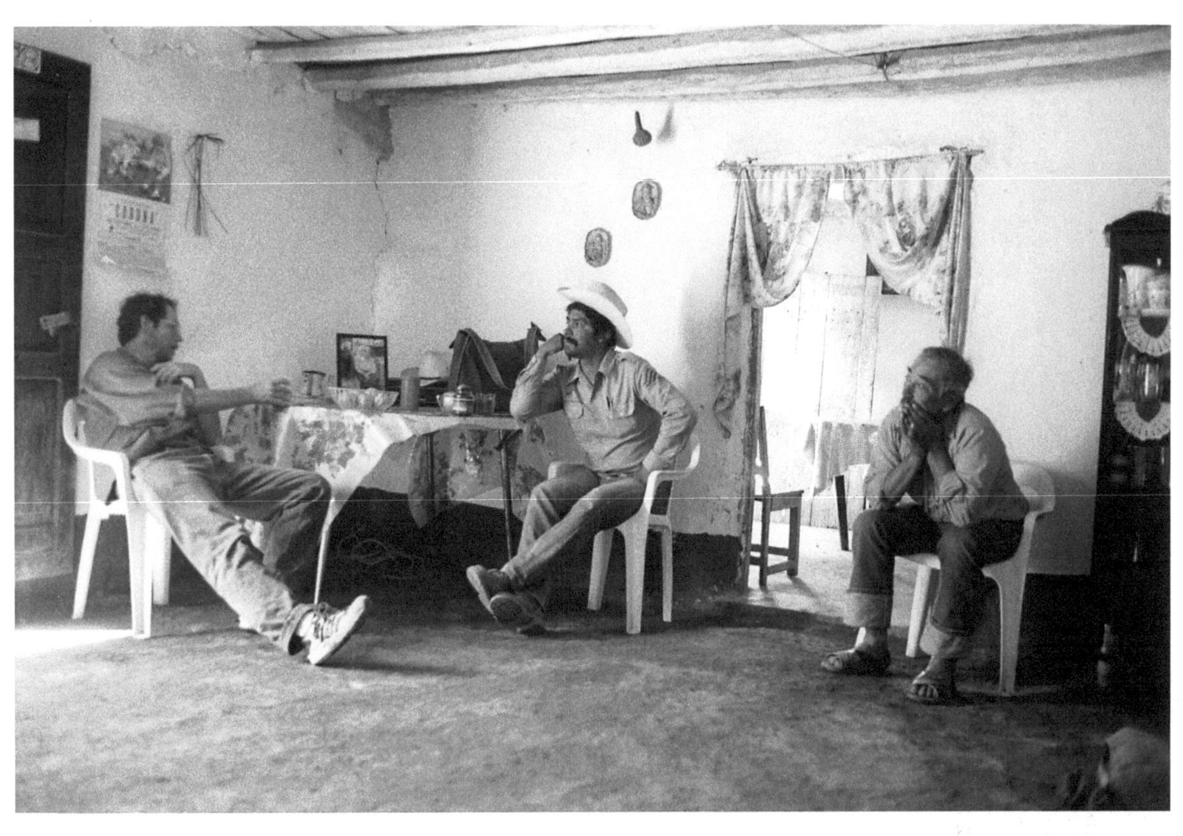

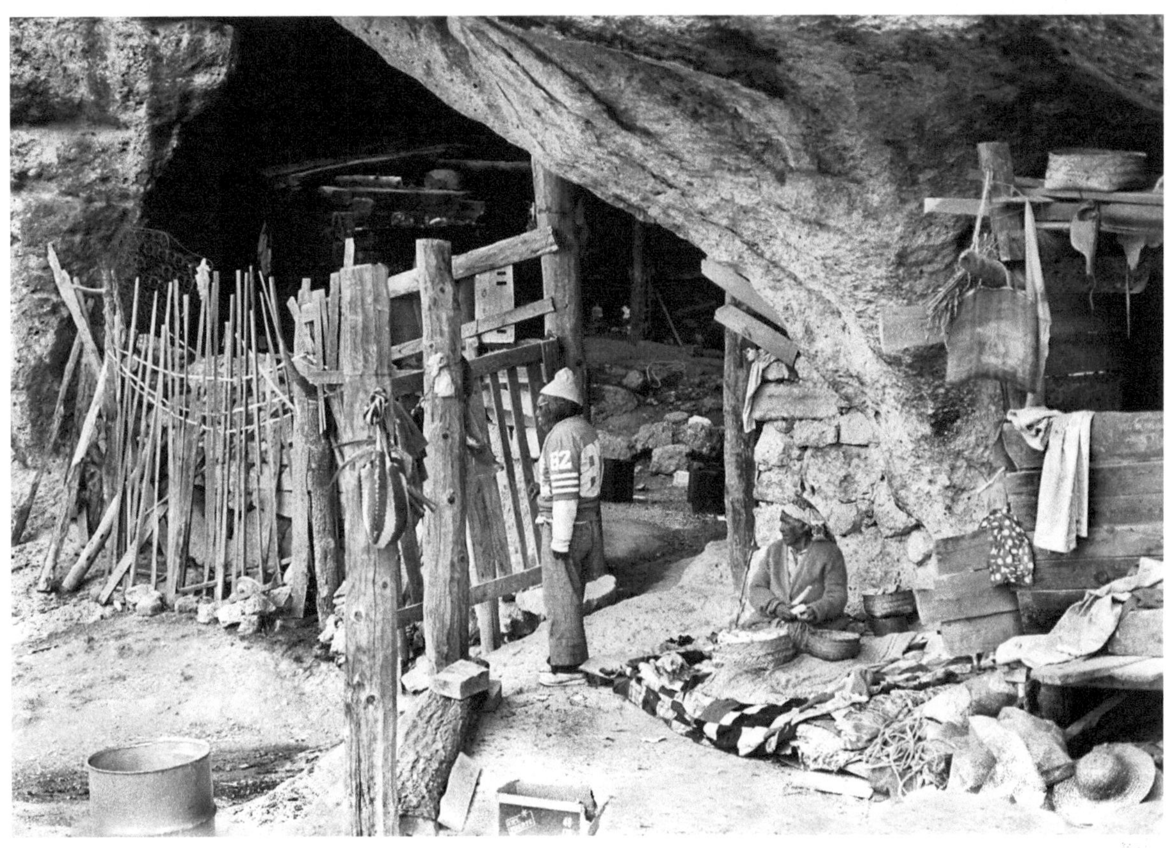
82

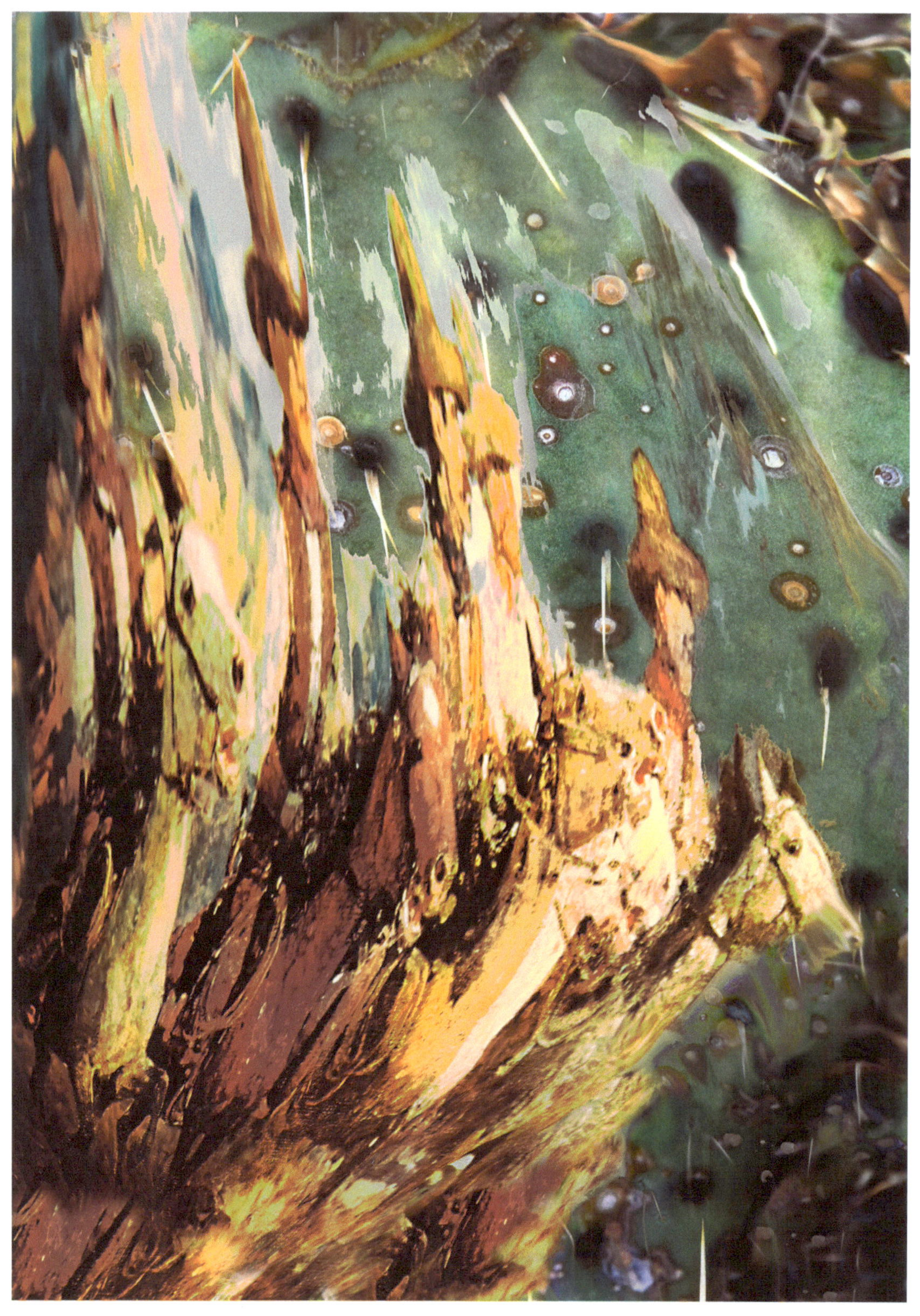

HISTORY

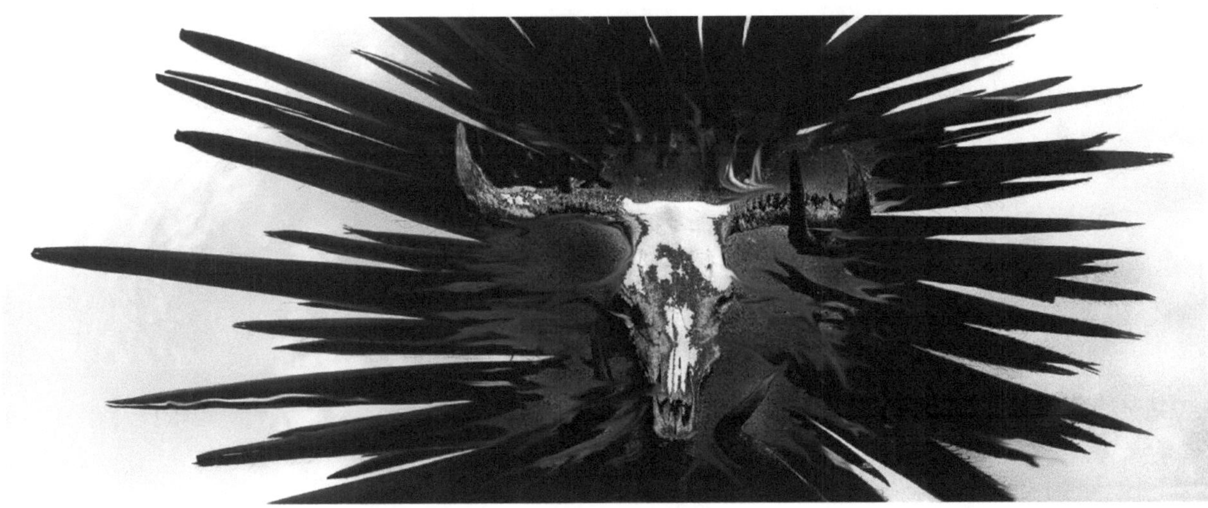

About 6,000 years ago, the horse became the fastest and easiest way to get around. Harnessing the animal marked a major leap in the history of travel. It meant the distance between points A and B could be traversed in a fraction of the time. As a means of transportation they created cavalries and cowboys. They became beasts of burden, and objects of art, and admiration. Wild horses came to epitomize the concept of freedom, and to this day kids drop a quarter into the mechanical pony for a taste of the feelings of liberation that horses inspire in humans.

Equines remained the most popular means of transportation until about 150 years ago, when machines finally won the race. Even so, mechanical means of transportation are still measured in horsepower, ensuring the horses' survival in the lexicon of travel.

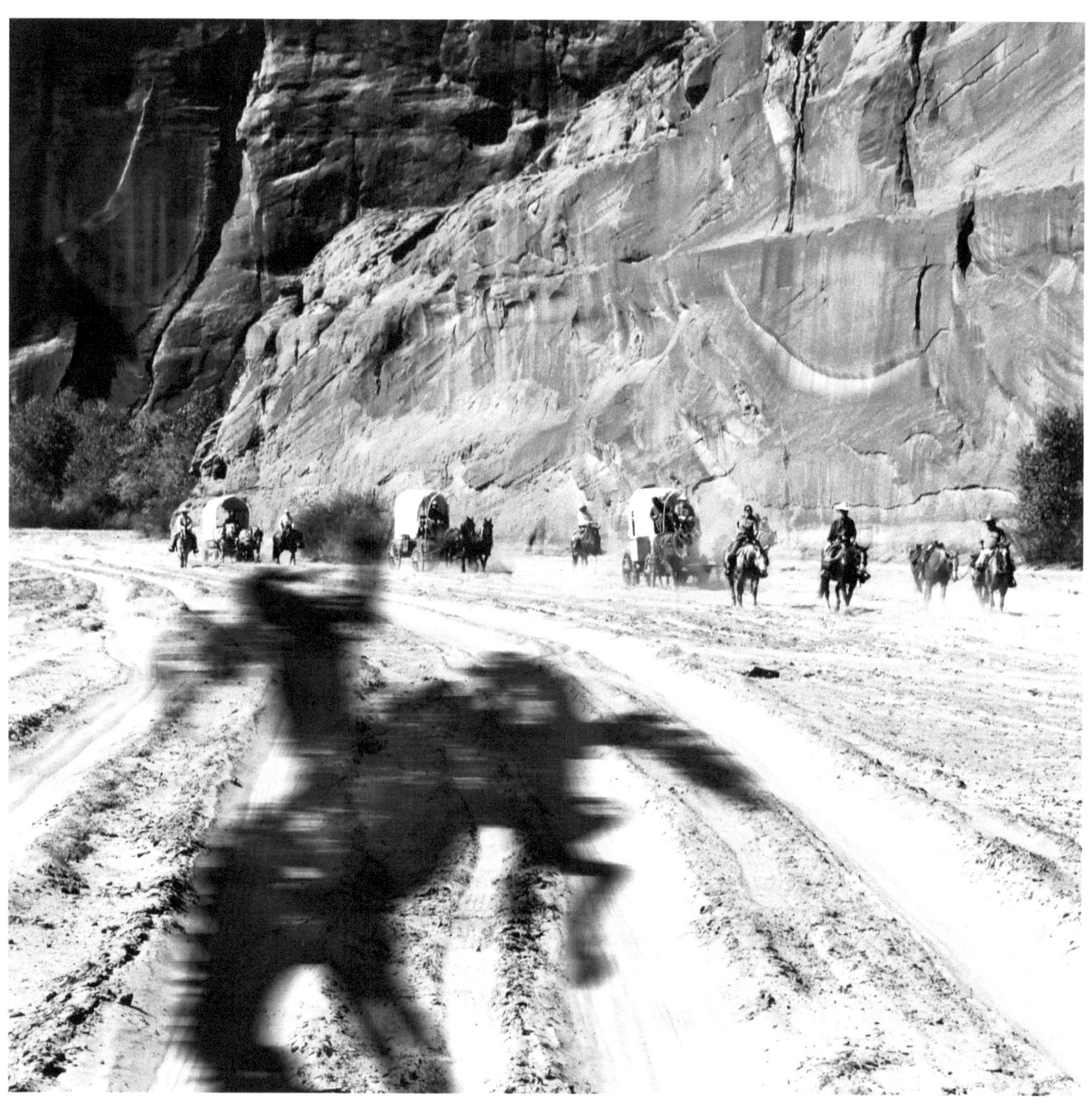

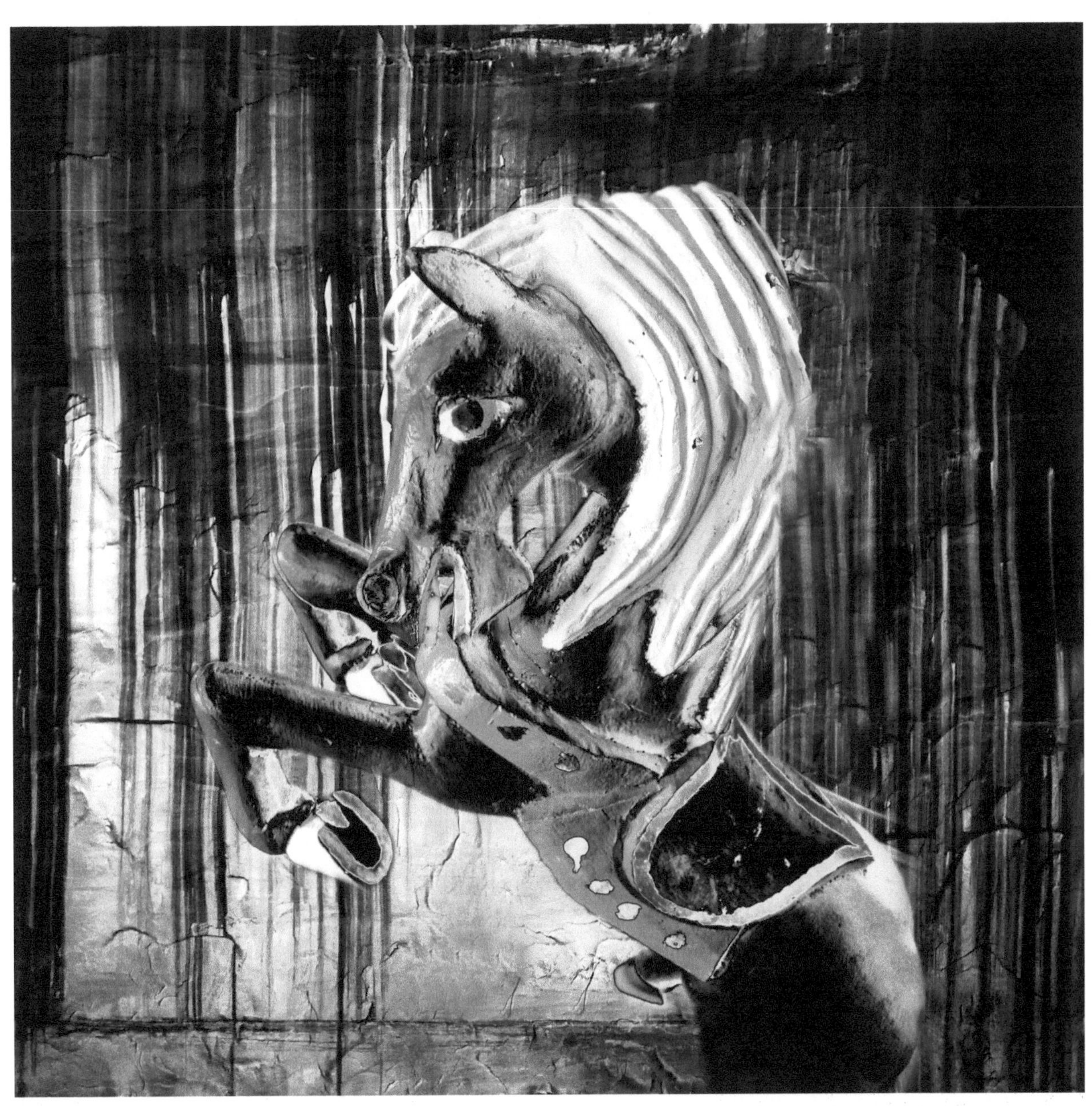

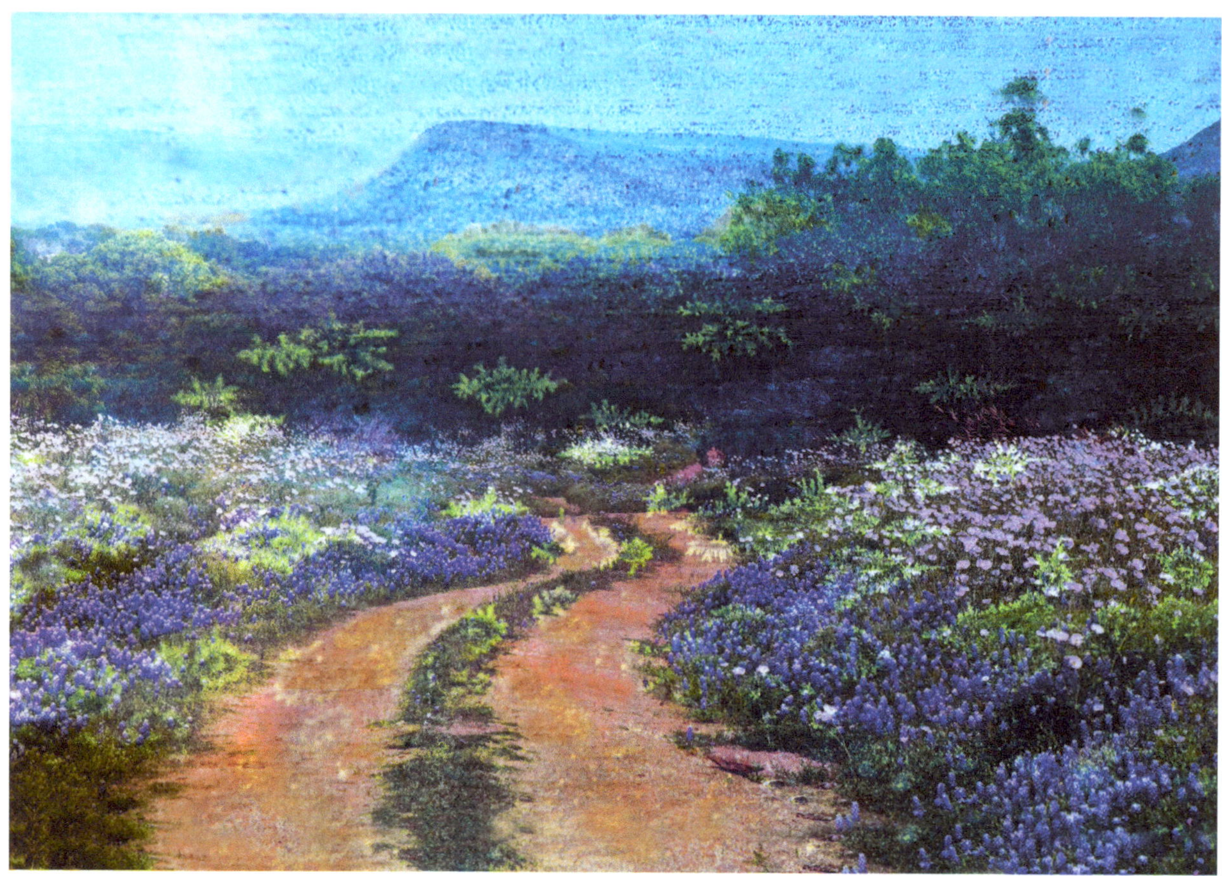

Long distance travel was still an act of commerce, or necessity. Water was the practical venue for travel, so civilization still clung to the coastlines and rivers. Roads were rough and unpredictable.

The steam engine was the next major achievement, allowing boats to travel upstream without being pulled. That invention led to the locomotive, and the rails they ran on moved people inland.

The gasoline engine introduced the automobile, which was in dire need of a decent surface upon which to travel. There were 8,000 cars in the United States of America in 1900, and by 1920 there were eight million. Without much of a road network they tended to bog down outside the city limits.

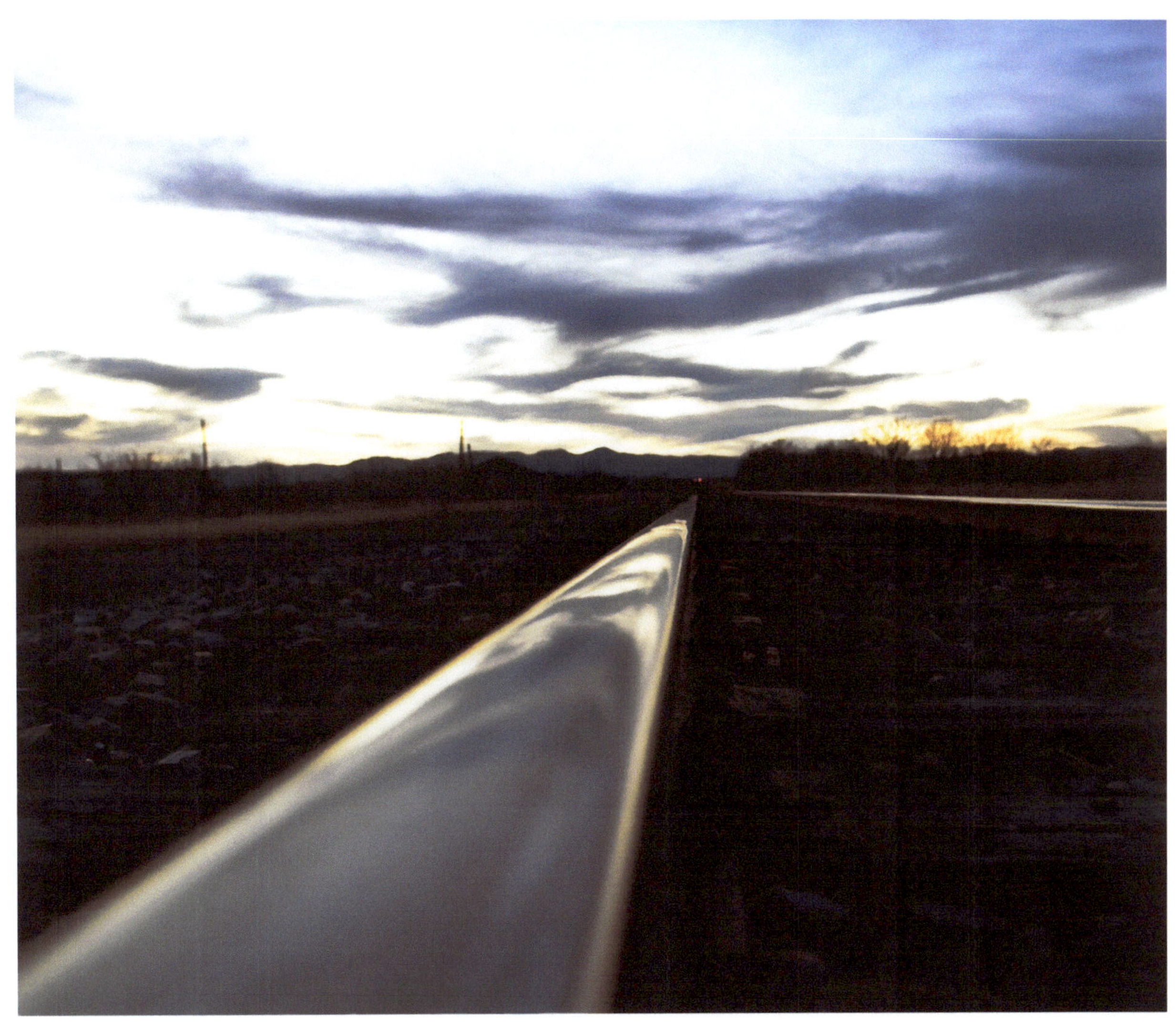

Distant lands have never been so close.

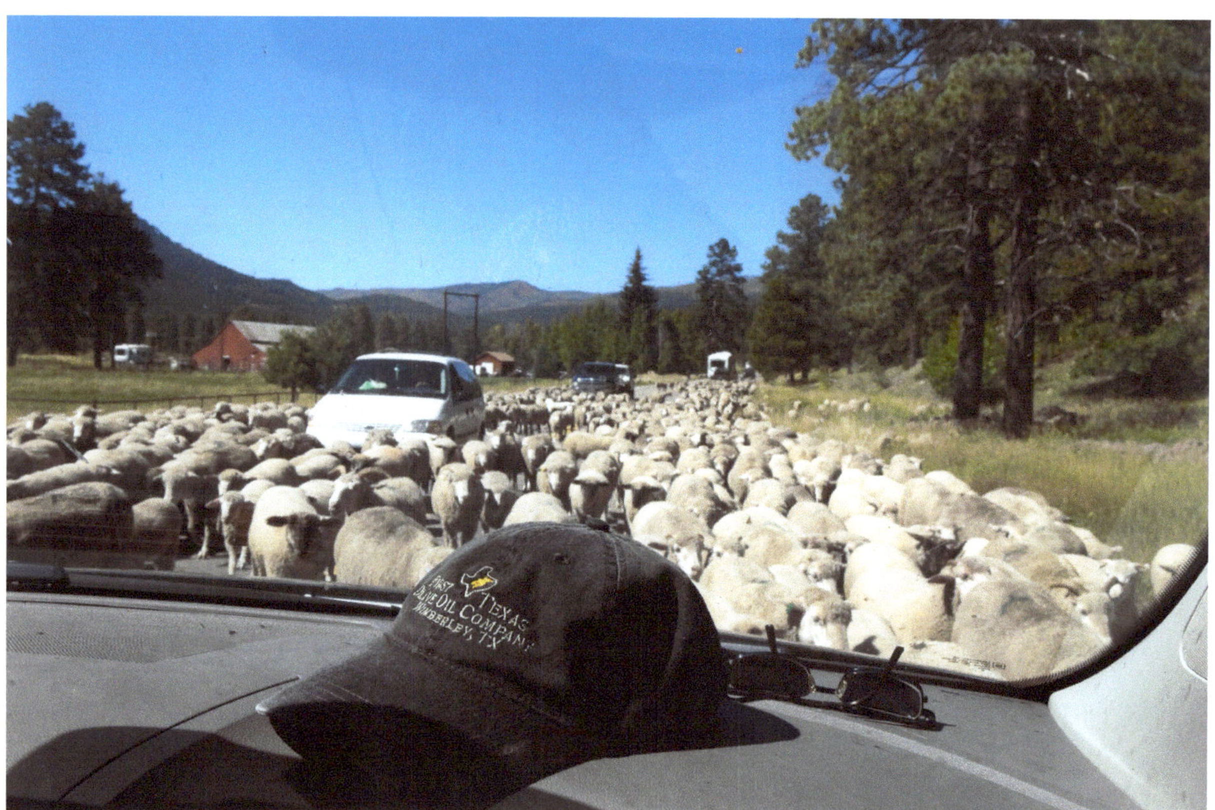

Thomas MacDonald ran the federal Bureau of Roads from 1919 to 1953. As one of the father figures of our Interstate Highway system, he gave our routes numerical order. When General Eisenhower returned from Europe after WW2, he lobbied for an American highway system similar to the Autobahn. As president, he made it happen. America was connected by asphalt, and the "road trip" became more pleasant.

In the twentieth century, man got his feet far enough off the ground to leap from one country to another. In the late 1920's regional airlines began offering regularly scheduled passenger flights. By the year 2000, 2 million passengers were flying out of America's airports every day. Continent hopping became possible for more and more people, and vacation possibilities were limited only to this planet.

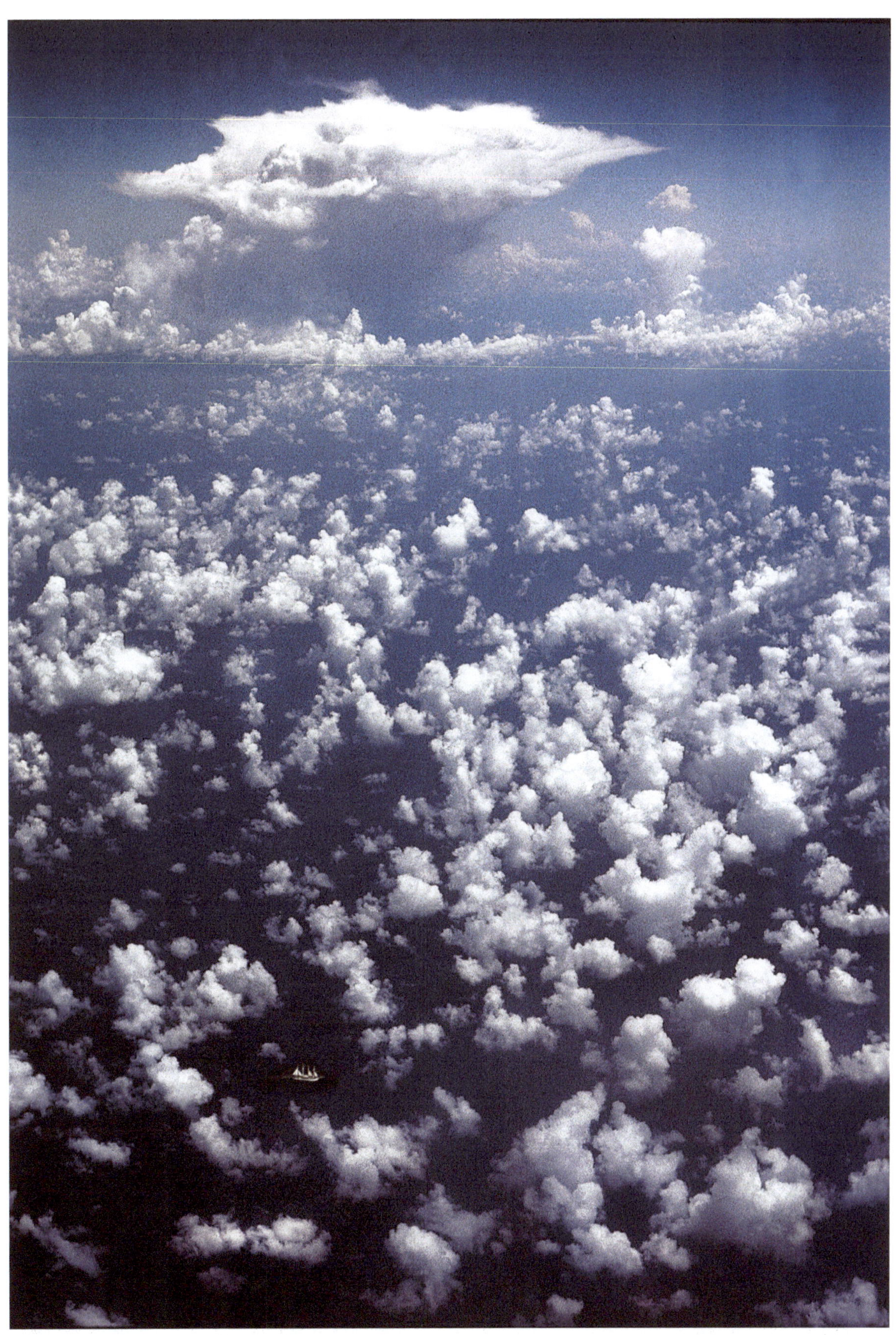

UNDERWATER

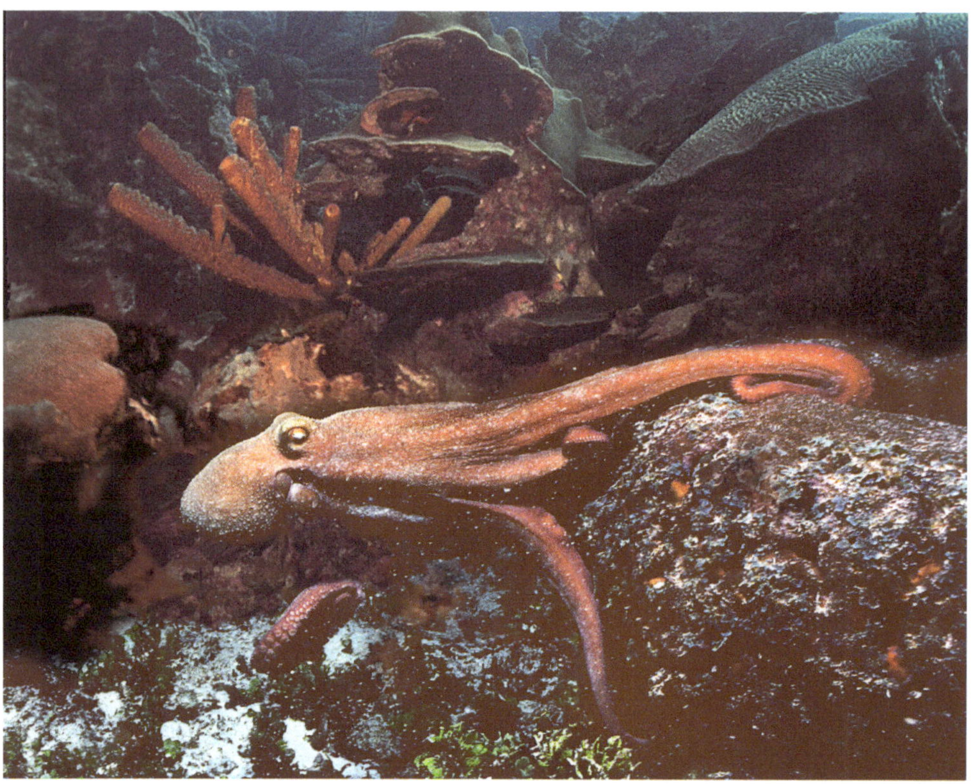

To achieve neutral buoyancy is to experience a form of physical freedom. Without the earth-bound constraints of gravity, or the anti-gravitational effects that occur in water, we are free to become the athletes we never were. We can summersault, back flip, and hover. Add the ability to breathe underwater, and then discount the physical effects of nitrogen narcosis, embolism, and the bends, and it might seem to the novice scuba diver that we could adapt better to the underwater environment than we have topside.

An alien terrain populated with creatures that seem too bizarre for reality enhances the ultimate travel experience.

On one of our trips to Mexico, Beth and I went snorkeling along the Southern coastline. We saw crazy shaped corals and sea creatures that resembled bad science fiction. I could not hold my breath long enough to take it all in.

Back in Texas I became scuba certified and began planning another trip to the Yucatan peninsula. Beth made it clear that she was not so enamored with the underwater realm, so I flew solo on more than a few vacations. I went to the Netherlands Antilles, the Bahamas, and the Galapagos with other divers. She joined me on trips to Honduras, and Belize and a couple more excursions to Mexico.

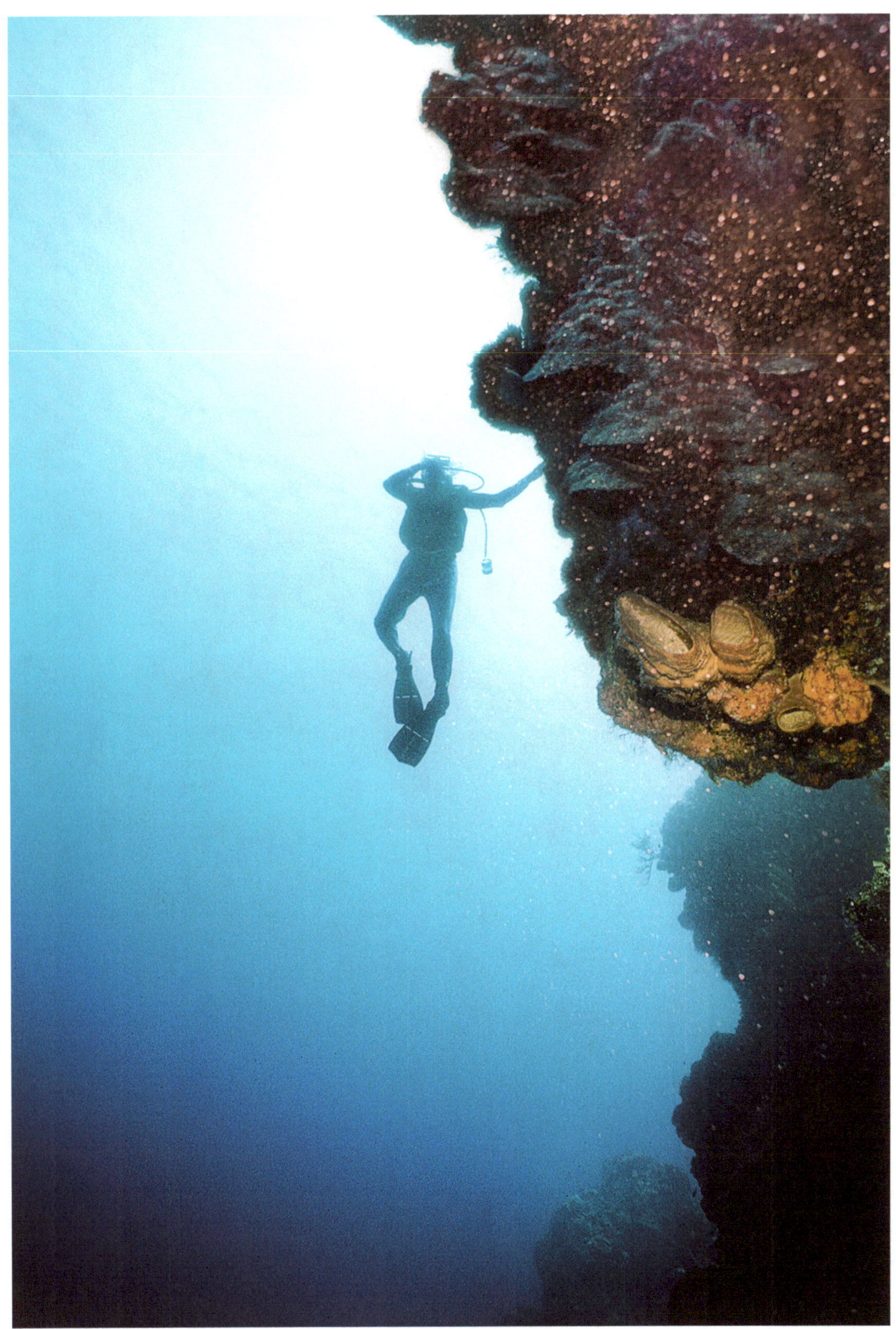

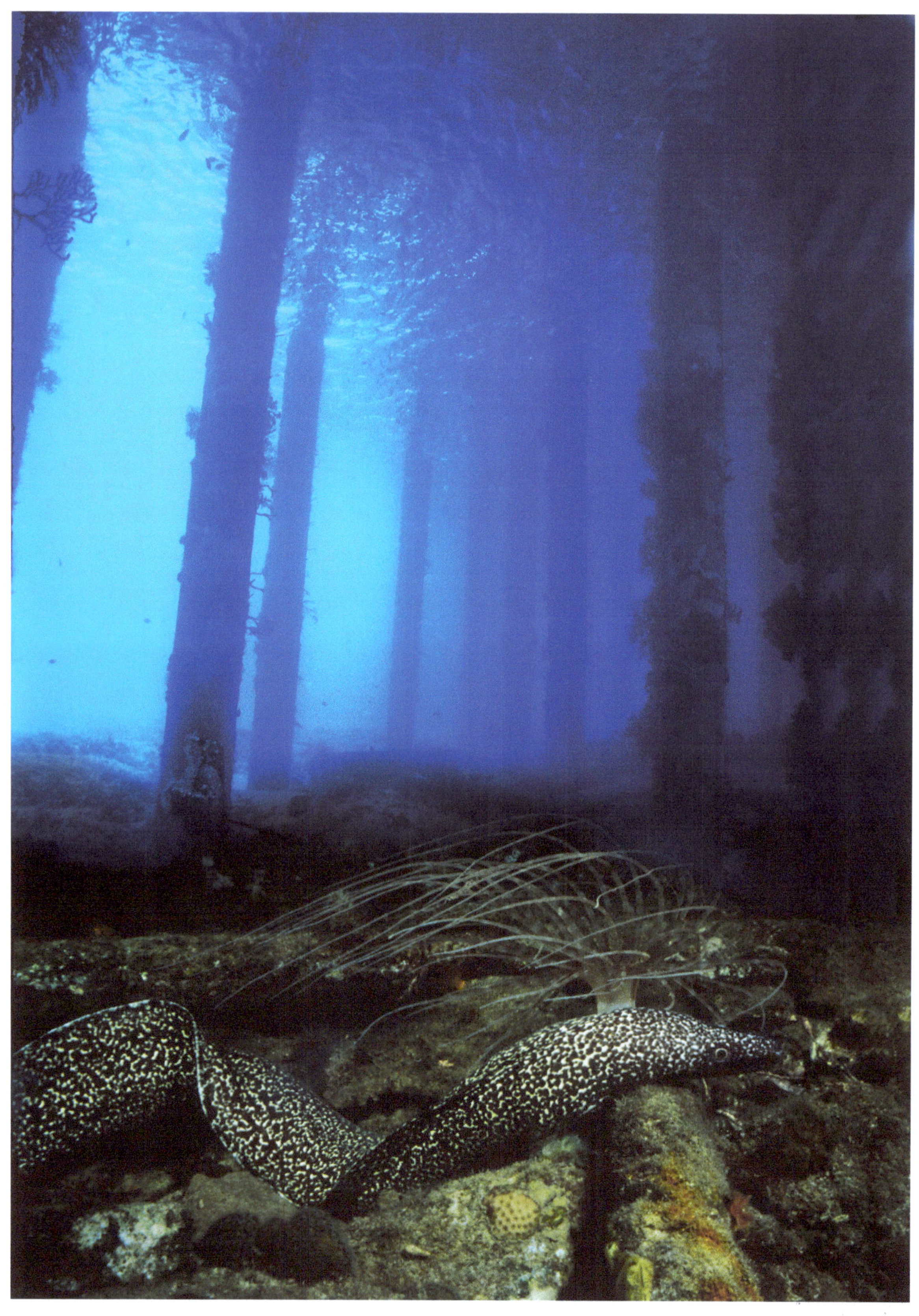

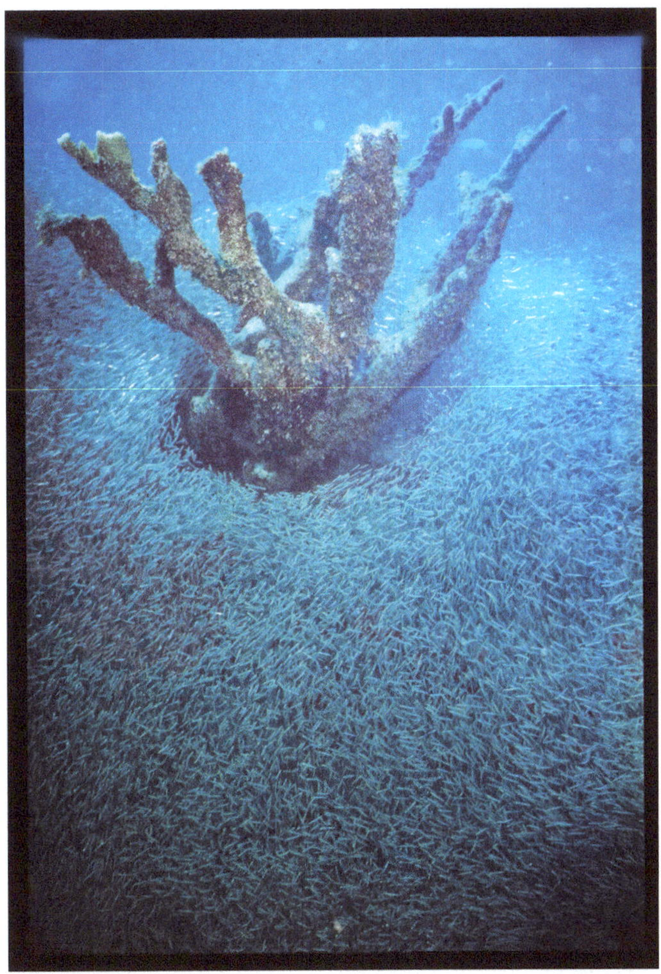

In the Yucatan Peninsula a friend and I dove in cenote's (watery sinkholes in the jungle), one of which led to a cave system that had stalagmites, and stalactites, left over from the last ice age.

Near Akumal, we witnessed an underwater phenomenon, a sardine swarm, feeding on plankton, that attracted sardine predators, that attracted the predators' predators, etc., etc., until the pelagic fish came in. It was a feeding frenzy from the bottom to somewhere around the middle of the food chain.

The ocean floor under the International Pier in Cozumel, Mexico is littered with debris. Eels take up residence in old tires, and sea anemones use piles of discarded rope and chain as a foundation on which to spread their tentacles, and snatch the living morsels that float through the currents. Octopi live in oil drums, and even the pylons that support the pier are covered with multi colored sponges and corals.

When the sun sets and the nocturnals emerge, the place really comes alive. Even the vertical pier supports seem to move as the polyps stretch out and sway in the currents.

The Galapagos archipelago is scattered along the equator in the Pacific Ocean, about 600 miles off the coast of Ecuador. The islands are volcanic, and although some of the older ones have disappeared below the ocean, newer islands are still being formed.

The terrain is dramatic and strange, both above and below the water surface, and provides an ideal backdrop for an equally odd array of wildlife. There are marine iguanas, and giant tortoise, penguins, albatross, blue-footed boobies, flightless cormorants, and about a zillion sharks. Sea lions are as playful as puppies.

The trip is difficult and expensive, and access to the area is restricted due to ecological sensitivity. It is a UNESCO world heritage site, unique enough to give Charles Darwin some special insight for his theory of evolution. Any place that strange and special is worth the extra effort.

In 1993 I joined a scuba tour on a live aboard dive boat for a couple of weeks in the islands. There were about a dozen experienced divers, and since I was swimming solo, I buddied up with a professional underwater photographer named Charley Waters.

The first thing I noticed about underwater Galapagos was the sharks. We saw a minimum of 20–30 every dive, (mostly hammerheads), and sometimes many more.

The thing I never got used to was the current. When it was advantageous, there was no way to stop other than to grab onto some jagged volcanic rock and when it was going in another direction, it was exhausting. The back and forth action felt like being caught in a washing machine.

There are several major currents that converge in the Galapagos, and the Humboldt is the strongest. Those currents are the reason the area is teeming with life. They carry an abundance of plankton, which attracts plankton eaters like killer whales, as well as smaller fish, which in turn attract larger fish, and so on up the aquatic food chain.

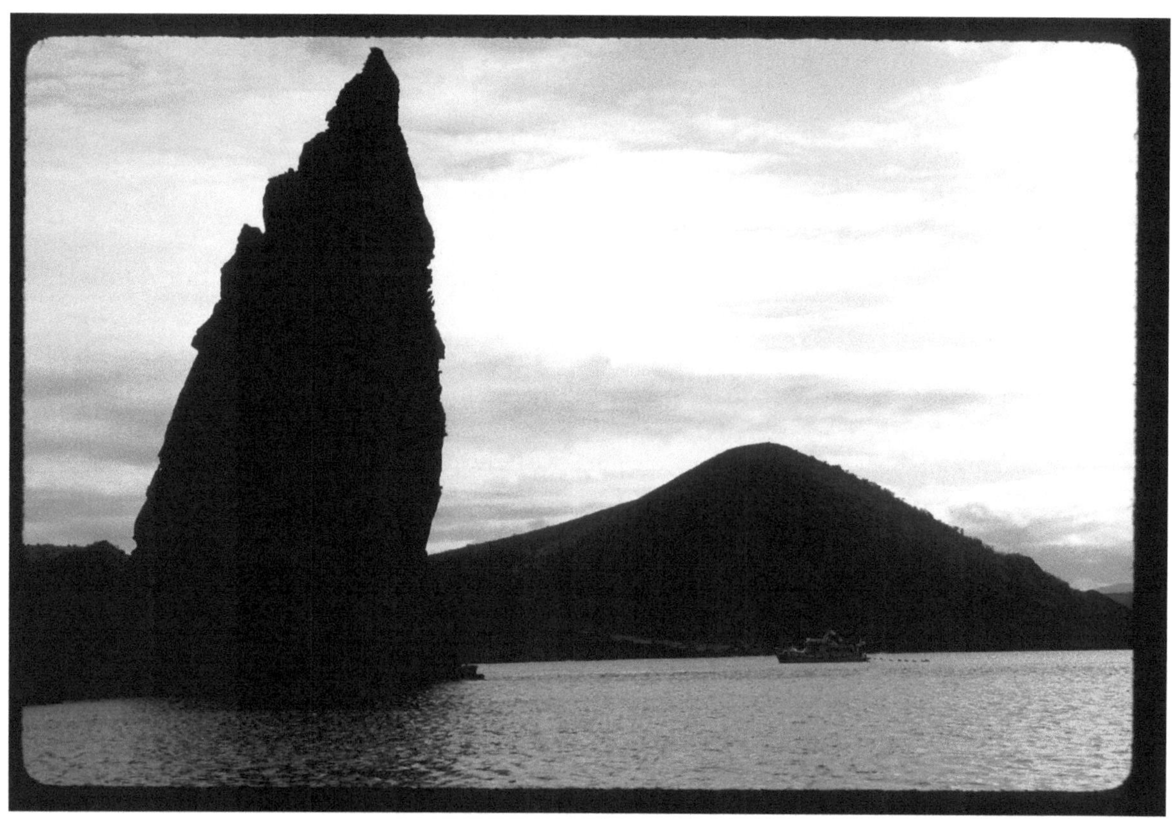

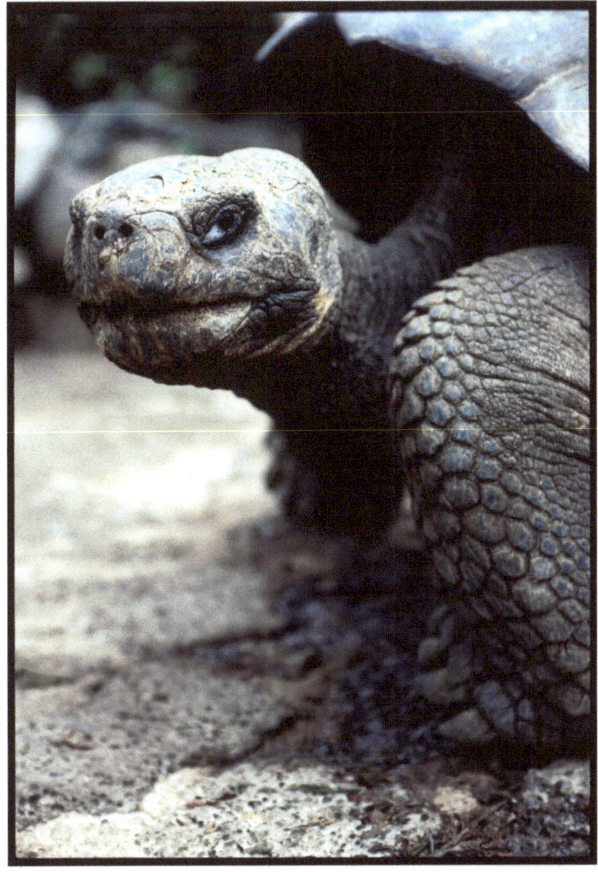

We dove mornings, afternoons, and nights, adjusting our depths and surface times to accommodate the nitrogen buildup in our blood. Pressure, due to depth, compresses nitrogen, and it accumulates in the body, especially with repetitive dives. It takes a while on the surface, or at least within thirty-three feet of sea level, to dissipate.

After a particularly grueling afternoon dive, most everybody decided to rest for the night excursion. Charley and I got one of the crew to take us in the dinghy to an island that was visible from where our mother boat was anchored.

Up close, the island resembled a giant white cake, about two stories high. The icing was birdshit that covered the top and dripped down the sides. Birds squawked at us from above.

Our plan was to dive the shallow side of the island, staying within one atmosphere, or thirty-three feet, so as not to add more nitrogen build up and jeopardize our chances of joining the night dive.

We eased over the side of the boat, and kicked once to get underwater, and I immediately felt the current pulling me away from the island. That was OK, but there was another sensation of downward pull, so I punched my B.C. button to shoot a blast of air into my buoyancy control vest. It barely slowed my descent, so I gave the vest another shot of air. I was over thirty feet down and still descending, so I filled my vest until the purge valve began releasing air on its own, a sign that the vest was fully inflated.

I was traveling down a volcano shaped slope. There was a rock out-cropping, and I grabbed for it and missed. Then the bottom dropped from under me as I slid over the edge of a cliff. The bottom was no longer visible underneath, and the surface seemed far above. I began kicking as hard as I could, and began to make headway, then just as fast as it began, the downward pull ceased, and my buoyancy stabilized, even though I was still being pulled outward so fast that my snorkel was fluttering against my face.

I started for the surface, then had a cautionary thought, and checked my depth gauge. 95 feet, not counting the distance I had risen in the last few seconds. Rushing to the surface would reduce the pressure on my body too quickly, causing dissolved nitrogen to enlarge, and form bubbles in my blood and body tissues. That causes the bends, which can result in paralysis, or worse, depending on where the bubbles are in the body when they expand.

Charley floated up in front of me. It was the first time I had seen him since we entered the water, about five minutes earlier.

I looked at Charley and pointed to my depth gauge. He looked past me and made a sweeping motion with his hand. That was the first time I noticed all the sharks. There were, at the very least, hundreds of hammerheads, maybe thousands. There was a wall of them that stretched from somewhere near the surface to somewhere below our position. They were curving around us, keeping their distance, but close enough to see the distinctive shape of their heads.

We watched them slide by, moving about twice as fast as we were, even though we were all in the same current. Then they were gone. Charley and I paced our ascent in accordance with his dive calculator.

When we surfaced, the island was a speck, barely visible between waves. I had the panic attack I had avoided underwater, and grabbed the plastic whistle hanging from my vest, blowing two long, shrill tweets. Charley looked at me like he was afraid he might have another problem to deal with, but I recovered quickly. "You see how far away we are?"

"Yeah. You see those sharks?"

"Yeah. Now what?"

We were much farther from the island than our fellow divers back at the boat, and still drifting. Swimming steadily toward the island helped us maintain our position, but it quickly became obvious that we would have to pace ourselves. Then the speck of land disappeared.

We dropped our weight belts and discussed doing the same with our camera gear, and swimming as hard as we could in the direction of the island, then decided there was no way we could make it. We decided to wait awhile before discarding the camera gear.

Our only hope was for someone to spot us, but there were only two dive boats in the area, one of which was ours. We had not seen an airplane since our arrival.

Charley remembered the rescue balloons that had been issued to all the divers at our first day orientation. When inflated, the bright yellow balloons form a four-foot cylinder that can be held aloft in case a spotter plane is in the area. We used our regulators to inflate the balloons, rolled onto our backs, and began steadily kicking in the direction of the island.

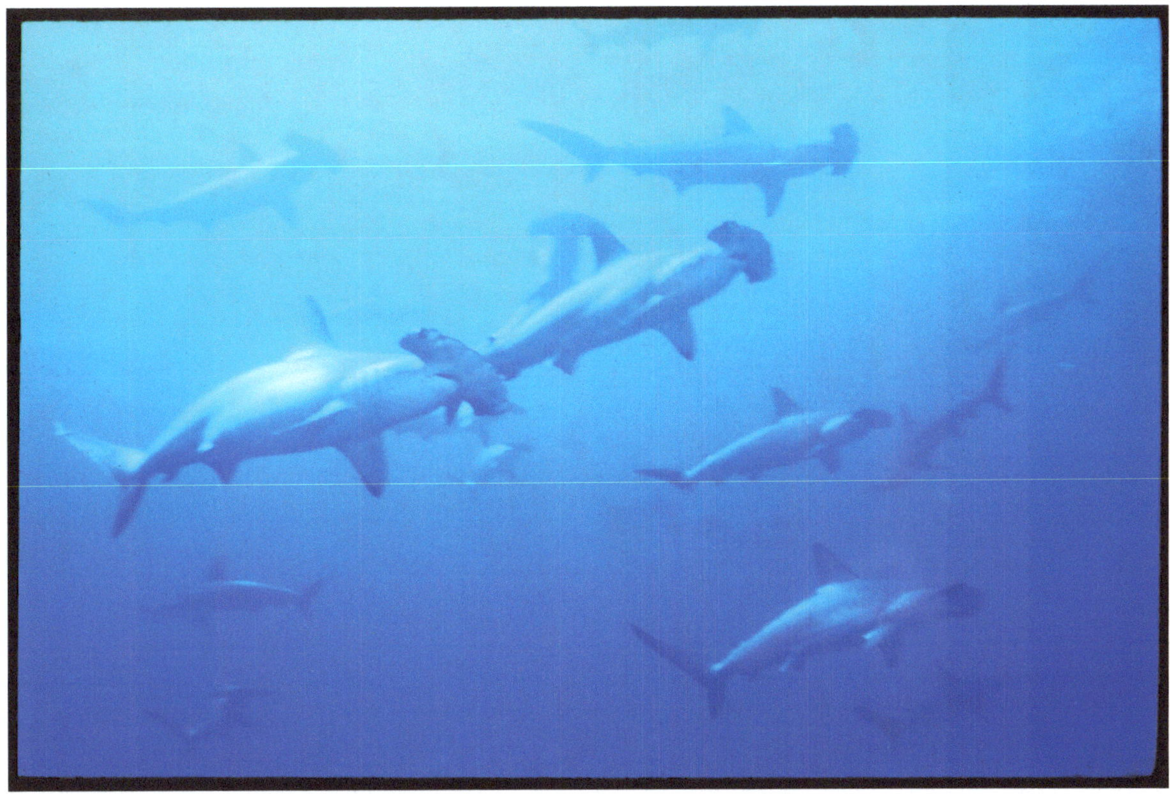

My greatest fear was breaking a fin strap, or getting a leg cramp. Either of those tragedies would leave me at the mercy of the current, and separate me from Charley. Being lost with somebody else is psychologically better than being lost alone, especially if the other person has a more positive attitude than you. Under different circumstances I probably would have laughed when he noticed my balloon deflating and told me not to go all flaccid on him.

After about an hour the equatorial sun began to fry our heads. We tried to protect ourselves by holding the balloons directly overhead, but then the sea birds discovered us. There were just a few at first, and every once in a while one would swoop down and try to land, and we would yell and shoo them away for fear they would bust our balloons.

In a very short time there were twenty or thirty birds hovering above us. Then it seemed like there were a hundred or more, flying in a circle over our heads, swooping in to land and then rejoining the flock when we waved our arms and shouted them away.

The birds ended up being our saviors. When our zodiac driver returned to the boat and reported us missing, another rescue boat was deployed, and a sharp eyed crewman on that boat saw what looked like a shadow above the horizon. They were half way to our position before anyone else on the boat could see what he was pointing at, and farther still before the shadow began to resemble a flock of birds. We had drifted so far out of the search area that had it not been for the birds and the sharp-eyed crewman, Charley and I would have become another diving statistic.

When I got back to Texas, I did the research I should have done before the trip. Other scuba divers have reported downward currents, and massive shark migrations have been documented. There have been a number of scuba divers swept away in the Galapagos currents. The unique environment deserves more respect than some of us realize.

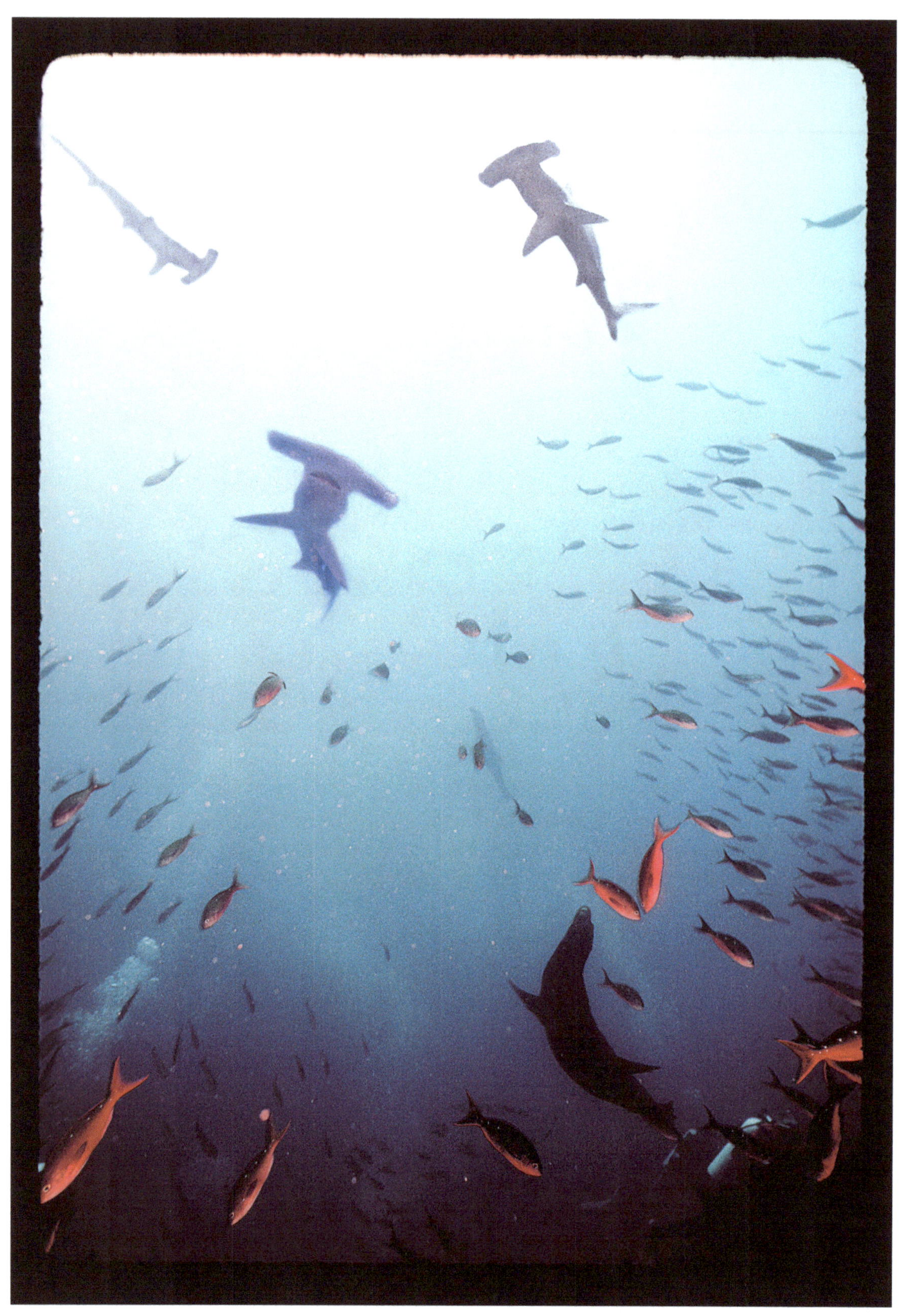

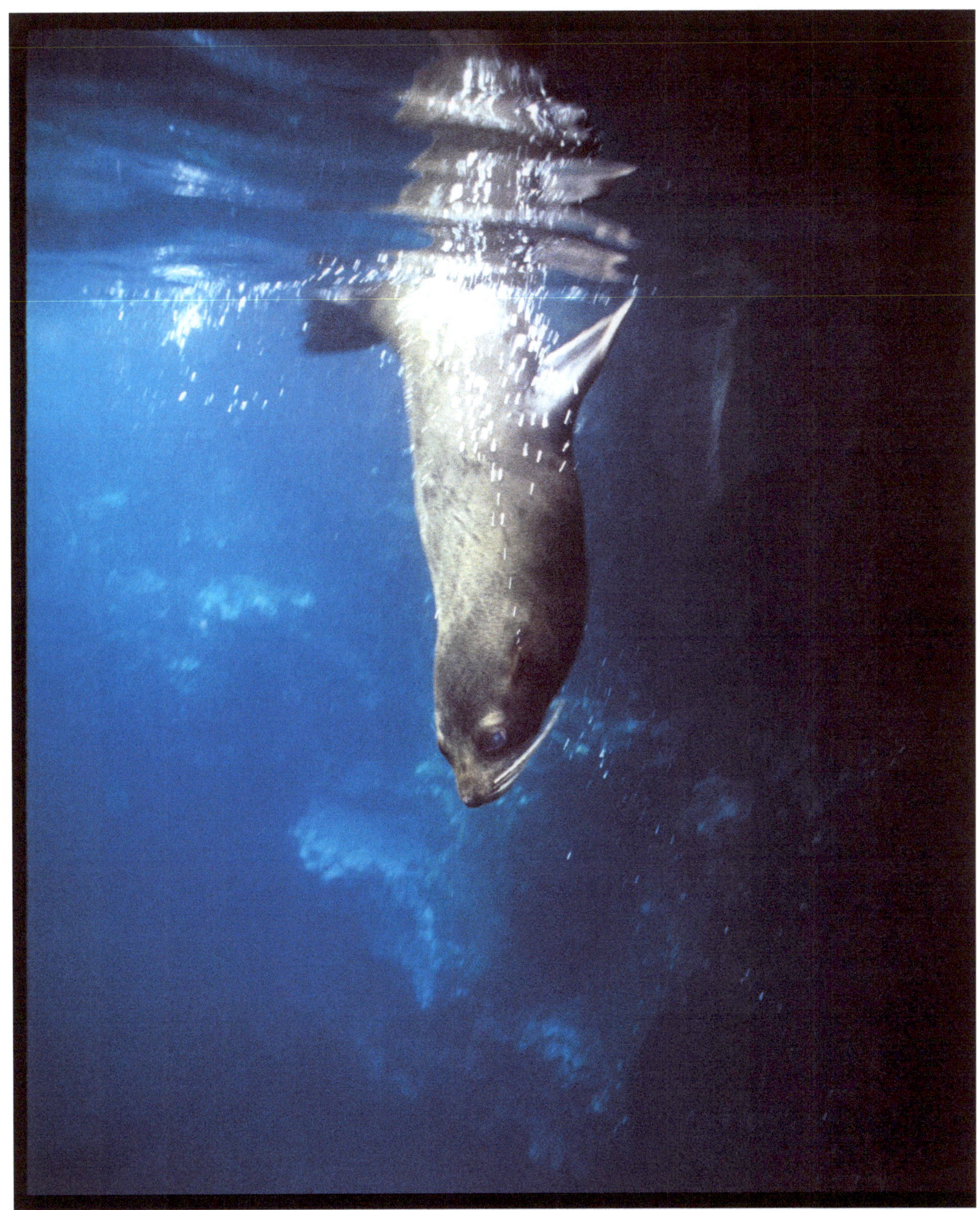

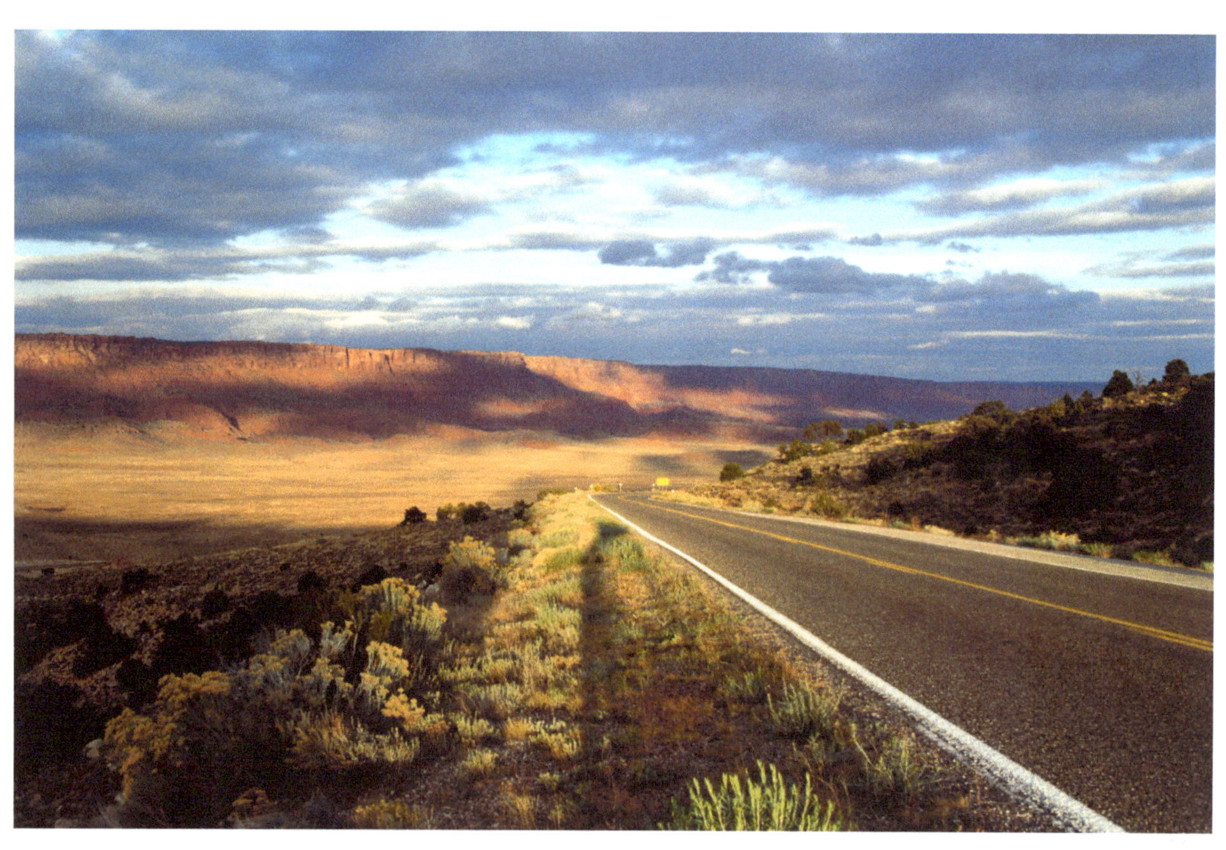

Travel becomes a strategy for accumulating photographs.
—Susan Sontag

LIFE IS CONSTANT

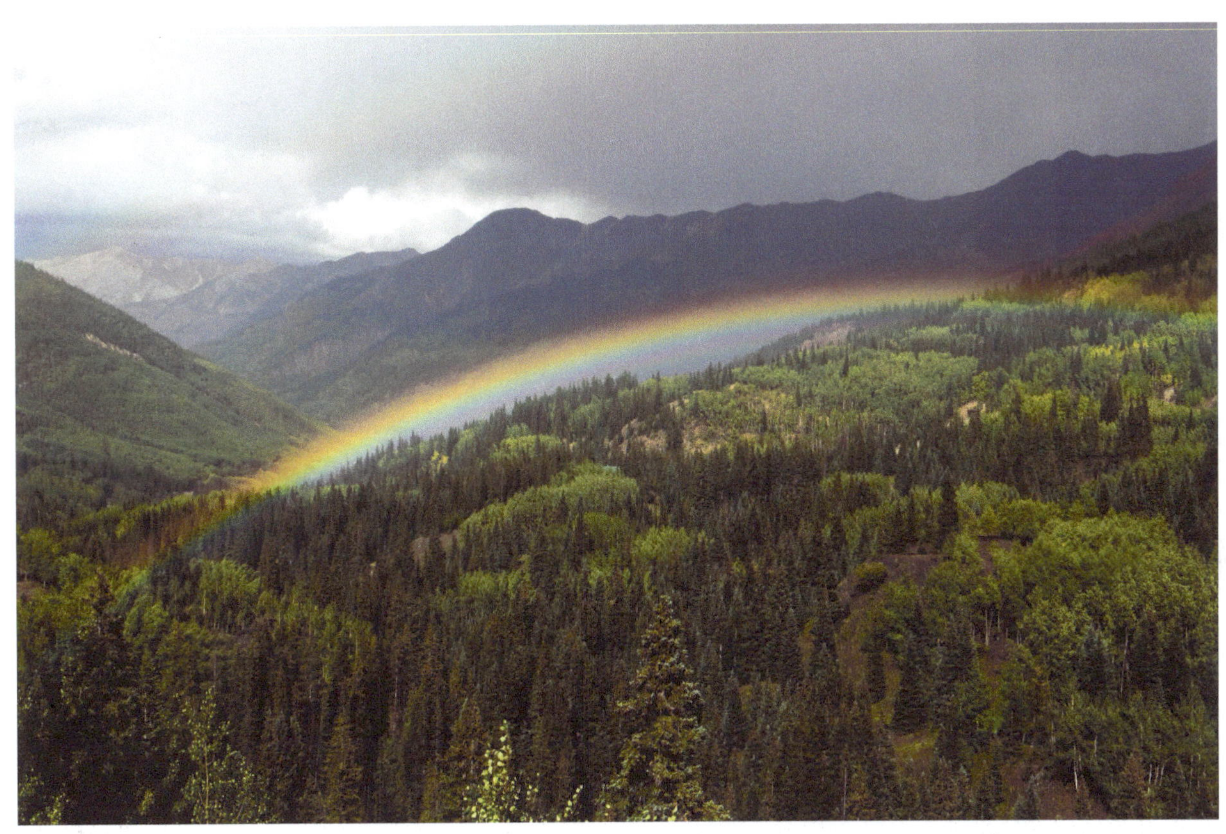

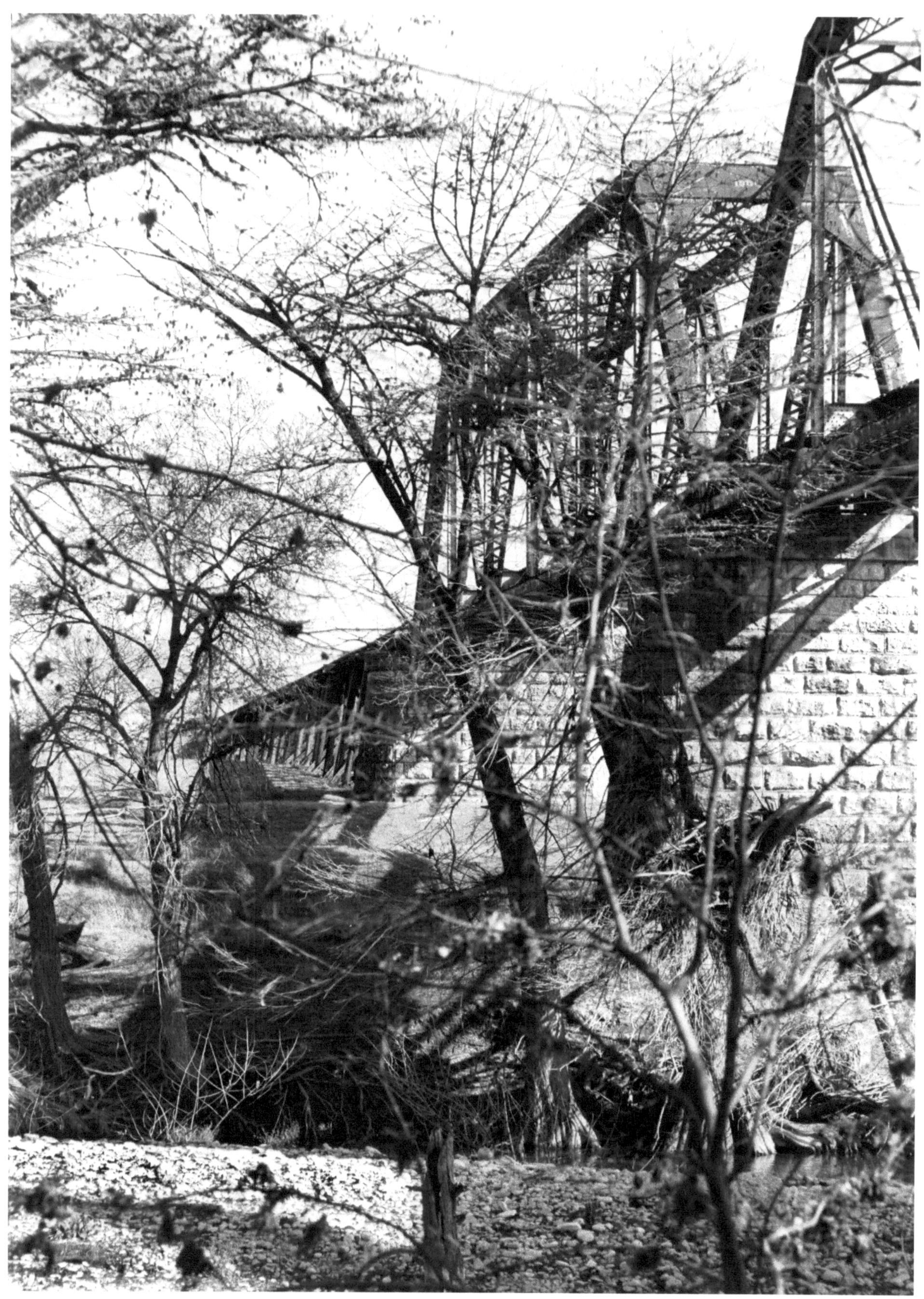

Life is what happens while you are busy making other plans.

—John Lennon

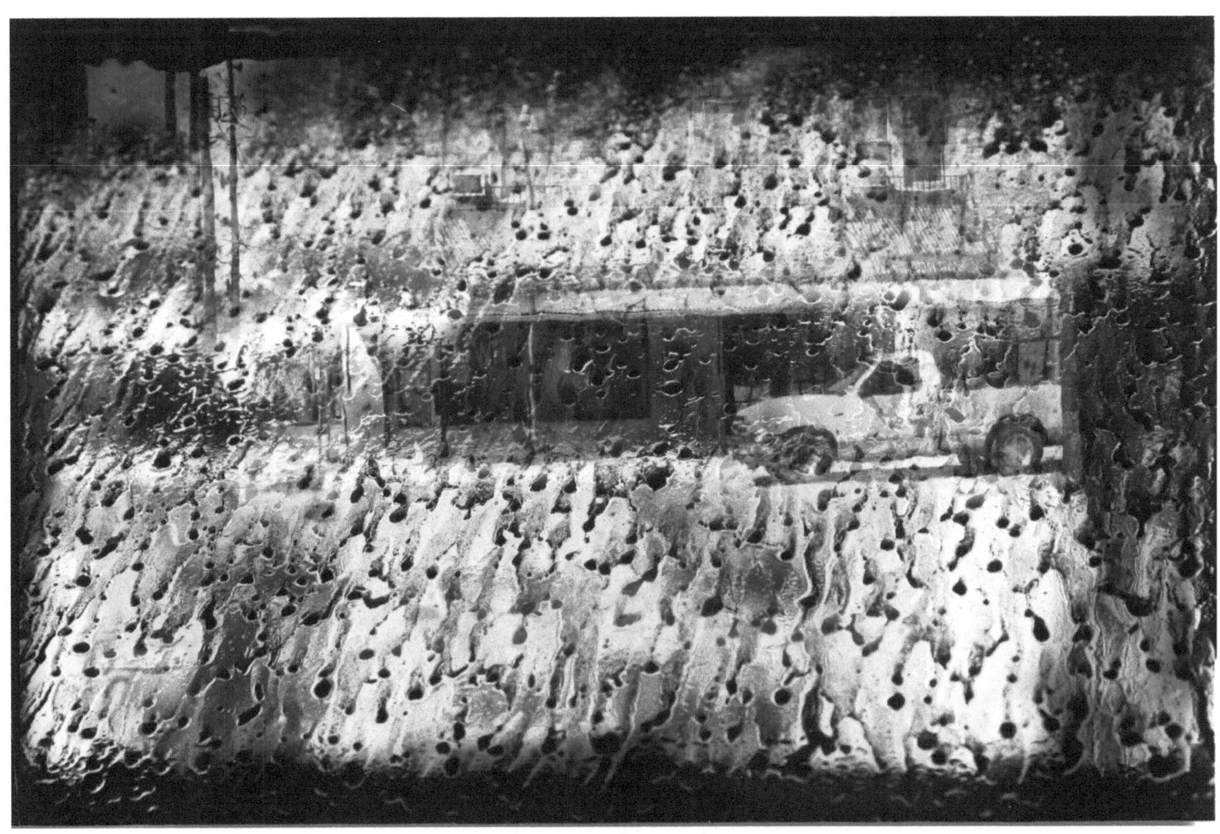

Luling, Texas – summertime, 2010

Beth and I were sitting in our car in the Luling car wash, watching soap suds slide down the front windshield. The street scene outside was distorted, and the blurry image of a truck rolled into our vision.

"Those suds are like our life spans", I said, "slowly sliding to a conclusion somewhere down around the windshield wipers. And that truck represents the thing we choose to do with our lives. You want to stagnate somewhere in the middle, or do you want to see what is on the other side? Adventure waits, and we should go there."

Whatever Beth said after that probably made more sense than my analogy, and in any case a blast of fresh water washed the suds away. The truck was gone too, but the idea was still there, because later that evening she brought the subject up again.

"It isn't like we never go anywhere. How about all those trips with Pat and June."

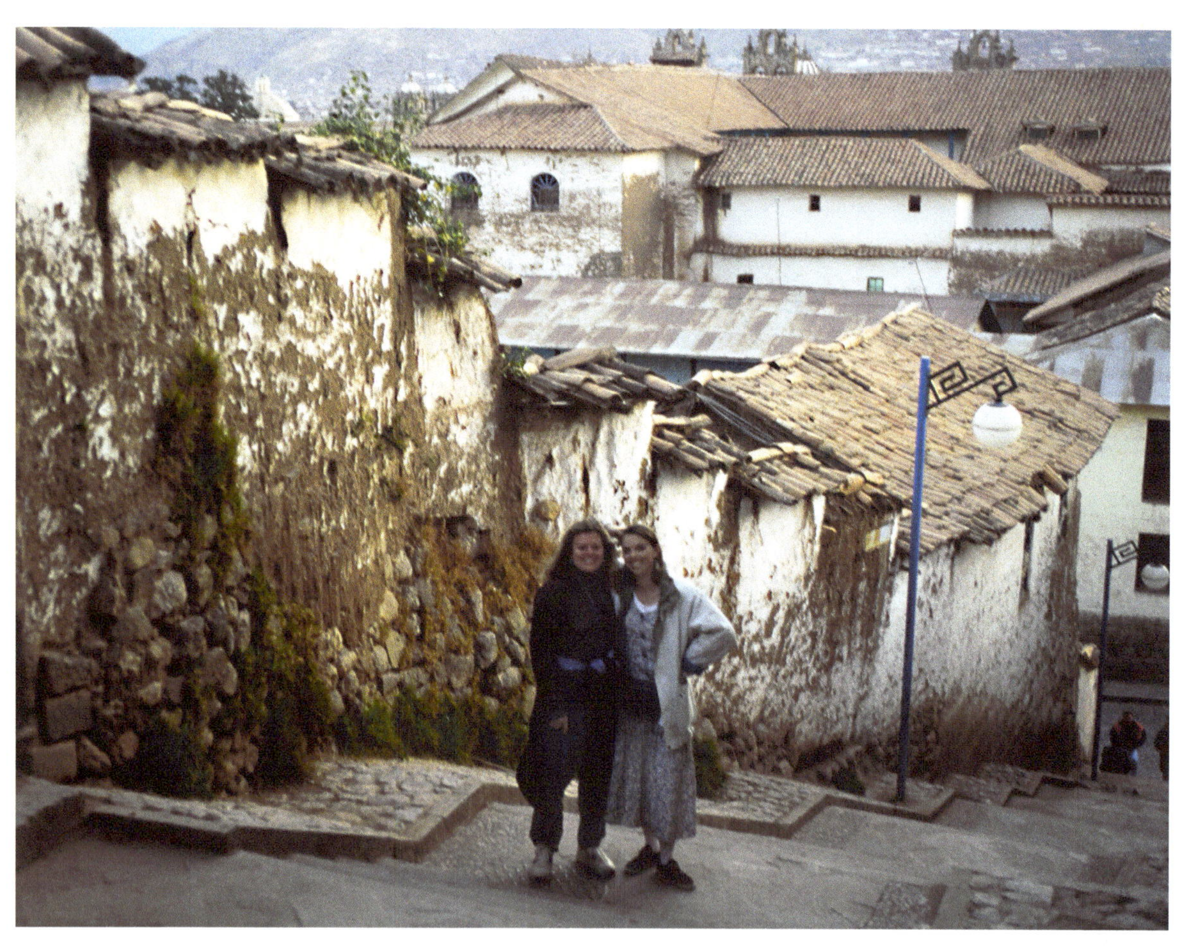

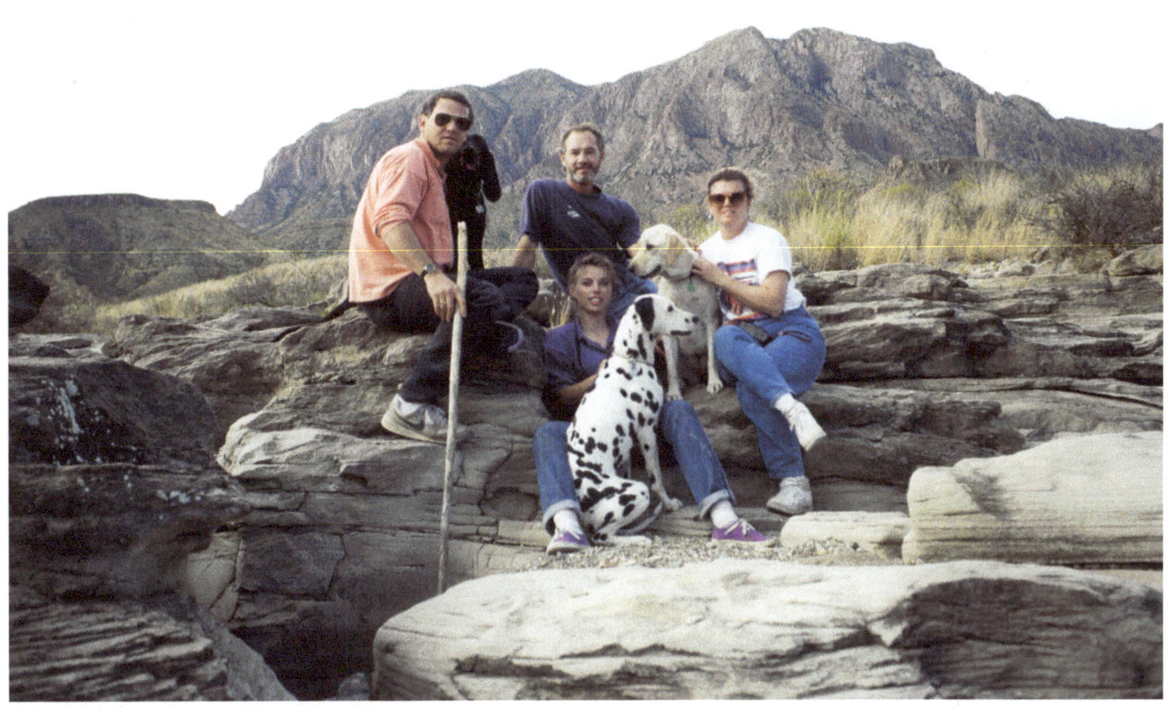

There was a guy who lived down the street from me in Denver, Colorado who became a traveling companion long before I met Beth. He is the guy with the duck on his shoulder, about twenty pages ago. Our fathers were in the Air Force, so both of us had lived in about half a dozen places by the time we were teenagers. Pat's family moved to Colorado from Puerto Rico. My family had lived in Okinawa for several years. Our early travel experiences probably had something to do with the wanderlust we developed later in life.

Pat and I took a lot of road trips together, before I moved to Texas and got married. I have pictures of Pat from some of the road trips Beth and I went on. He is also in most of our Christmas pictures.

Then Pat married June, and they began to travel the way I always thought Beth and I would. June's job as a computer programmer for United Airlines provided them with ultra cheap tickets to exotic locations. They usually asked us to join them, but our vacation allotments, and travel allowances kept us closer to home.

Now, even though we live a thousand miles apart, and do most of our traveling separately, the four of us still occasionally meet in some part of the world we have never seen.

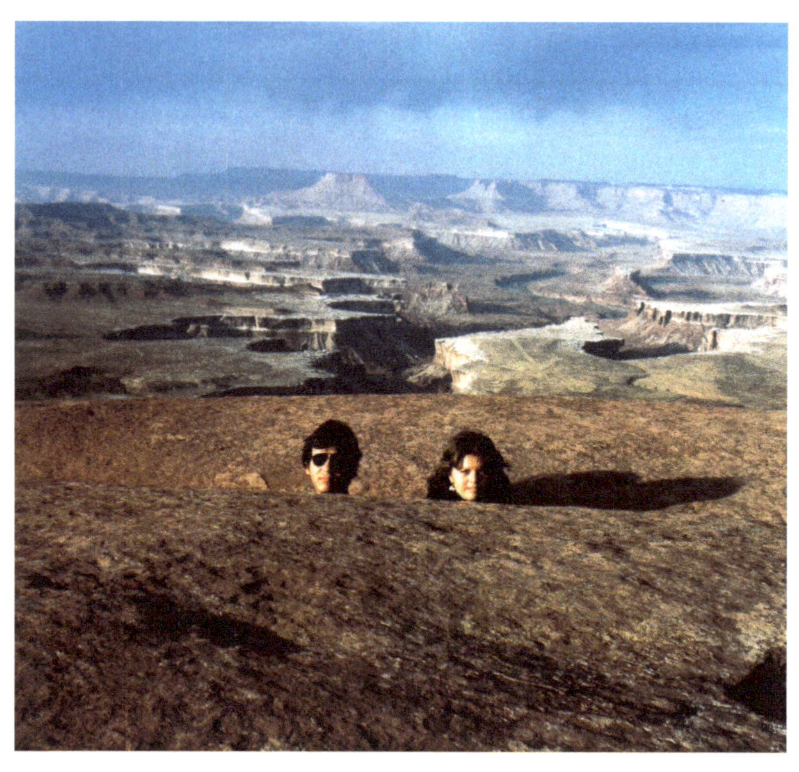

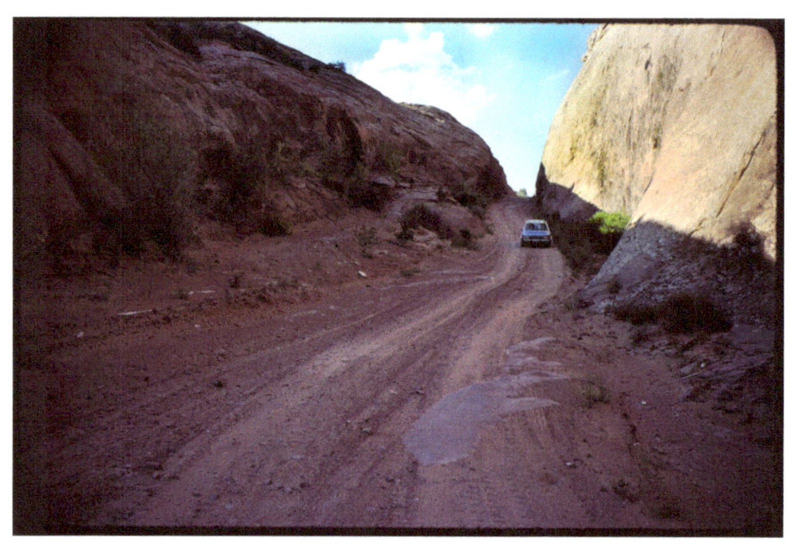

Denver, Colorado – September, 1979

Beth and I rented a small economy car at the Denver International Airport. We picked Pat up and the three of us headed for Moab, Utah. Pat supposedly knew the area like the back of his hand. We took our time, hiked the canyons, and camped along the way.

Two days later – mid morning.

About thirty miles from the turnoff to Moab, Pat led us down a gravel road that intersected with a poorly maintained dirt road that he was pretty sure eventually led to Moab.

As luck would have it, there was a man on a backhoe grading the gravel road. Pat and I got out of the car and asked if the dirt road led to Moab. His gaze shifted from us to our economy car and back. "Well, I never been that way myself, but some say it does, and some say it don't."

We decided to chance it, and headed down the road that quickly became more of a trail that led down an embankment before turning into a footpath and disappearing altogether.

Looking back the way we came, we all realized there was no way our car could negotiate the embankment from the opposite direction. "We can hike back to the road and pay that man to pull us out," Beth suggested.

"Or we can make it to that next rise," countered Pat. From there it's downhill to Moab.

That part of Utah is sparsely forested, and for the most part the terrain is smooth sandstone, laced with dramatic surprises. It looked doable.

For the next four hours, Pat and I rolled rocks and generally cleared a path as Beth inched the car along behind us.

Pat and I argued about splitting the cost of the car, and Pat decided the worst-case scenario would require dismantling the vehicle, and hauling it out in pieces. "I have a job, Pat. I'm here on a one week vacation."

We did make it to the next rise by dusk, and although Moab was not as close as we had hoped, we could see it's lights twinkling on the far side of a ravine that looked too steep for our car to negotiate.

"This car is going to be one of those rusting hulks that you see outside small towns like this and wonder how they got there," I said.

"You can't think about that on the way down," Pat said.

The worst part was the last several feet, where our side of the ravine dropped straight down. We piled enough rocks around the bottom to make the transition less severe. The car was still upright when it hit the bottom with enough impact to make the passenger window slam down and never roll up again. We rolled down the dry creek bed until we found an easier way up the other side, and from there it was a slow but uneventful ride into town.

Moab, Utah – after dark.

We came into town through the garbage dump late in the evening. The bar was still open, but the friend we were supposed to meet much earlier was gone.

I mentioned to the bartender that we had entered town through the dump.

"I know that trail", he said. My 4 wheel drive couldn't make it."

"You need a Dodge Horizon," Pat said.

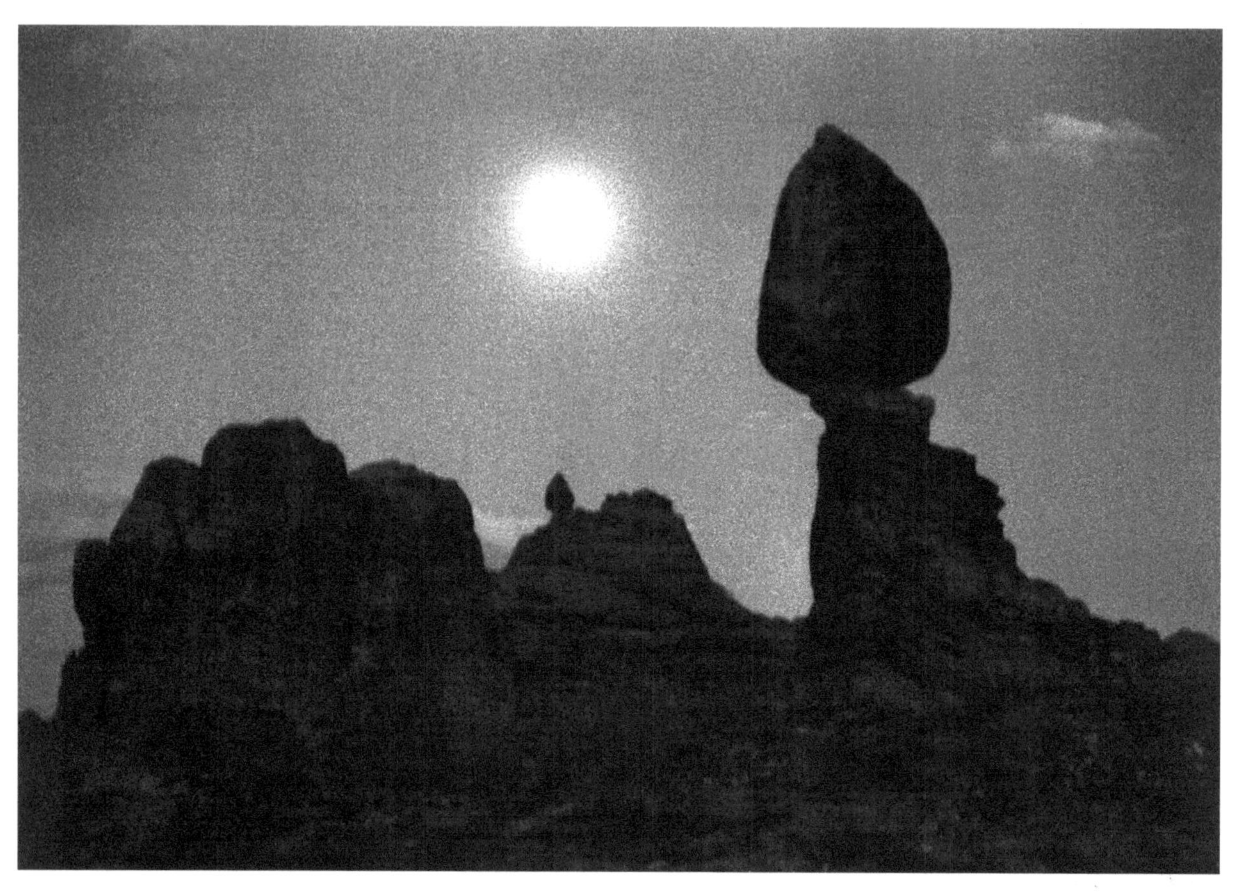

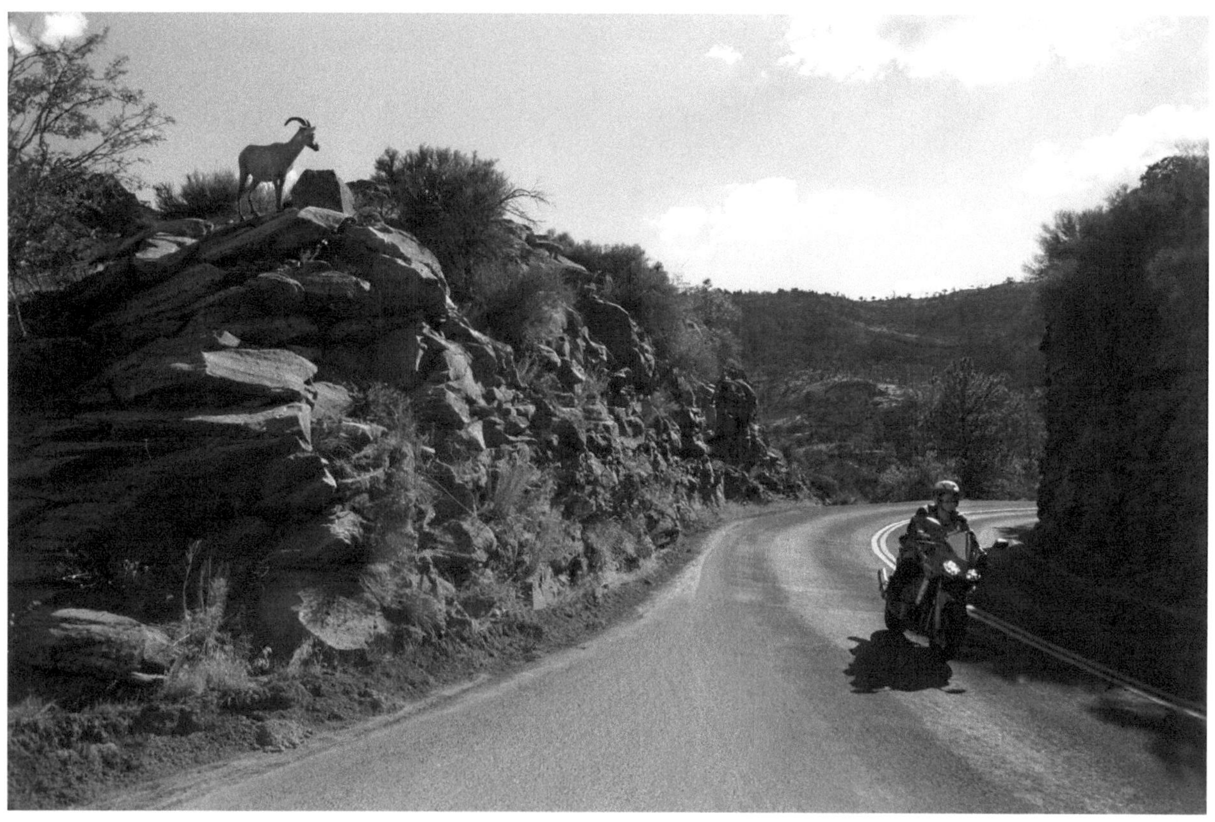

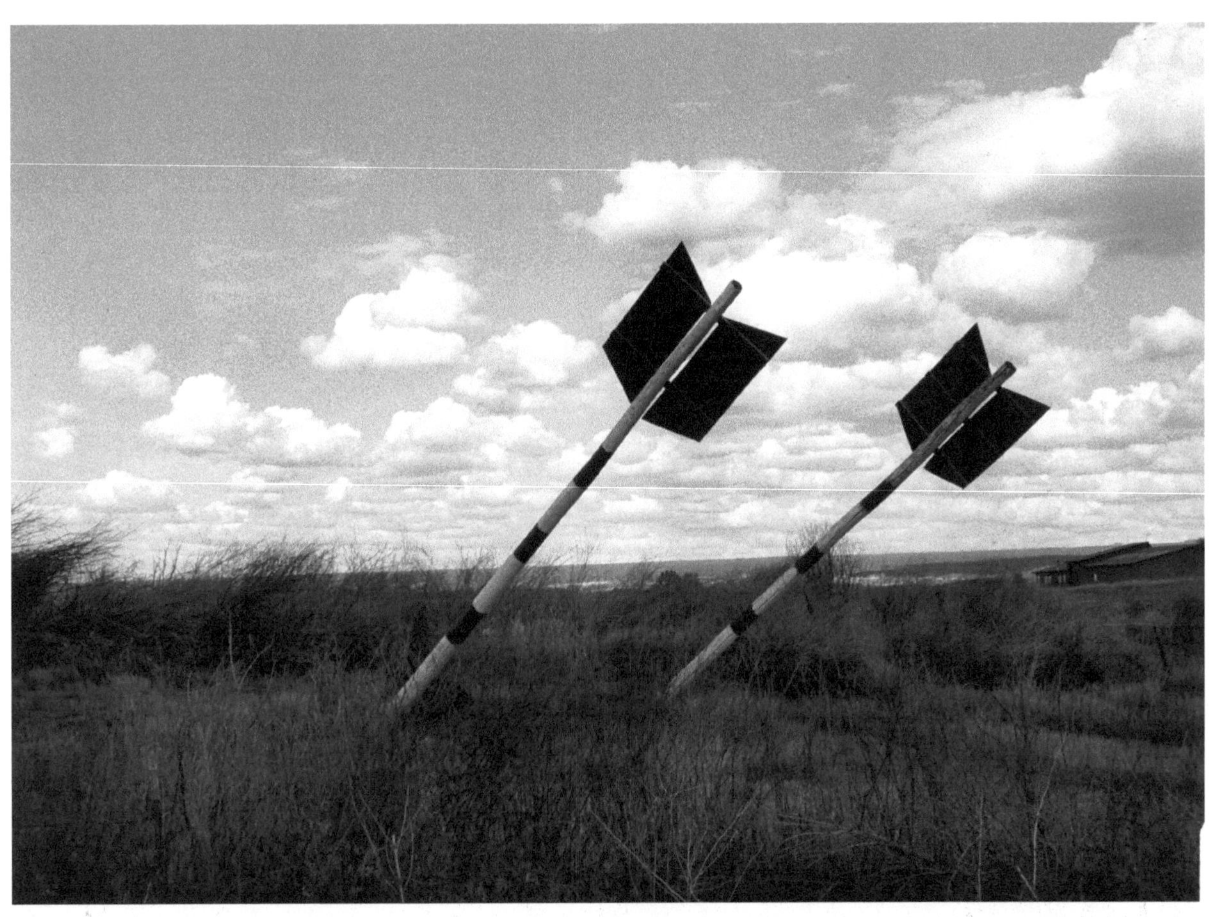

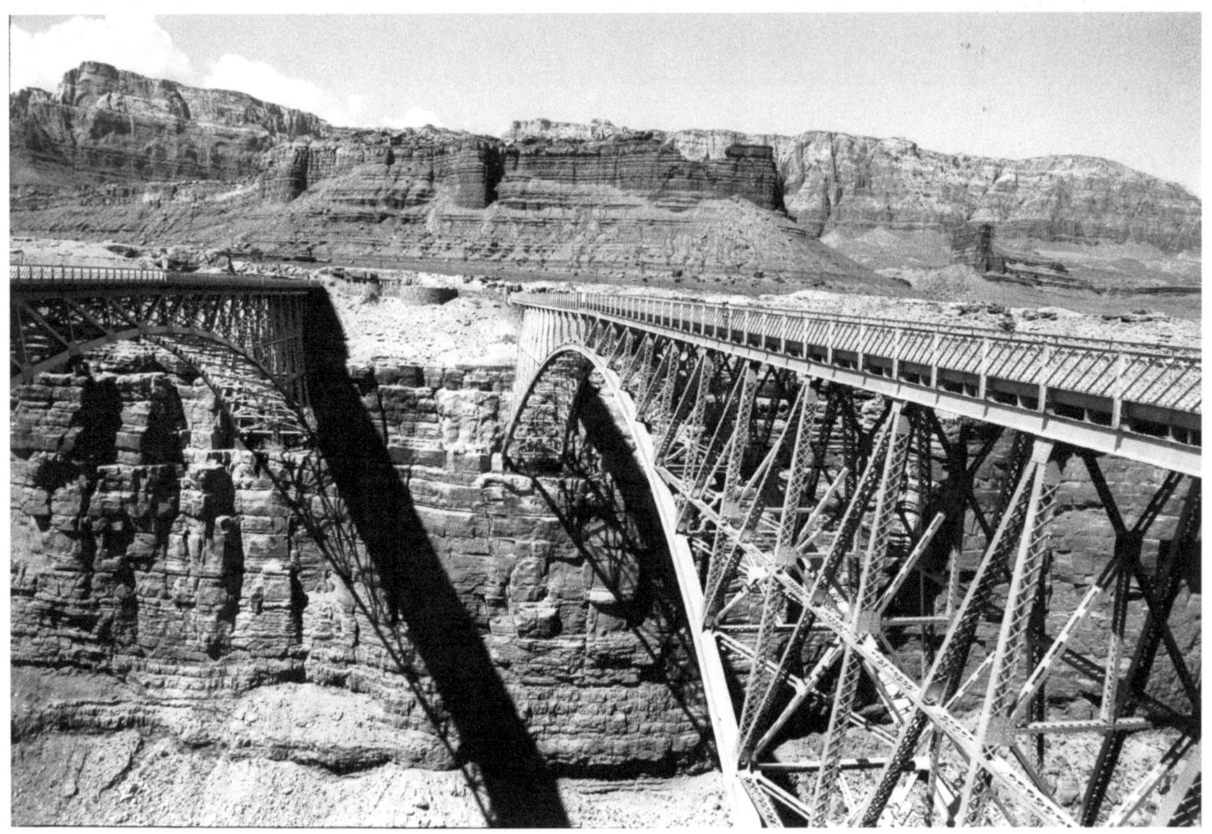

LOCATION

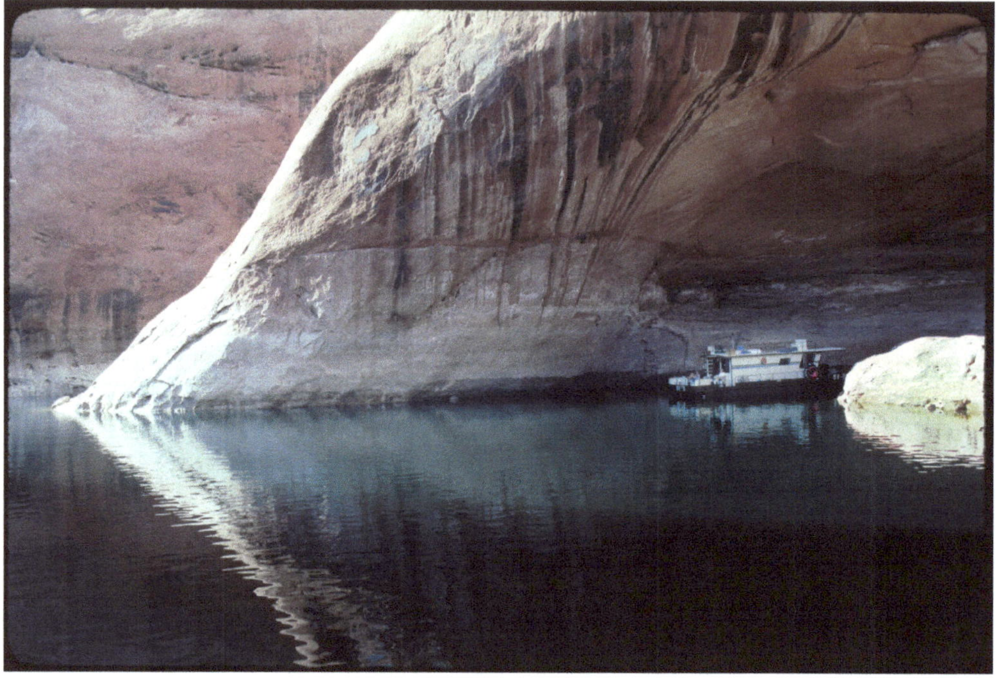

About eleven million years ago the Colorado Plateau rose to its present height. It took the Colorado River another five million years to carve Glen Canyon down to its present day depth. In the more recent part of that history ancient Americans came and went, leaving a few artifacts and some dwellings wedged into the shear rock cliffs.

In 1869 a one-armed civil war veteran named John Wesley Powell led an expedition through the canyon. About a hundred years after that, the Glen Canyon Dam was built, Glen Canyon was flooded, and Lake Powell was created. About twenty years after that, Beth and I met Pat and June at Bullfrog Marina, on the shore of Lake Powell. We rented a houseboat and set course for the Escalante River arm of the lake.

Lake Powell has 1,900 miles of shoreline, which sounds like too much for a 161,000-acre surface area, but looking at a map it is easy to understand the discrepancy. Watery fingers branch off the main channels and then vein off again and again as the water seeks out every gully and dead end canyon that allows its passage. So it is easy to get lost, especially if your map gets blown off the pilot console, along with a brand new pair of prescription sunglasses. Luckily, getting lost for a week was one of our objectives.

Lake Powell was so much fun that we went back a couple of years later, and then again a couple of years after that. We explored a different area each time, and they were all so dramatic in their various formations that I would have a difficult time picking a favorite location.

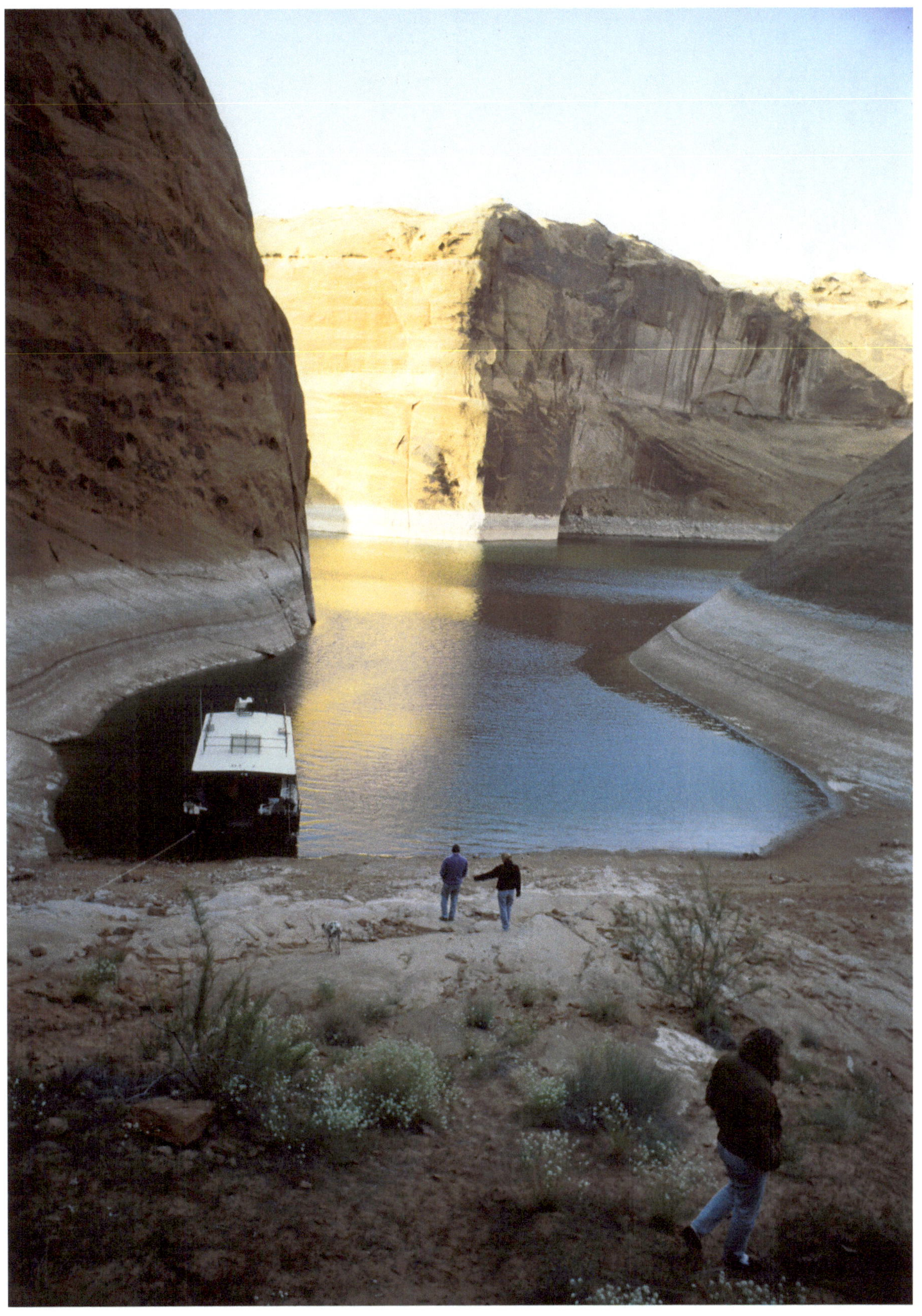

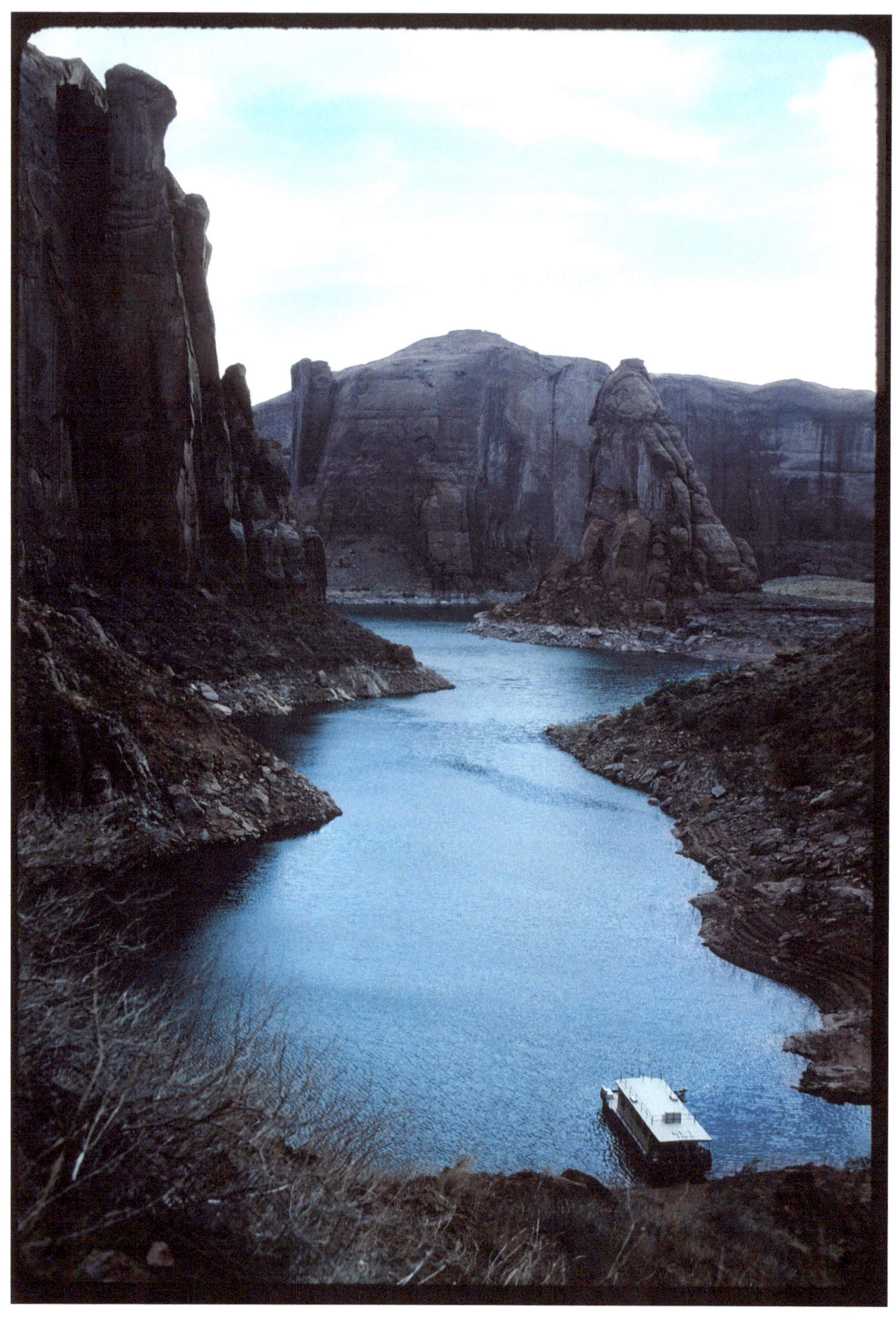

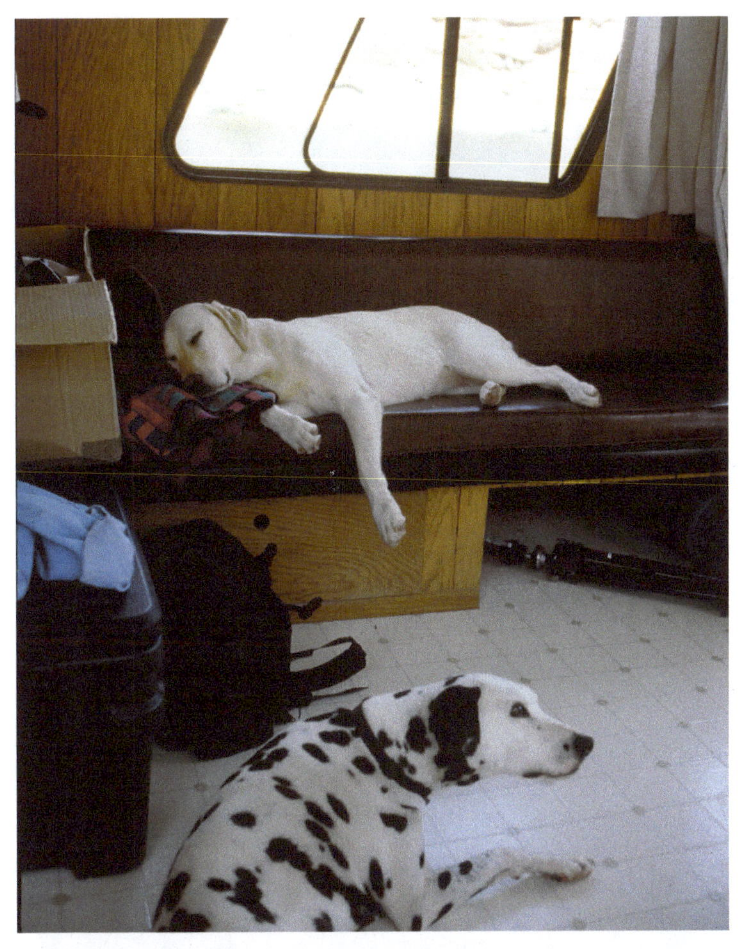

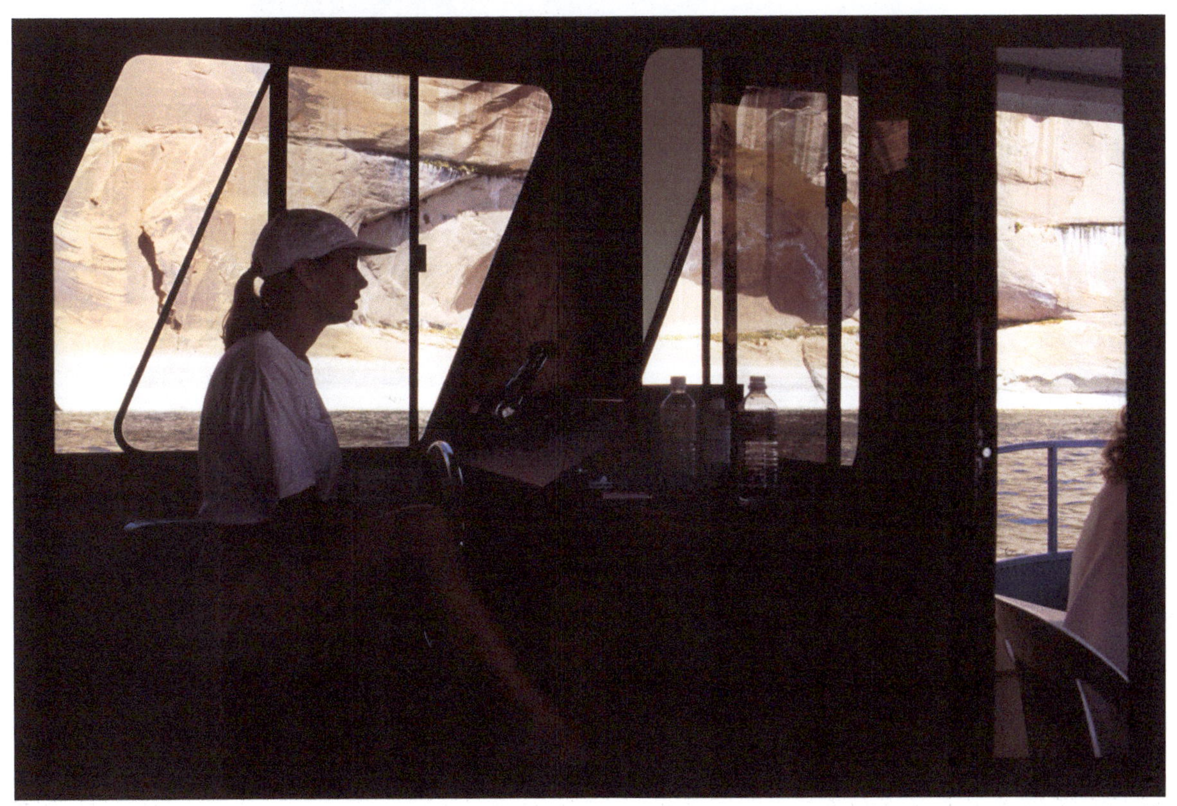

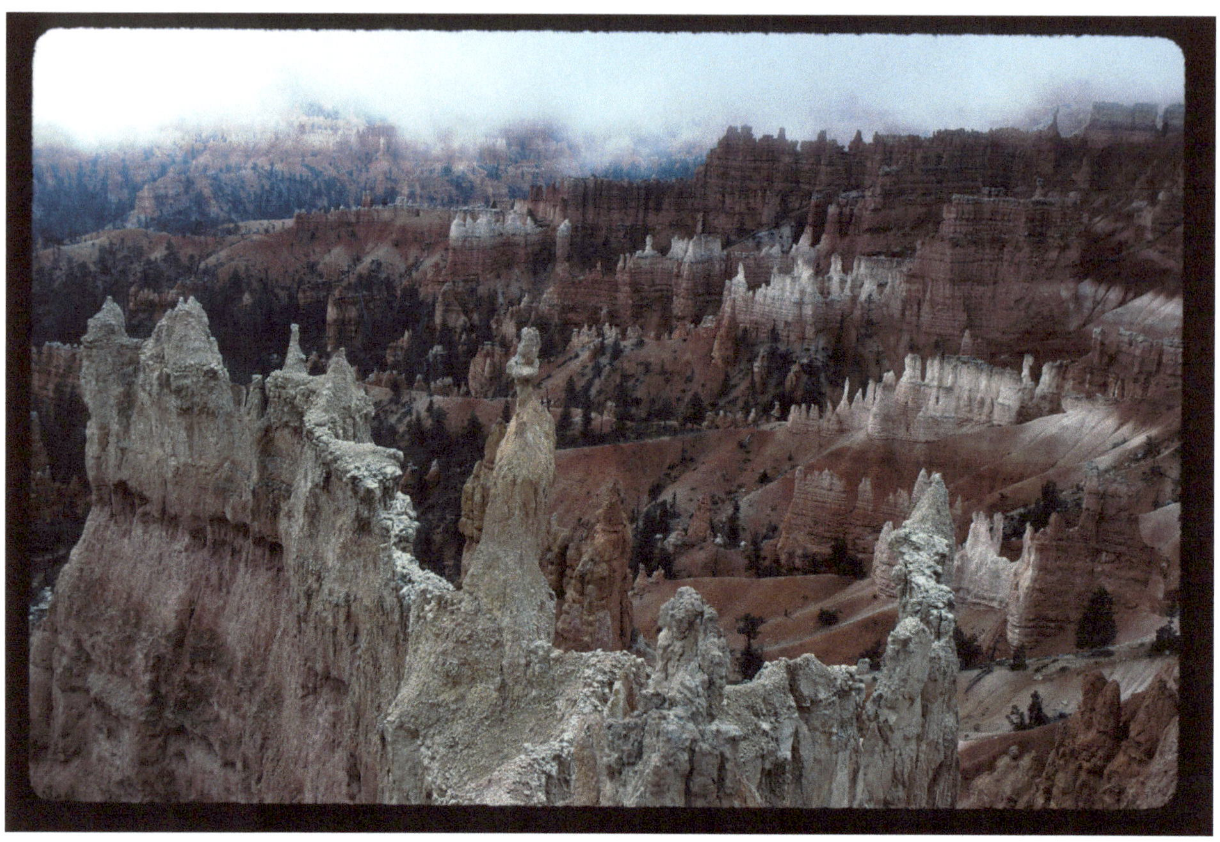

For a place that is not exactly on the way to anywhere, Lake Powell is not far, (by Utah/Arizona standards), from some other out of the way locations.

Antellope Canyon is a slot canyon that was etched out of the limestone topography by water. It is located within the Navajo Nation, near Page, Arizona. The Indian name for the upper portion to the crevice, (which is not printed here because it looks and sounds like a typographical error), translates as "the place where water runs through rocks."

In the mid-90s Pat and June, and Beth and I paid a Navajo guide about five dollars each to show us the entrance to lower Antelope Canyon. He pointed to a slit in the ground, narrow enough to step across, and meandering out of sight in two directions, then returned to his makeshift shady spot near the gated entrance. We climbed down a series of homemade ladders to the sandy bottom.

The walls of the crevice were smooth and undulating, twisting in every direction, and the earthy colors alternated hues, contrast and saturation with every passing cloud. We were underground for about three hours, but the afternoon sun arcing overhead caused the canyon walls to appear to change shape as well as color, like we were wandering through a three dimensional light show.

In 1997, several years after our visit, a thunderstorm occurred seven miles uphill, creating a rush of water that flooded the canyon and washed eleven tourists through the slot and over an embankment at the lower end.

We have not returned to Antelope Canyon, but from what I have heard and read, weather warnings and a secure ladder system have been installed. Tourist fees and attendance have increased dramatically, but the mesmerizing spectacle of the underground light show is as good as it ever was.

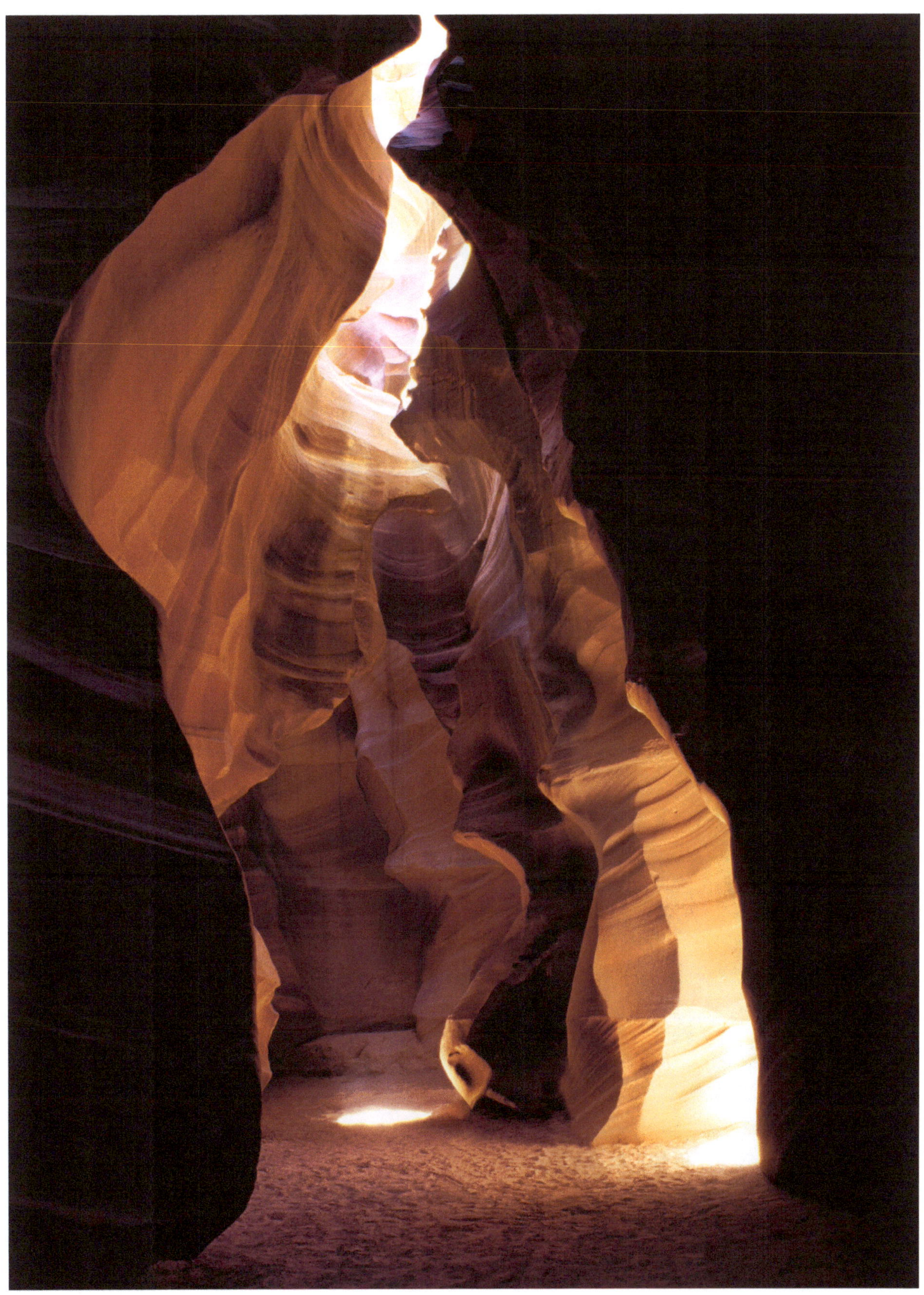

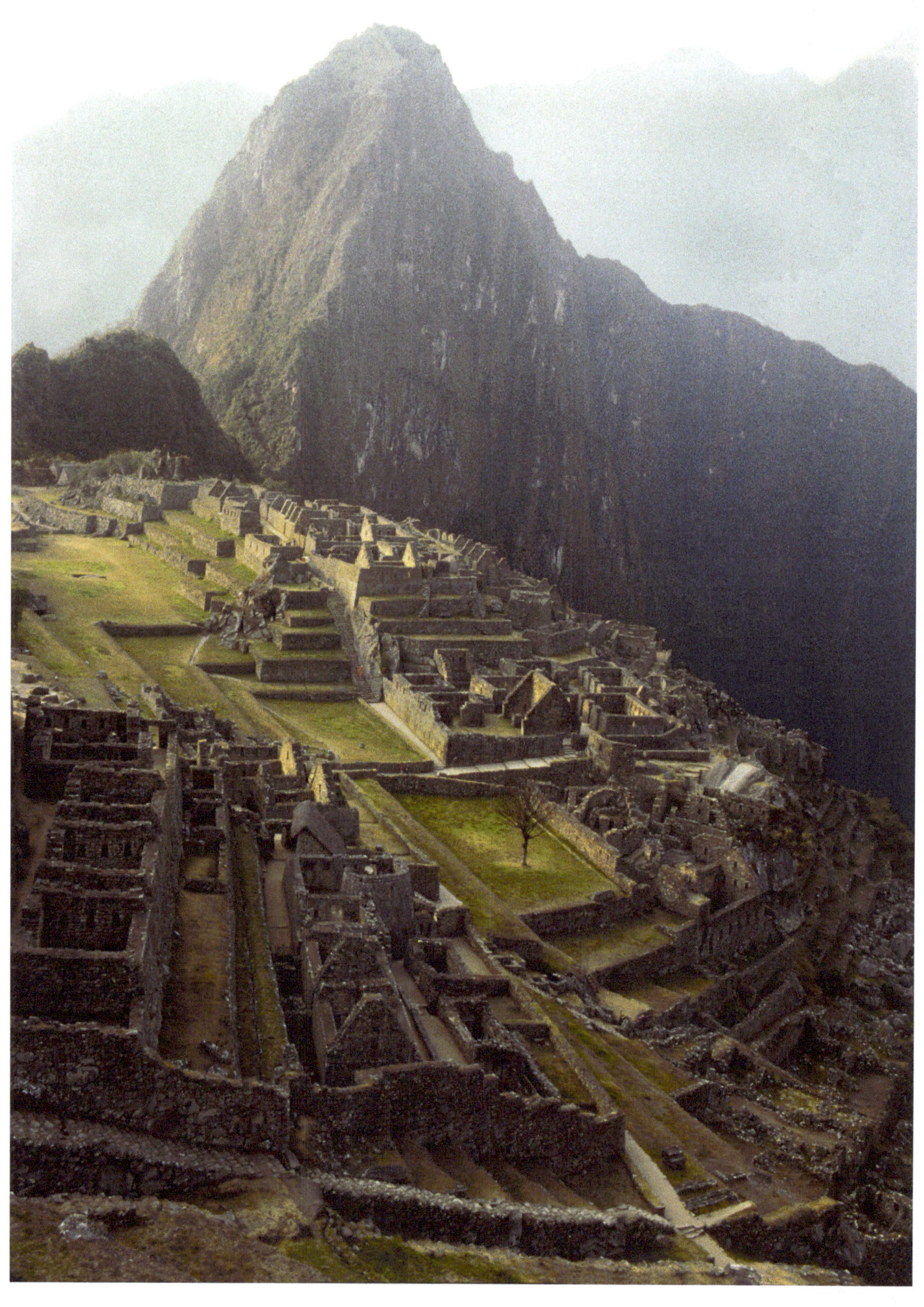

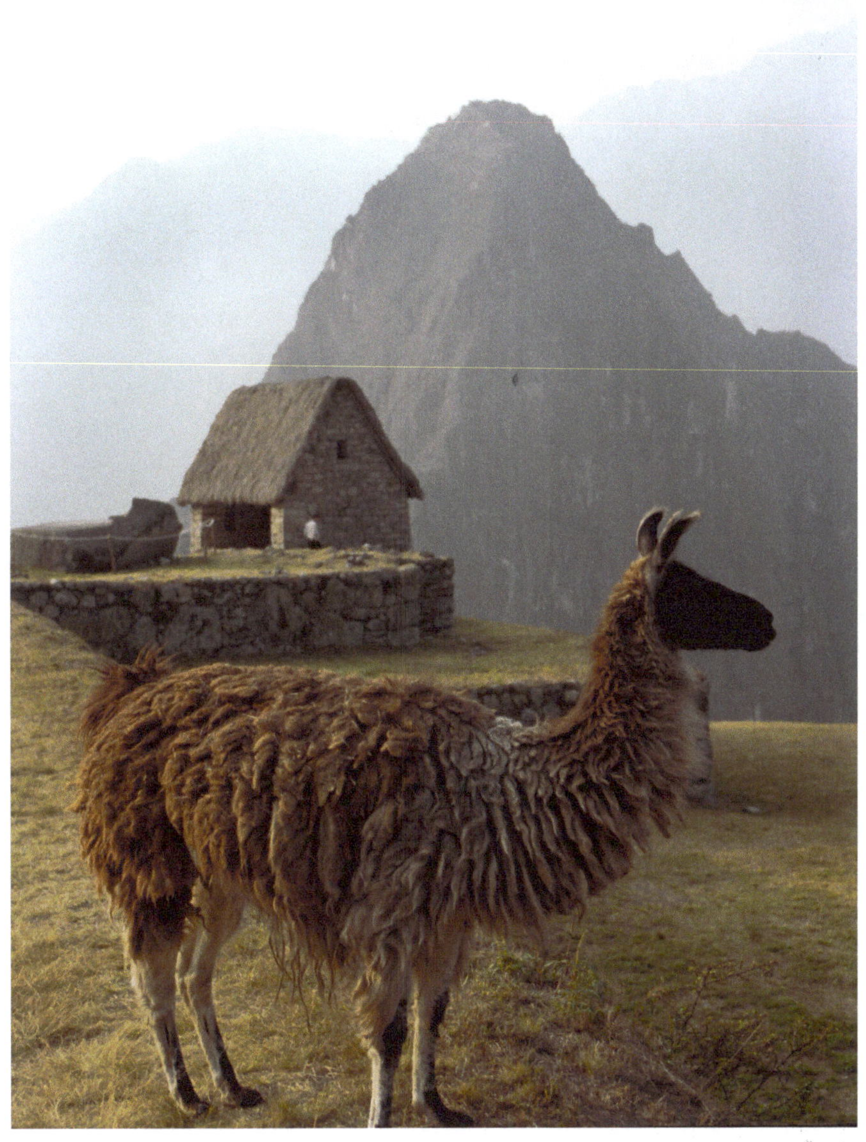

In Peru, the four of us joined another couple of friends, David and Phyllis, and climbed Huana Picchu, the mountain that looms over Machu Picchu. Sections of the climb were almost straight up, with steps dug into the side of the mountain, and a rope to hang on. We found a bag of coca leaves along the trail, and each of us chewed a mouthful. We were hoping for a shot of energy, but it never happened. The leaves tasted like dirt, and we spit them out, but the chewed greenery stuck between our teeth, causing fits of laughter whenever any of us showed their enamel, which was hard not to do with everybody laughing. None of us chewed enough coca to produce a narcotic effect. The source of our laughter was thin air, exhaustion, and the camaraderie of good friends having an adventure. We struggled to the summit of what looked like the top of the world.

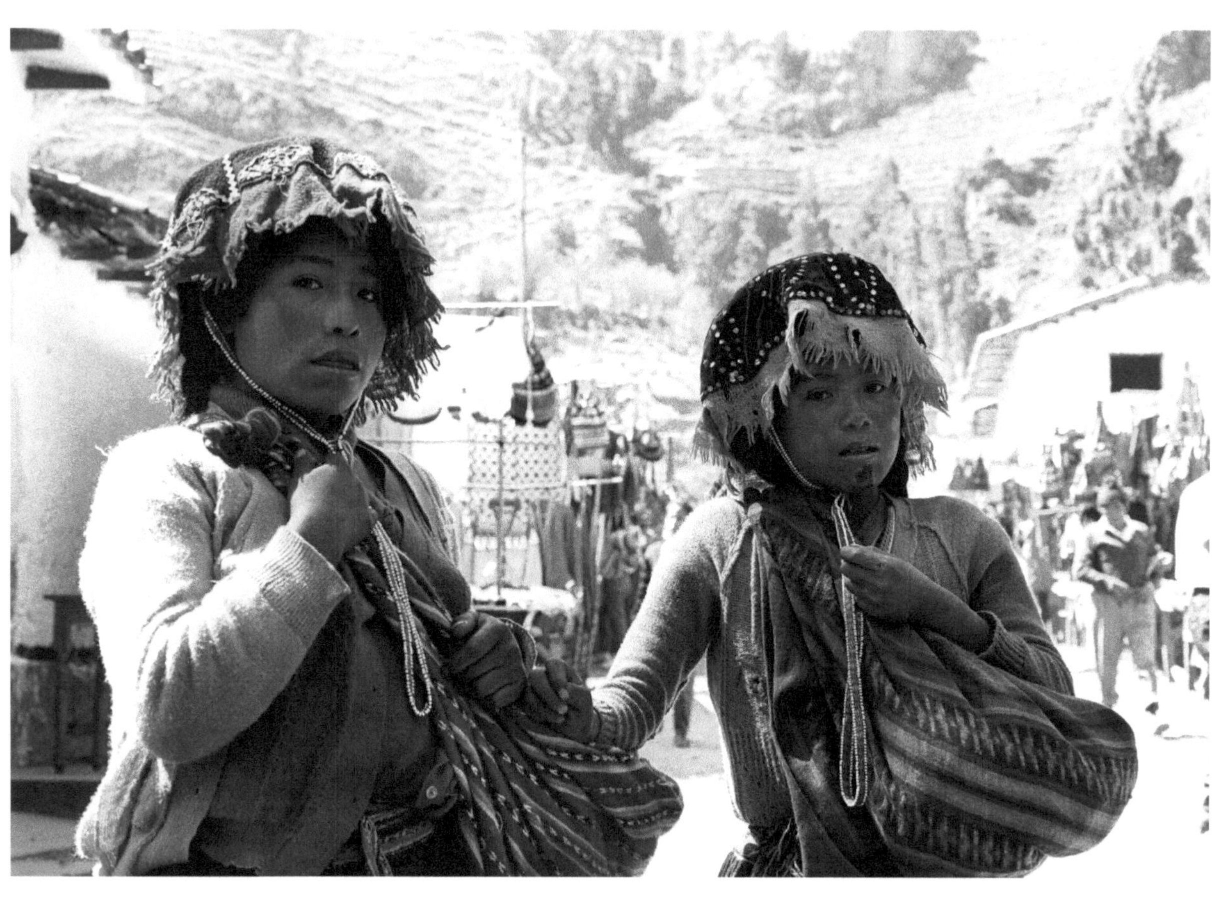

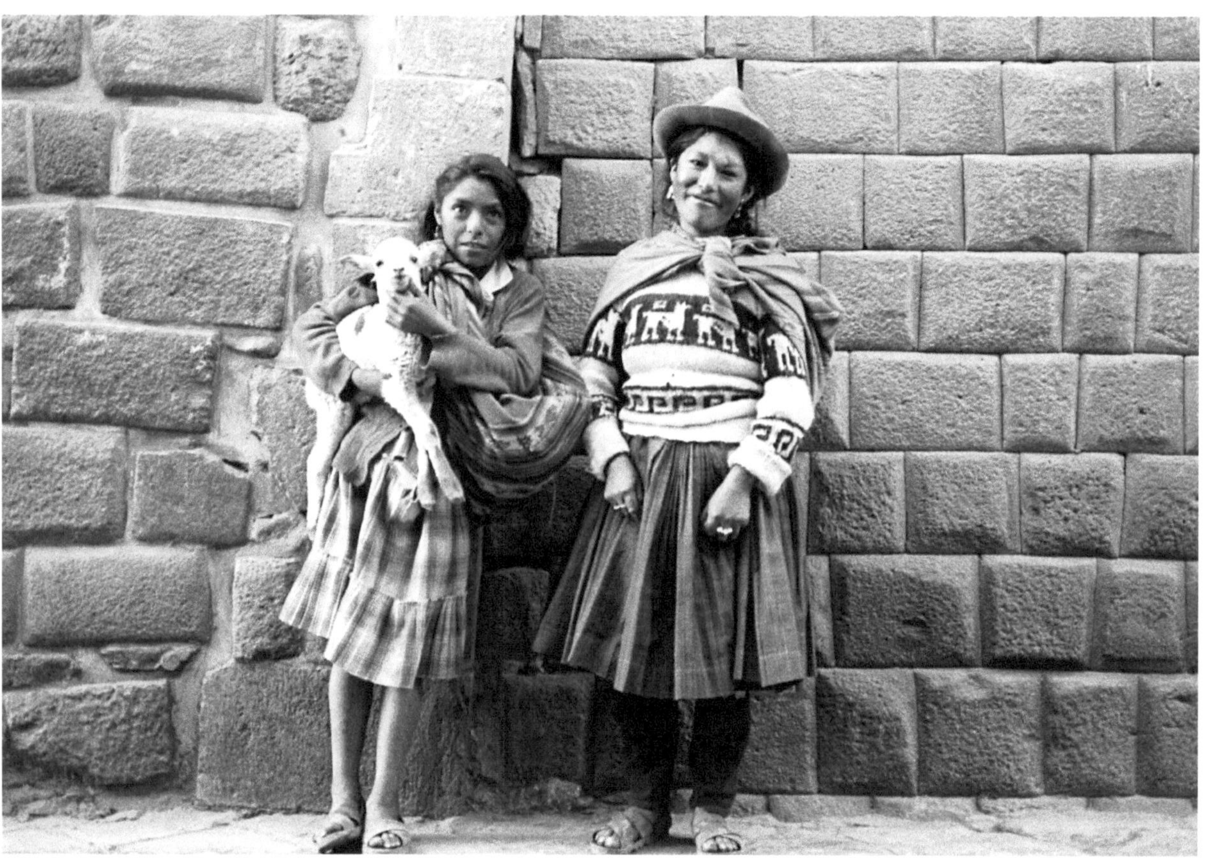

Most of the people we met were friendly, and seemed at least as content with their situations as anyone I knew back home. And yet many of them were obviously struggling to meet life's daily needs.

What do they think of us? I wondered. They must think we are rich. Then I remembered that we are rich. Not by U.S. standards, or any measurement of fortune of any other part of the world. Anyone with the ability to travel across the globe is rich, no matter how long they had to save for the trip. They are rich in money, and luck, and being born in the right place at the right time. Travel has a way of generating introspection.

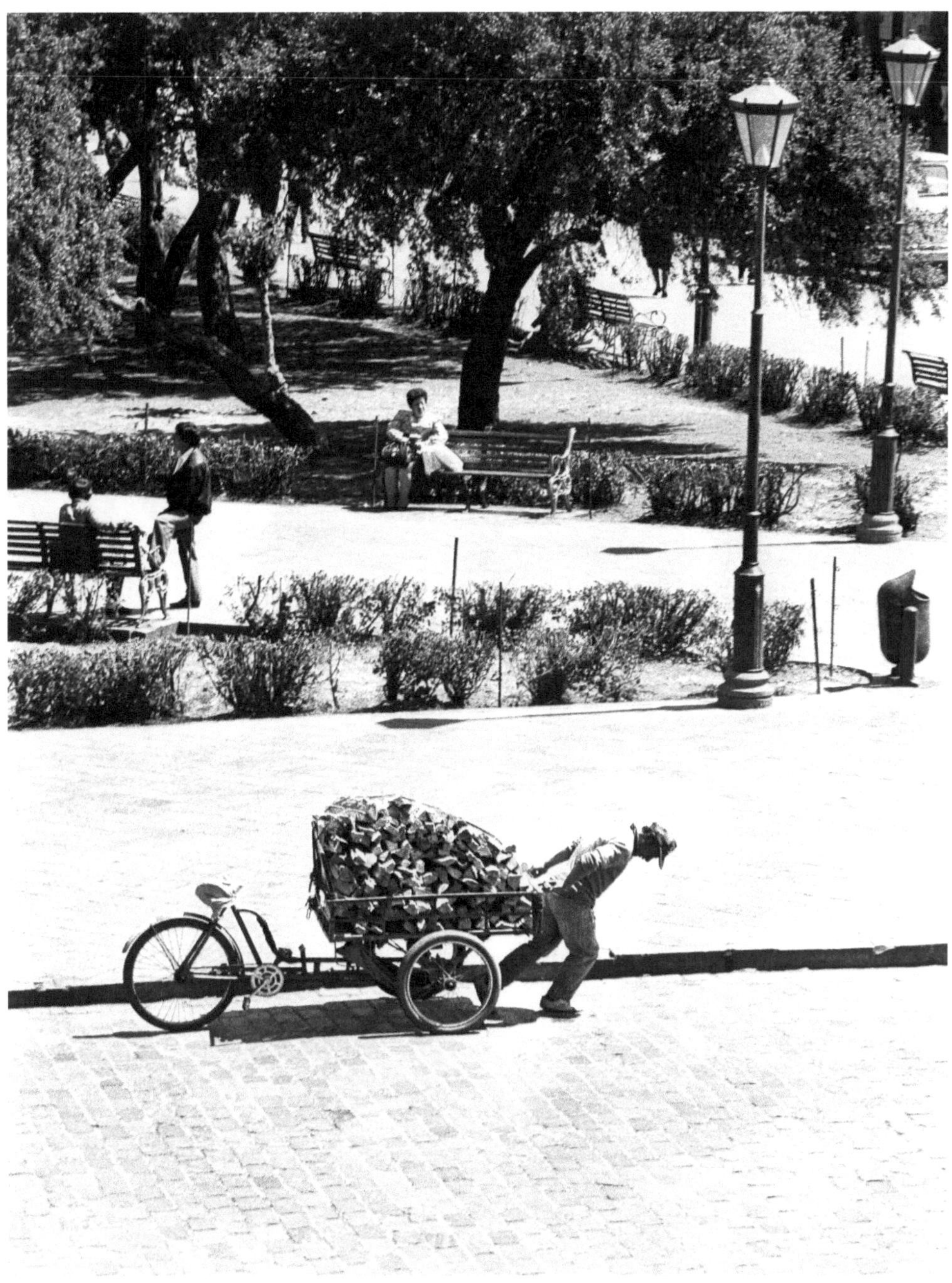

Travel is glamorous only in retrospect.

—**Paul Theroux**

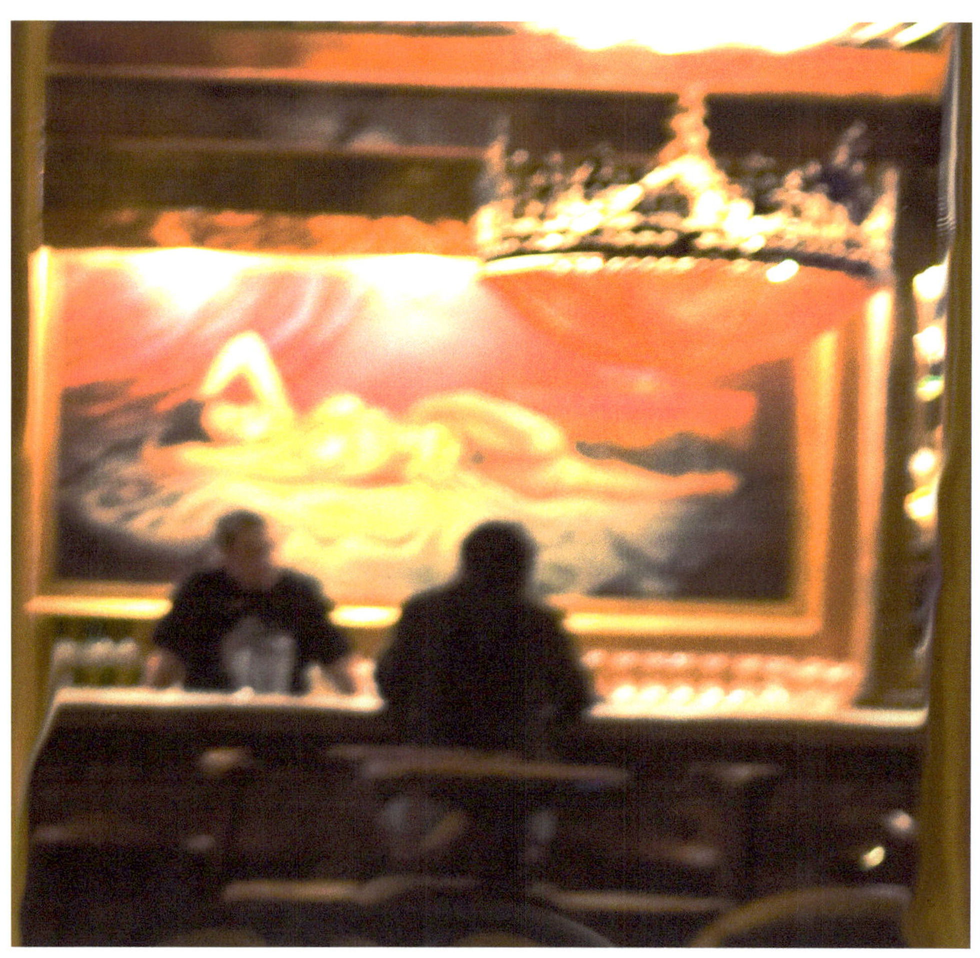

It takes too long to drive out of Texas.

—**Beth McJunkin**

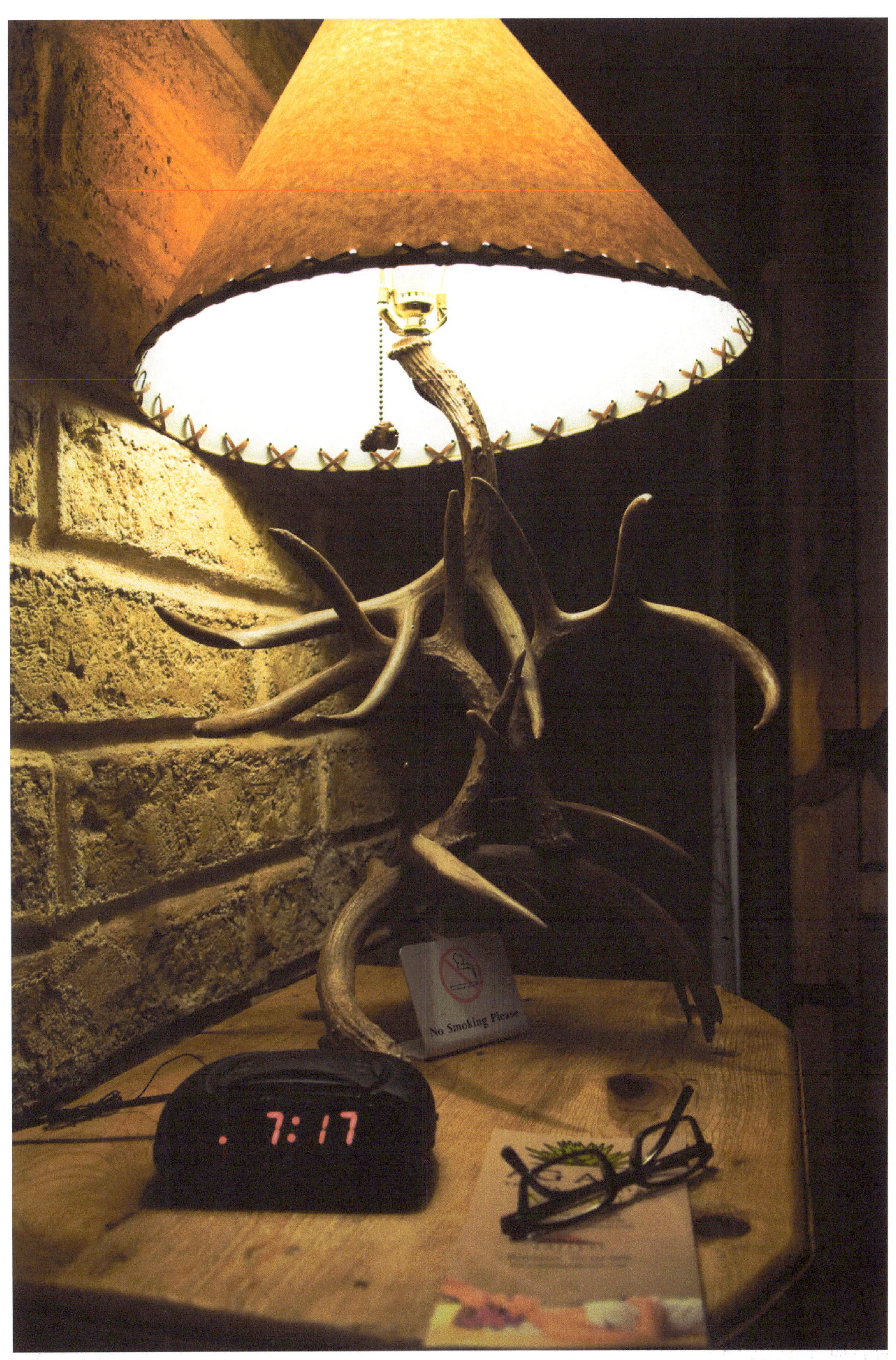
No Smoking Please
7:17

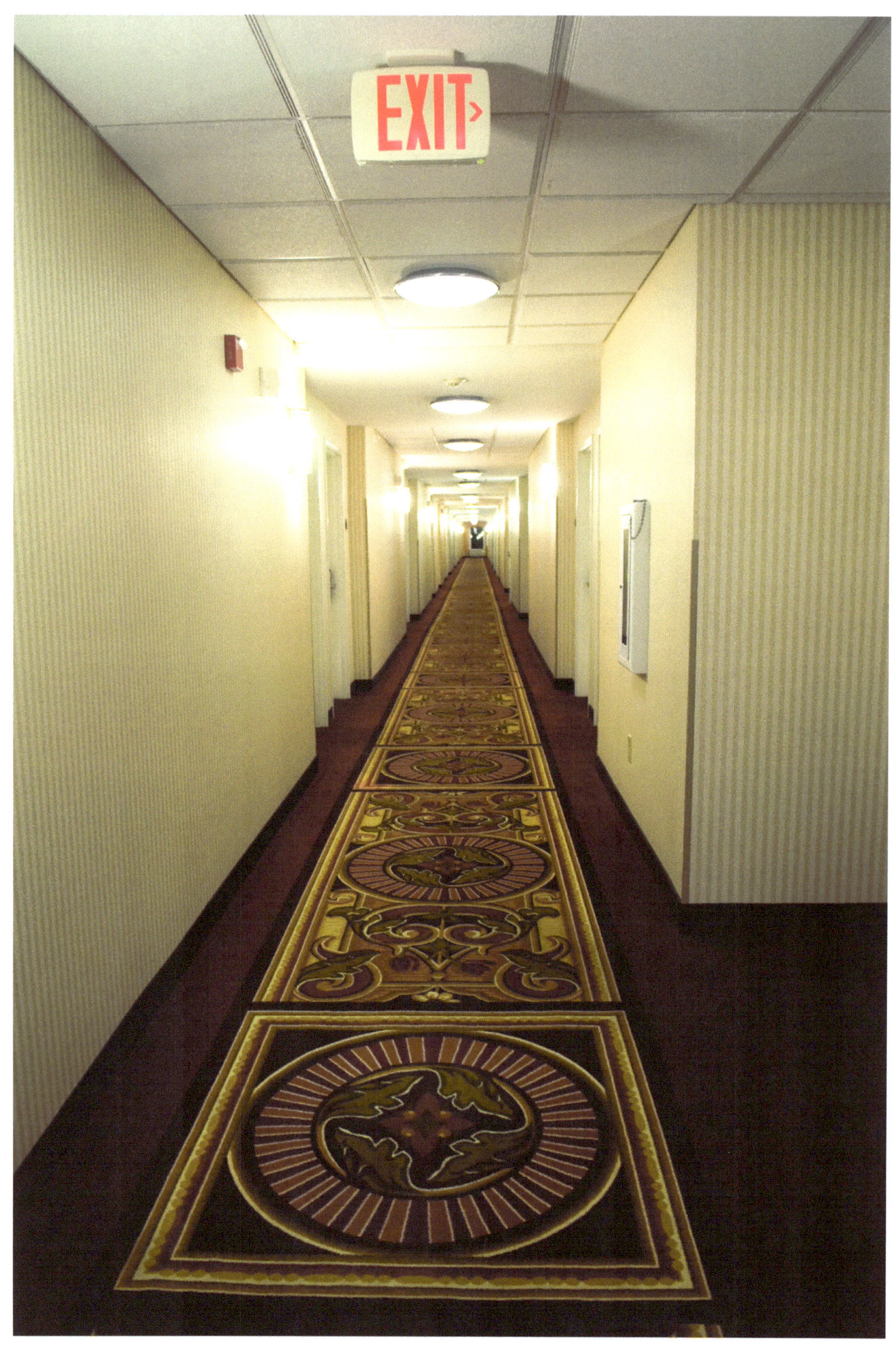
EXIT

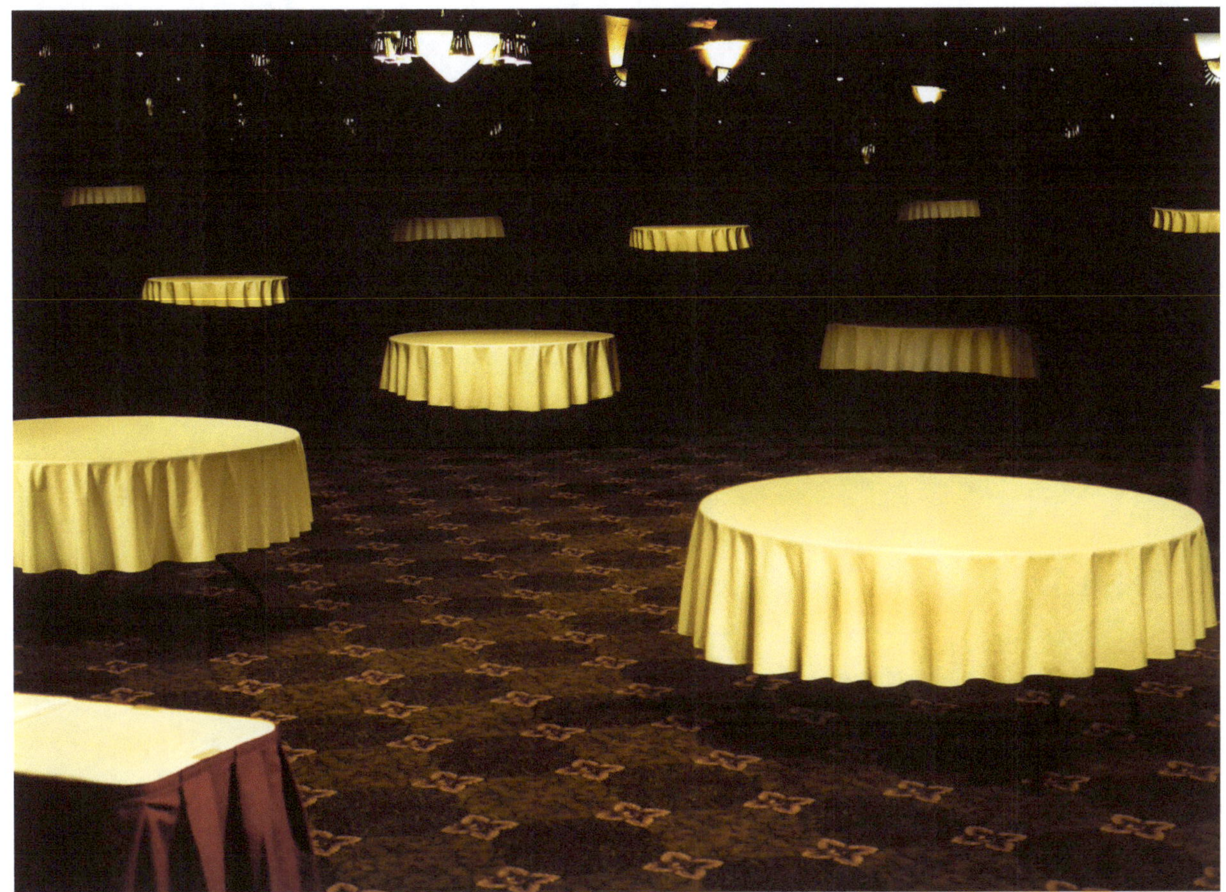

Beth and I reminisced about all the trips we had taken, and congratulated ourselves on completing those excursions without much mishap. So far I am the only one who has suffered from travel. Two bouts of food poisoning, and one instance where I was washed out to sea taught me a thing or two about taking chances. Barracuda and guinea pig are no longer part of my diet, and I am much more careful about swift water.

The fact that Beth was even talking about travel again was a good sign. Sometimes even negative talk is good. She was softening, and I could see adventure in our future. I could see Europe on the horizon.

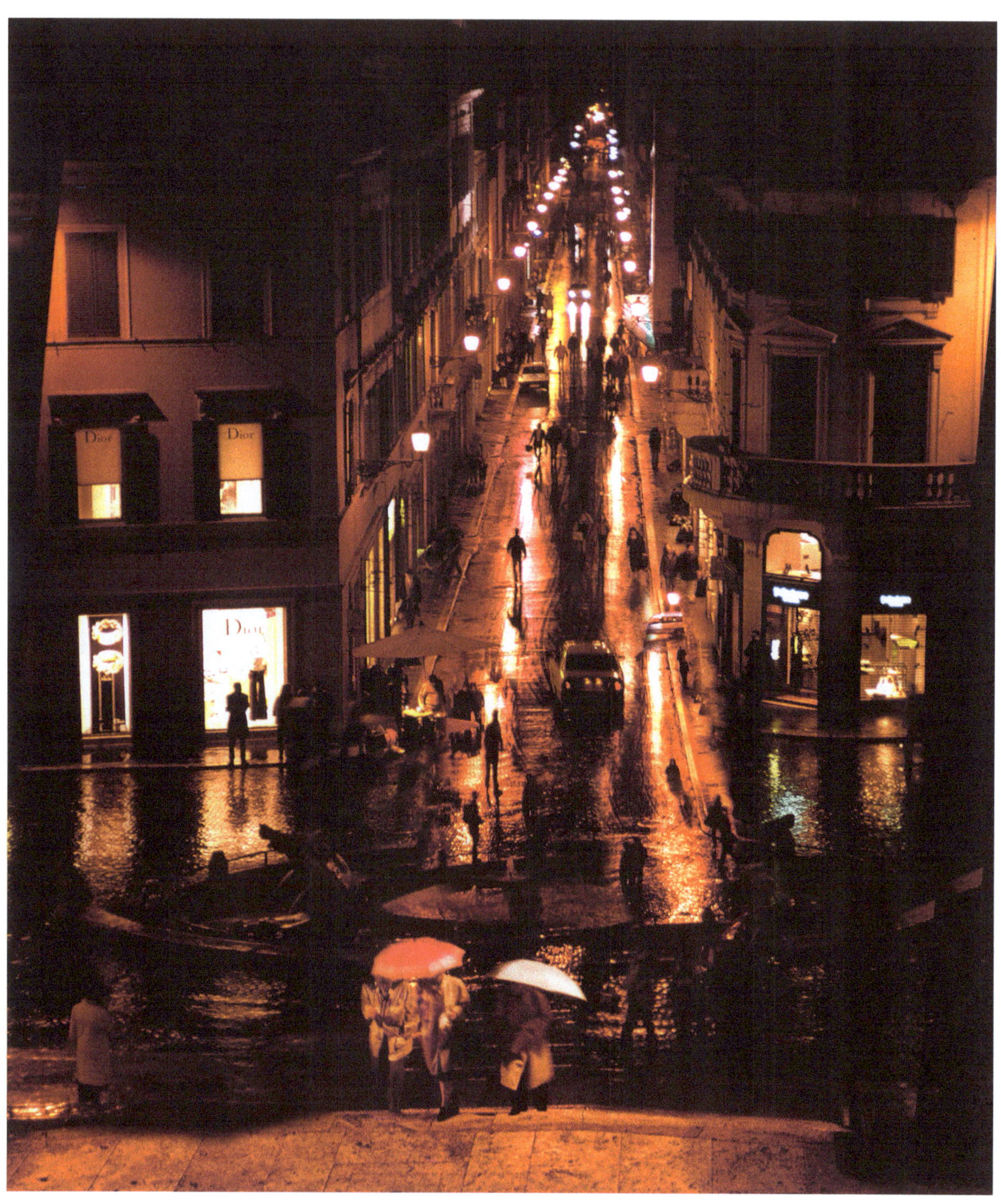
Dior
Dior
Dior

EUROPE

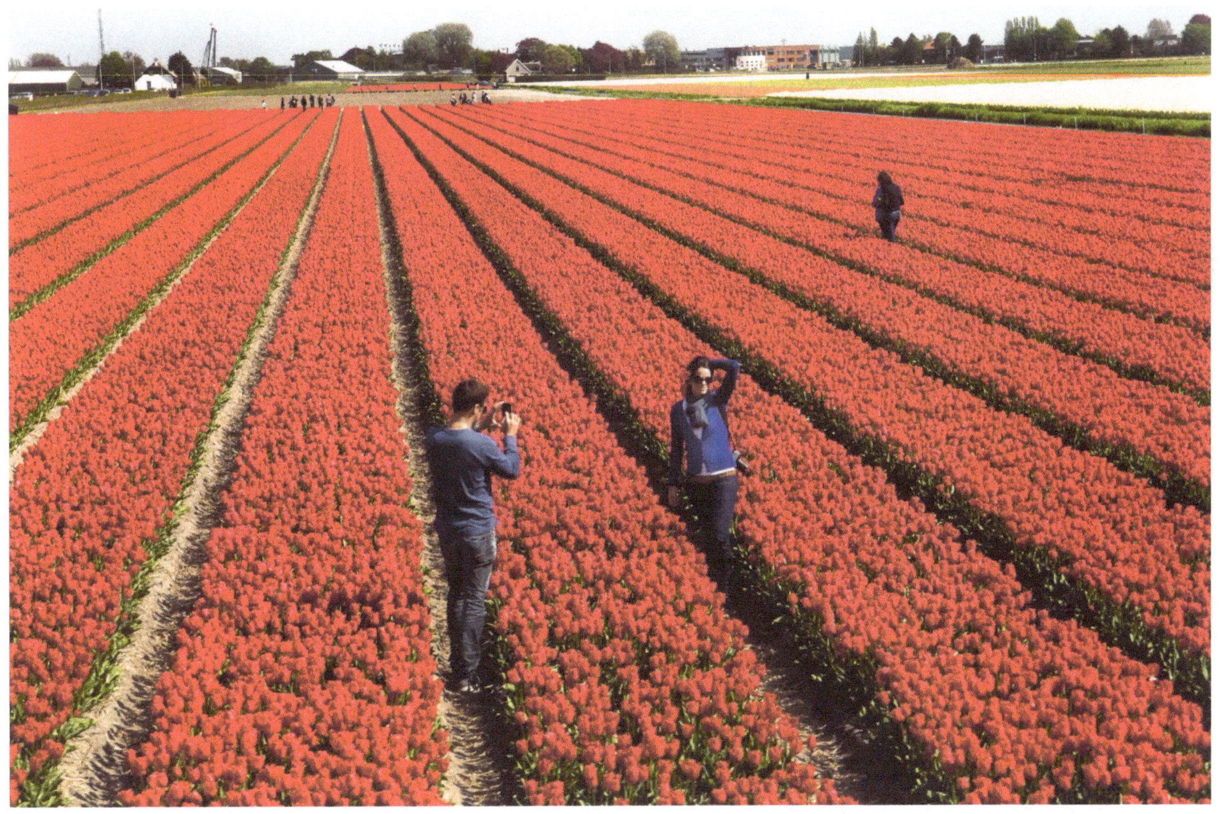

Travelers never think they are the forigners.
—Mason Cooley

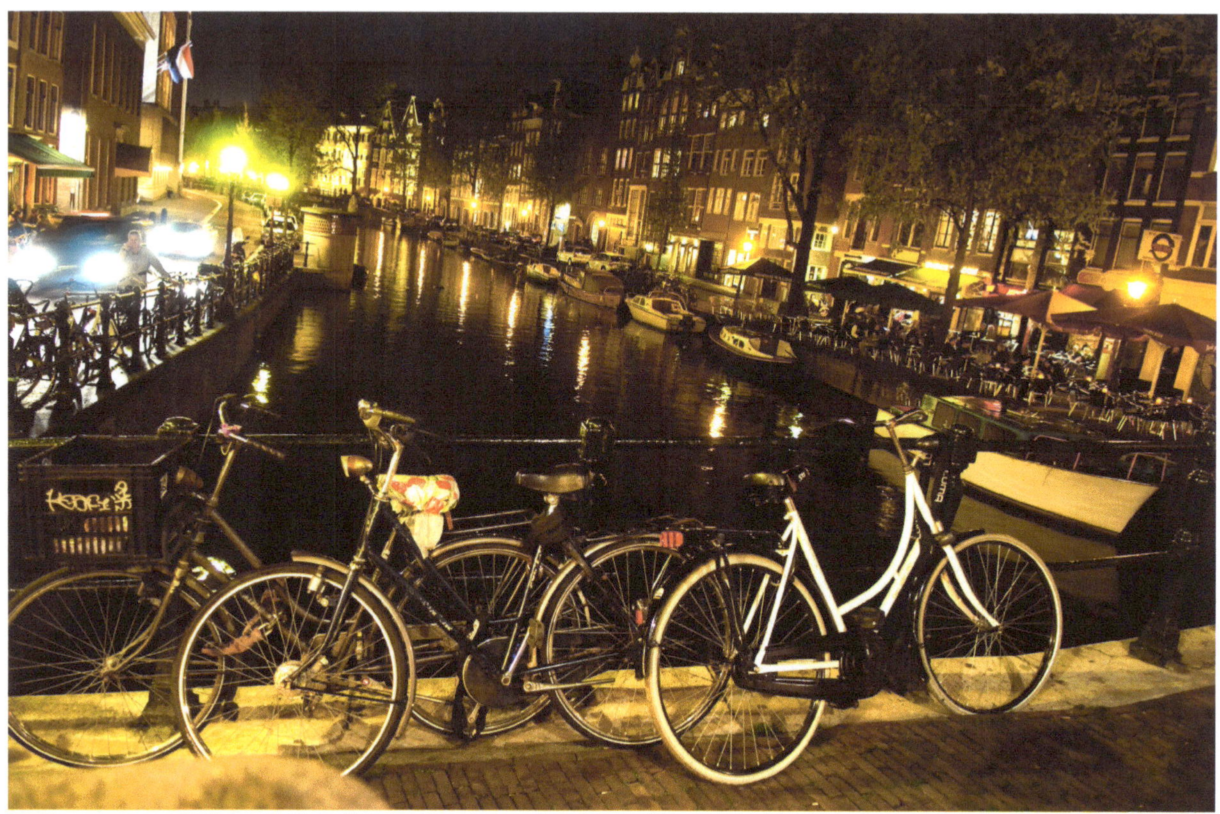

We took a slow boat from Amsterdam to Budapest and saw a multitude of castles in various stages of collapse, perched high above the Rhine, the Main, and the Danube Rivers. We walked down cobblestone streets that have been traveled by knights on horseback, plague wagons, mechanized armies, and digitized tourists.

We drank beer in Cesky Krumlov, in the shadow of a castle, built on the edge of a steep rock cliff that rose from the side of a trout stream. The first castle in the vicinity was built around c.1250. The town began to prosper and grow by 1302, and did not change much in appearance until after Hitler invaded. By that time the city belonged to Czechoslovakia. After the fall of the iron curtain, many of the buildings fell into disrepair, and were taken over by gypsies, before being rescued by commercial interests and becoming a UNESCO World Heritage Site.

Farther up the Danube we crossed the border into Austria and toured Vienna. A few days later we crossed another border into Slovakia, and stayed a couple of days in Bratislava before moving on to Hungary.

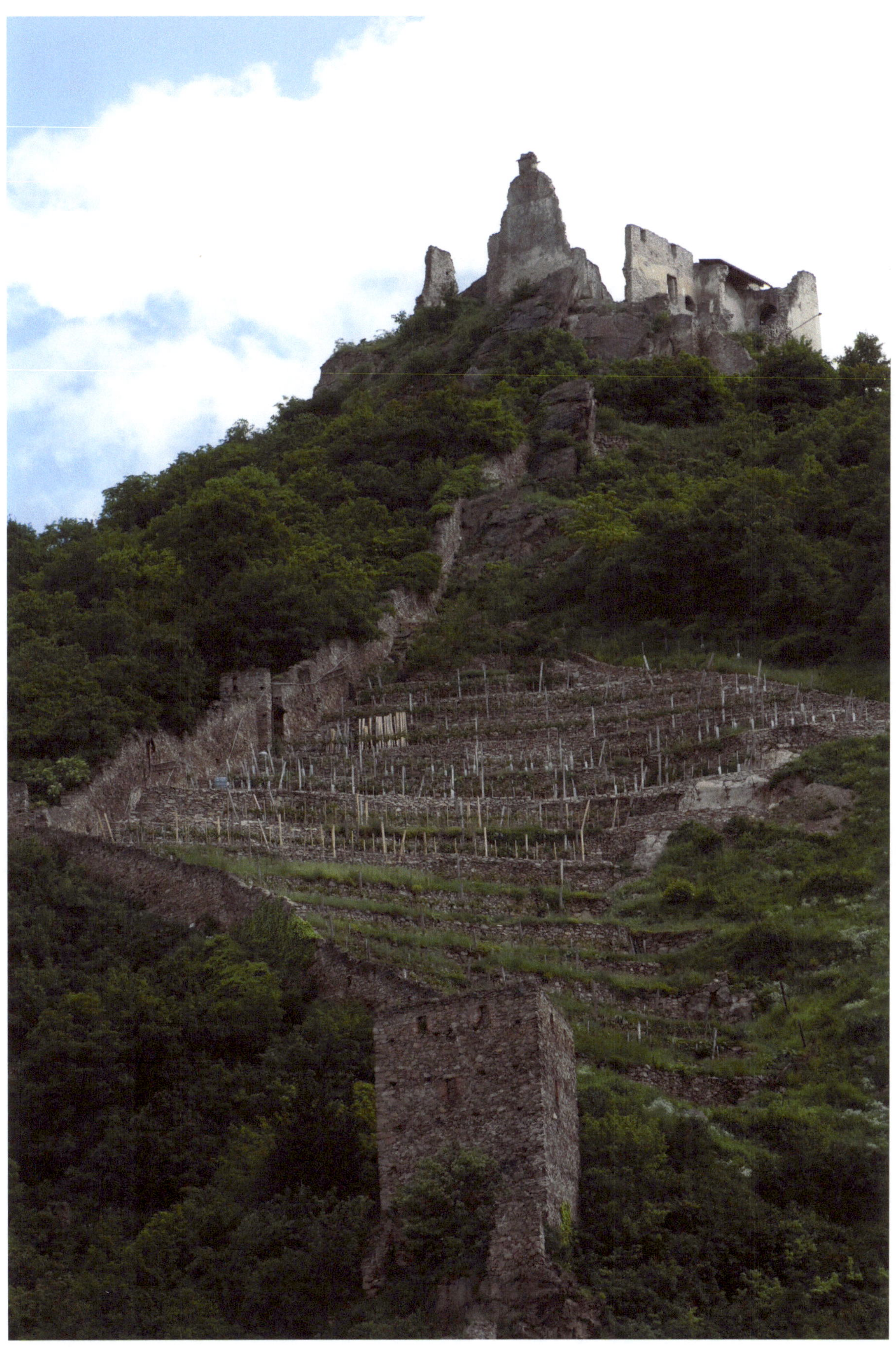

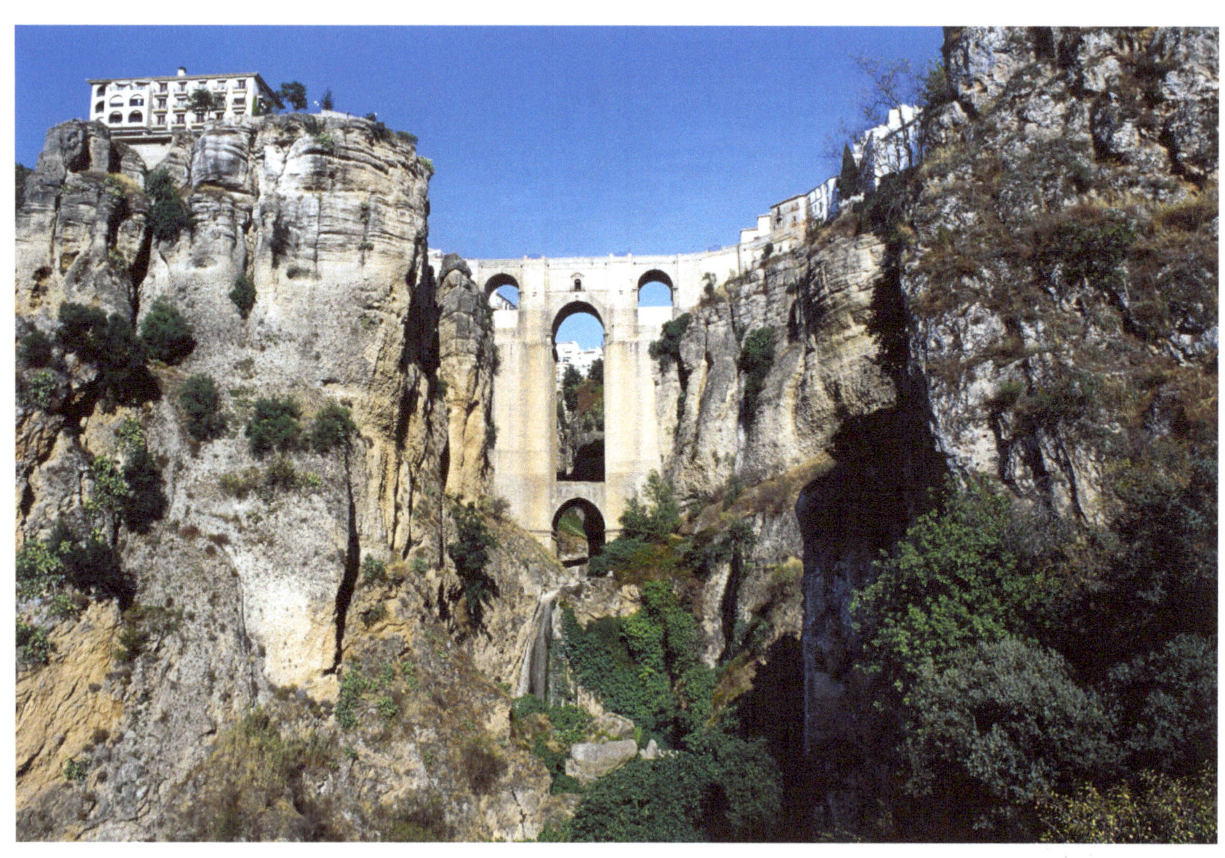

Civilizations are built on the bones of previous occupants.
—Jim McJunkin

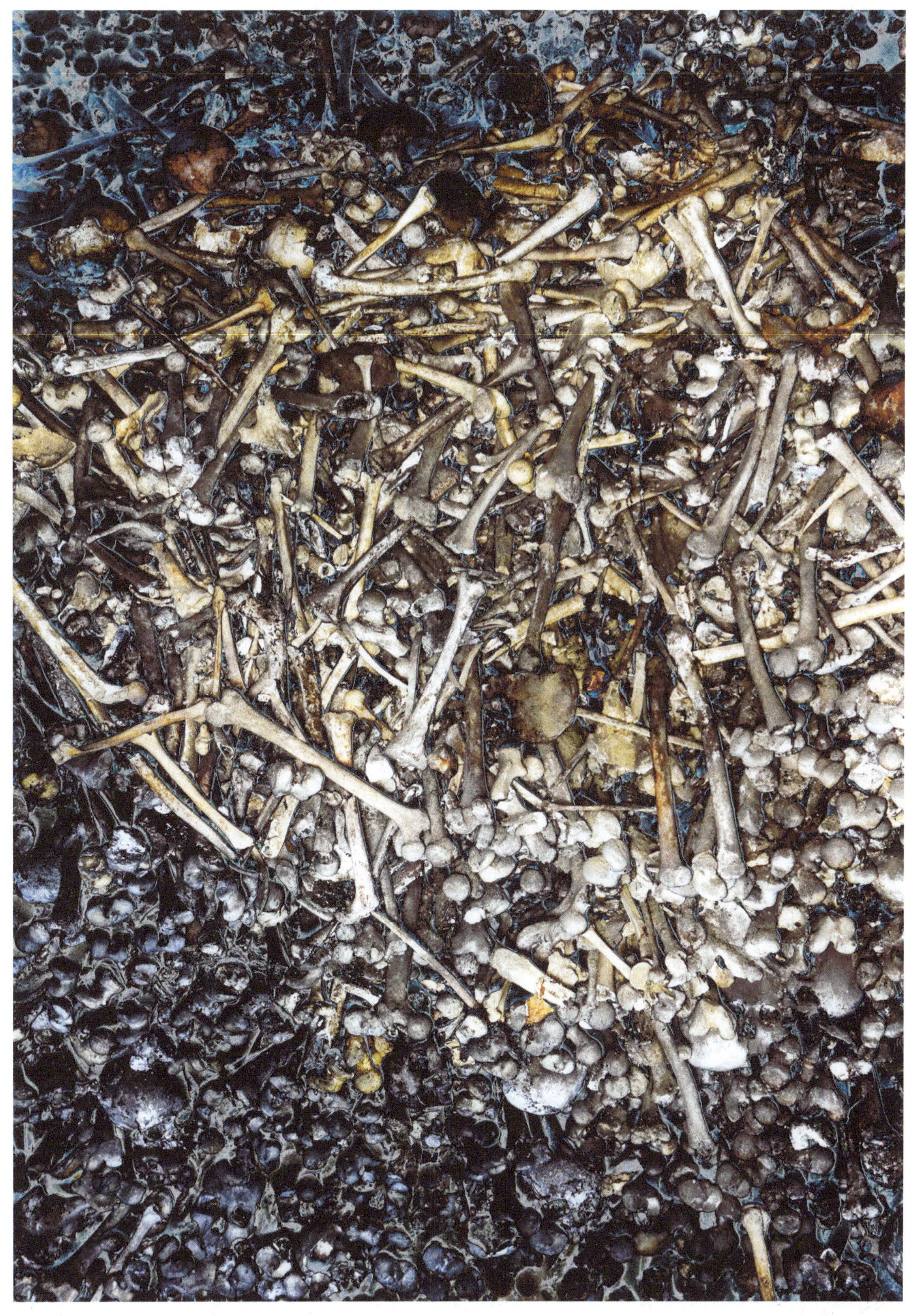

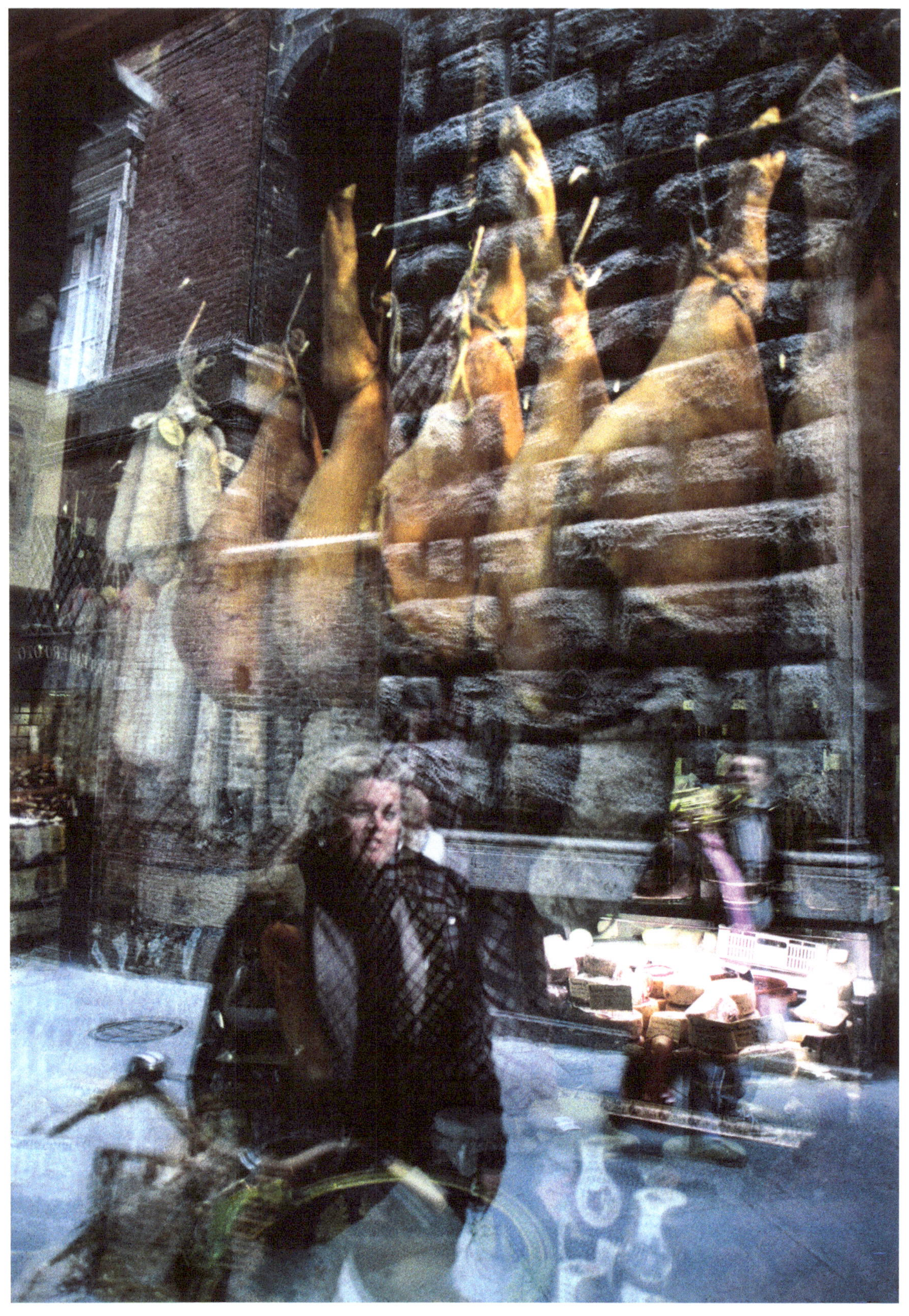

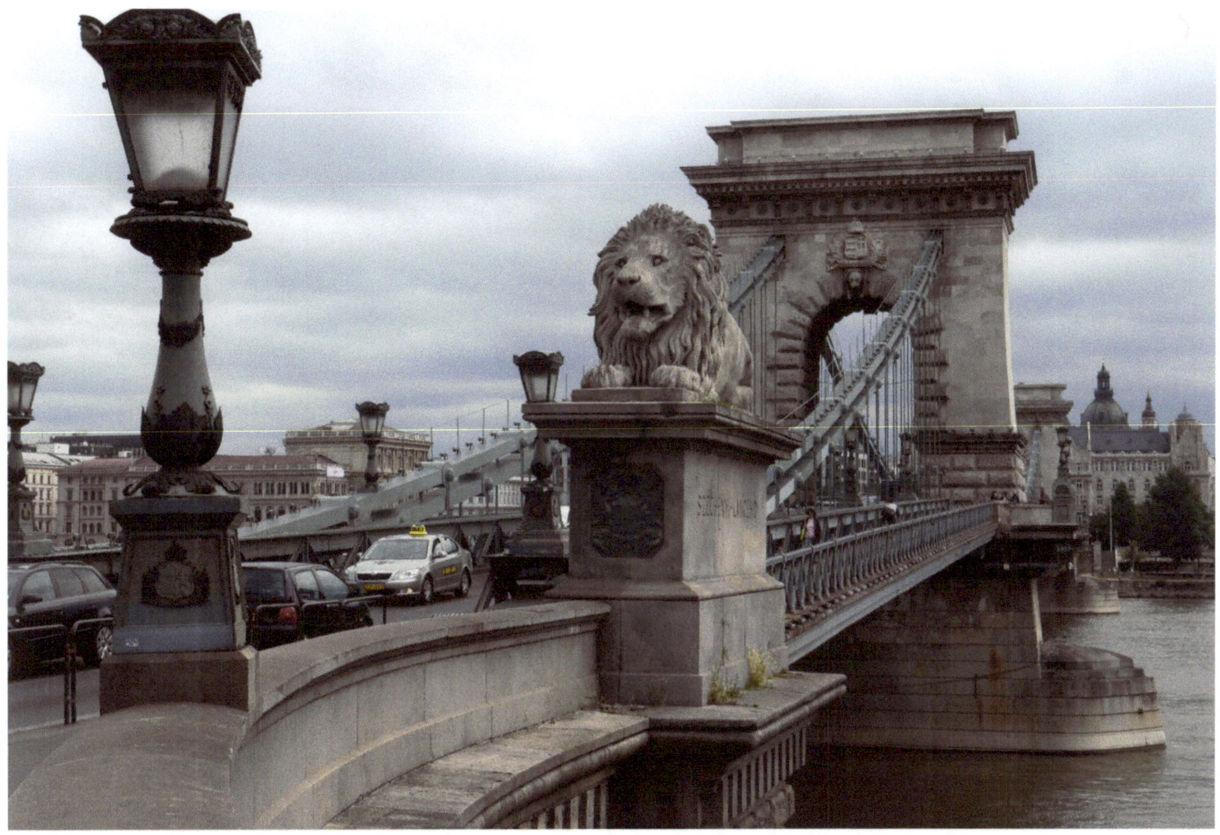

Budapest is actually two cities. Buda is on the western bank of the Danube, and Pest is an easy walk across any of a series of impressive bridges that span the river. In the Hungarian market I was confronted by one of the all time worst pick pockets. On the other side of the river I lost twenty dollars in a side street money exchange. It was our last evening in Hungary, and I was out of the local currency. We just needed enough for a vernicular ride down the mountain where we could walk back to our hotel.

I was at the back of a long line at a money exchange when an honest looking man offered to help. He offered nineteen dollars worth of Hungarian Florins for my twenty-dollar bill. If not having to stand in line was worth a dollar, then we could both benefit from the transaction, and small gestures such as this sometimes blossom into more significant cultural understanding, etc, etc.

I was having some difficulty doing the math in my head, partially due to the fact that my wife was tugging at the back of my shirt, saying, "Don't do it. It's counterfeit. All the guide books say never exchange money on the street." The bills looked authentic, so I made the exchange.

Back at the vernicular we learned that the money had actually been authentic about 40 years ago, but only in Russia. "Sorry. We do not accept the Euro or out of date Russian Rubles," the attendant said without even trying to suppress laughter.

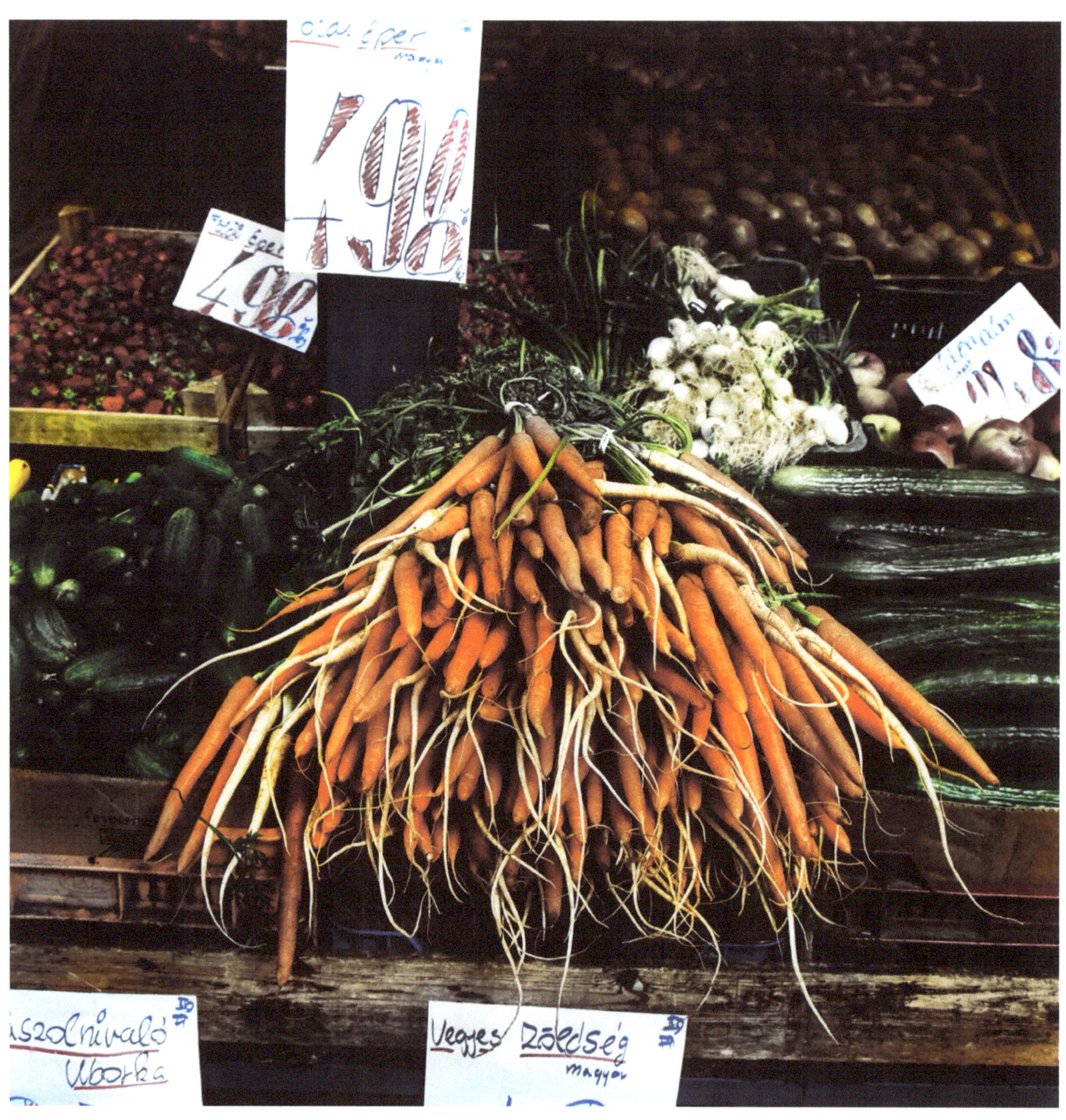
498
Uborka
Vegyes Zöldség
magyar

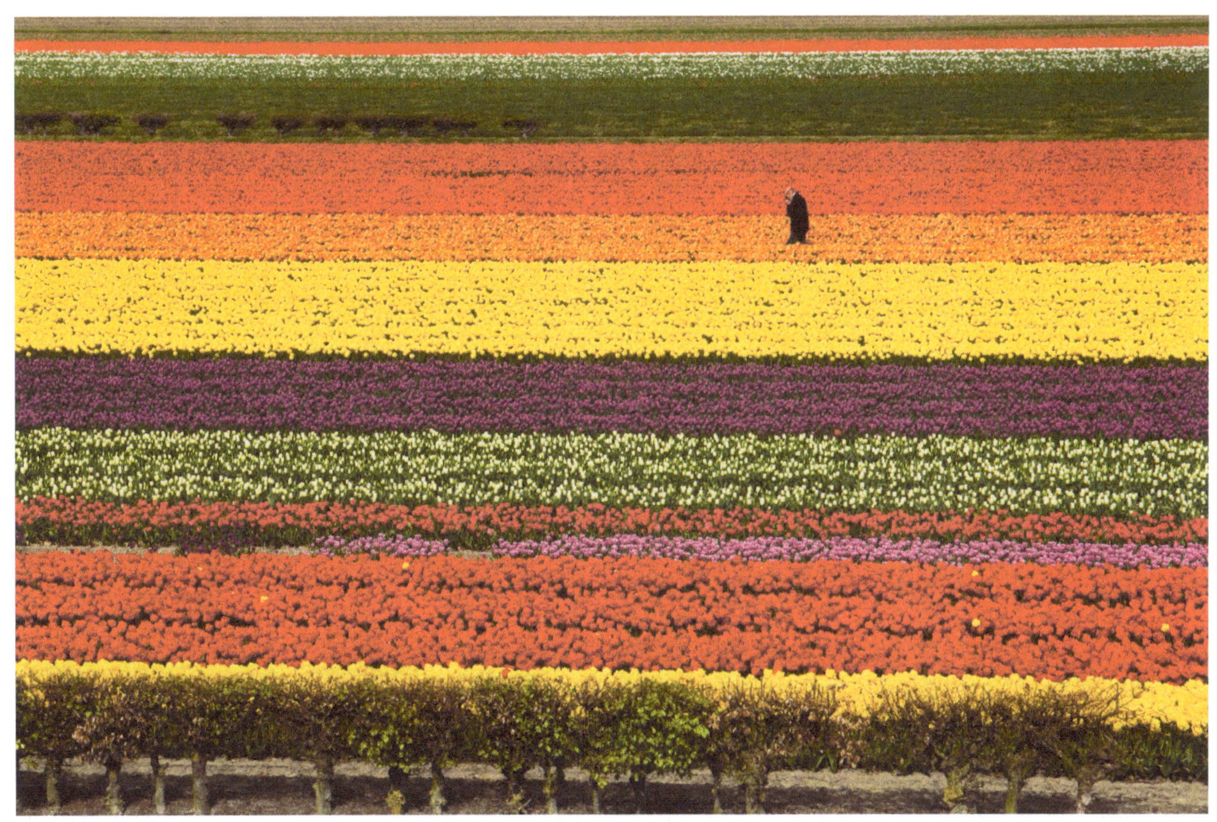

It is better to travel well, than to arrive.

—Buddha

The waterways Beth and I were floating through were the venues for some of humanity's earliest evolution. We were aware of some of the regions history, and would learn more later. So much happened before our boat trip that a full accounting is not possible, so here is a synopsis with omissions and overlaps. Prehistory, including Neolithic cultures, the stone, iron and bronze ages. Germanic tribes, Alexander the Great, Julius Ceasar, and the Roman Empires northern border. The Ottoman, and Hapsburg Empires, World War I, and World War II, when allied bombers blew up most of the bridges. There are a number of history books that can be consulted for a more detailed analysis.

The idea of connecting the North Sea to the Black Sea via the rivers in between was first attempted by Charlemagne in 793, without success. Then, in the 19th century, a series of locks and weirs were inserted into the rivers. Problem solved.

Beth and I passed through 68 locks on our trip from Amsterdam to Budapest. The first 48 locks raised our boat until we crossed the Continental Divide. The rest lowered us, and provided a much more gentle excursion than Charlemagne could have ever imagined.

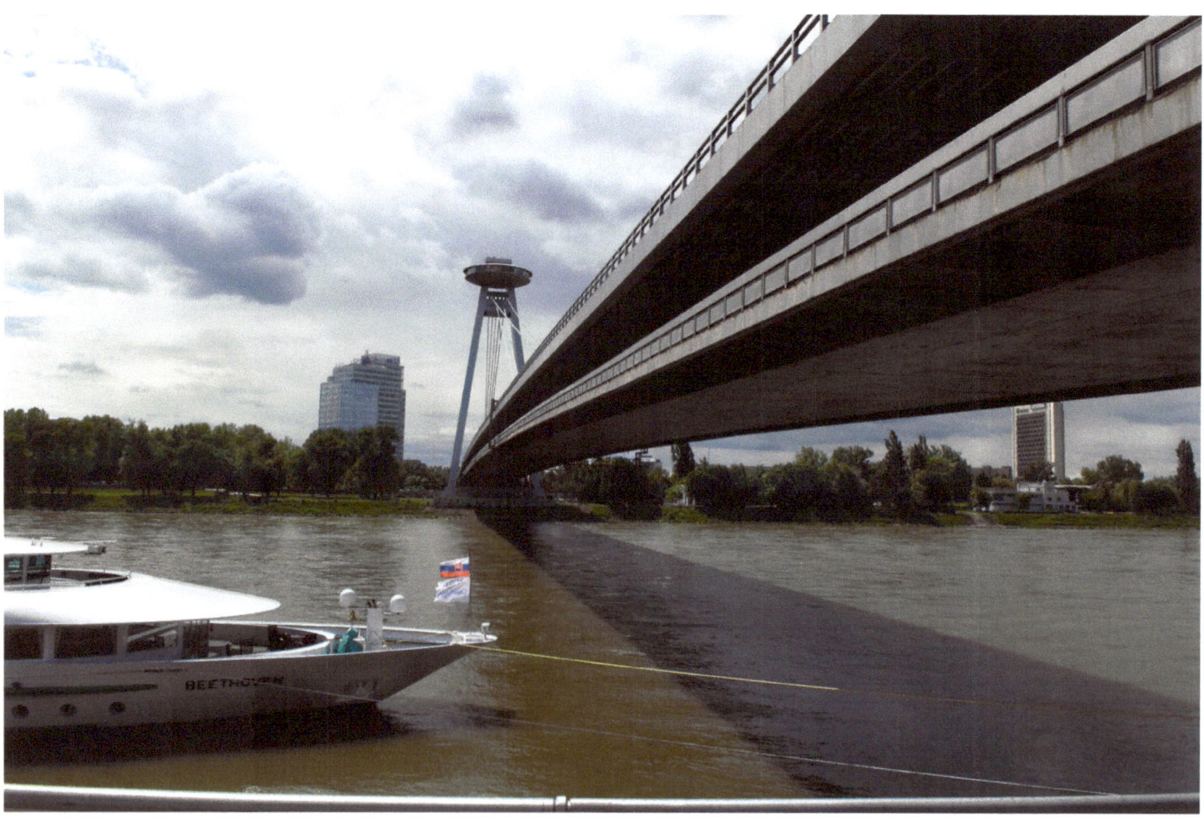

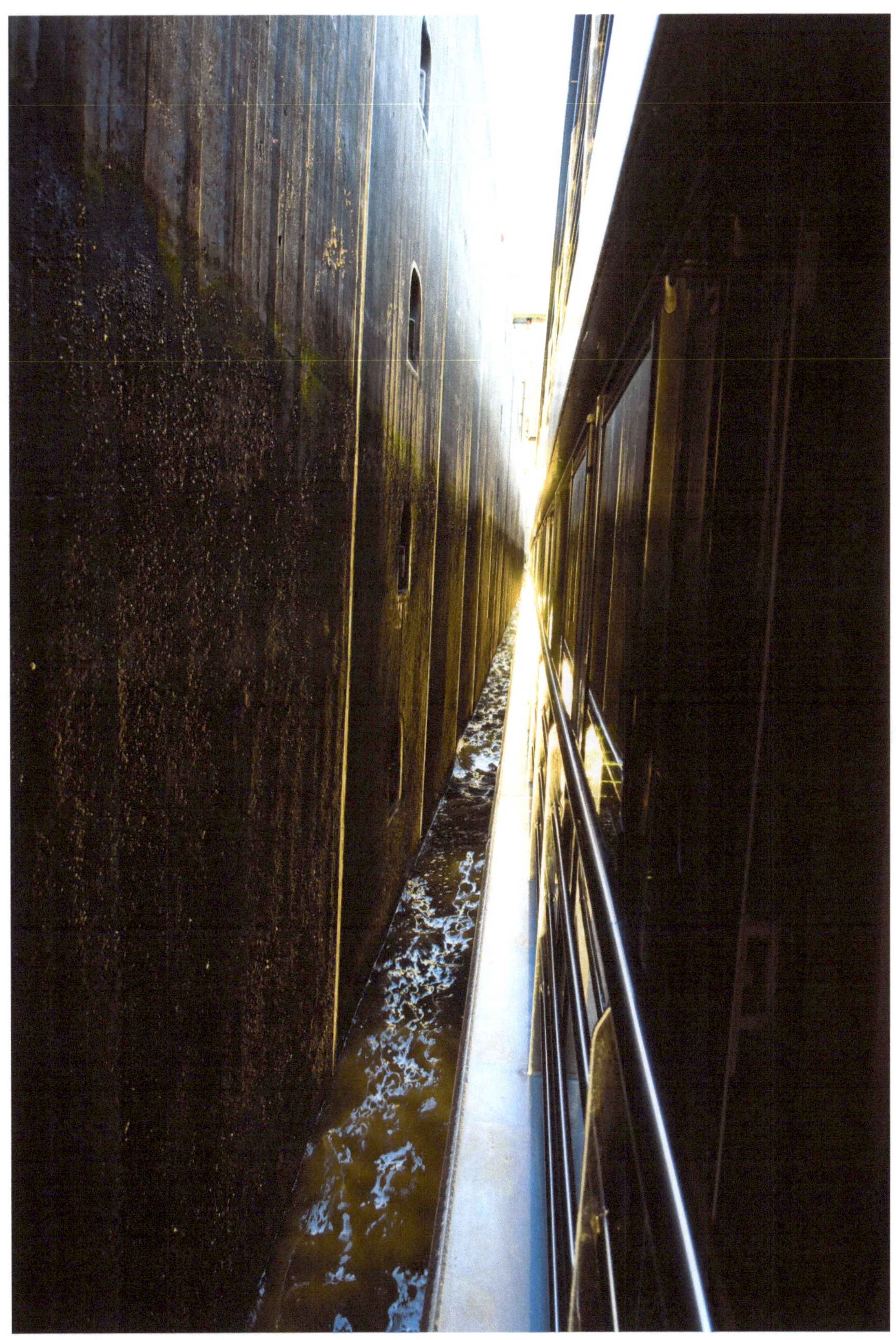

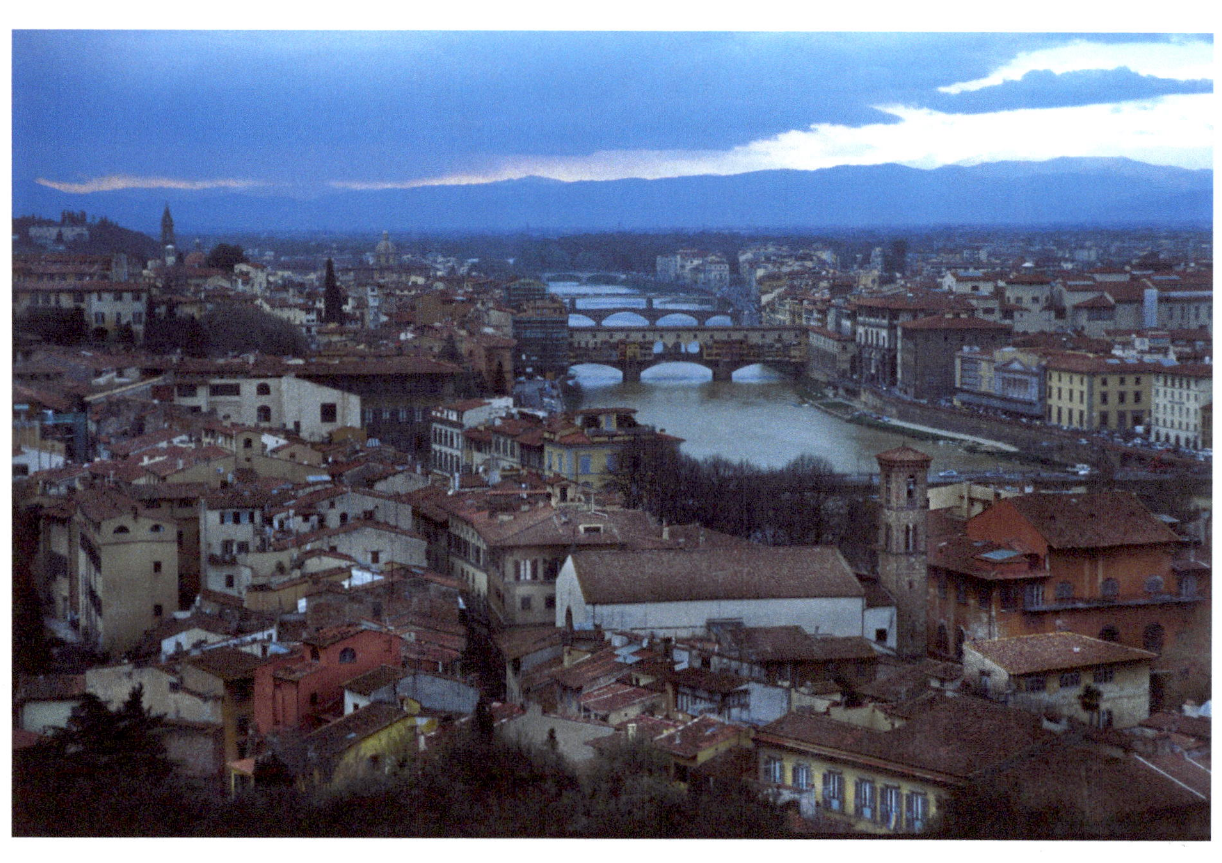

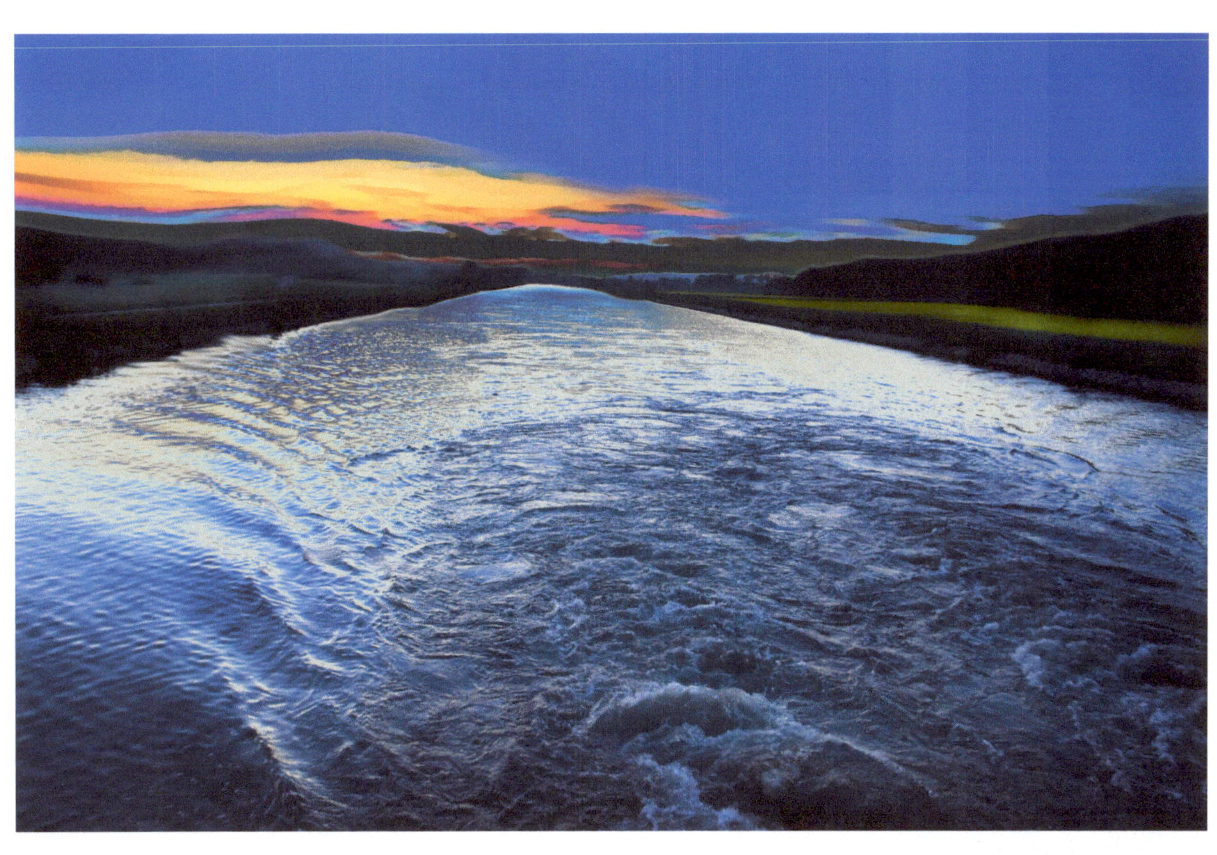

We continued our journey across Europe, experiencing as much as we could in a limited amount of time. We visited Spain, Italy, and Portugal, and even made a day trip to North Africa.

We traveled like there might be no tomorrow, which is probably not the best way to experience the other side of the world. We saw so much art in such a short span of time, that I caught myself scanning masterpieces the way I might scan advertisements in a magazine. We saw enough religious art to get religion, and enough architecture to understand the difference between Baroque and Gothic. We absorbed enough about Rococo architecture to mention it in a sentence.

When I think about the people we met, I'm struck by how similar we are in spite of our cultures. Aside from the pickpocket and the money exchanger in Budapest, and a rug merchant in Tangiers, everybody seemed truly interested in America, and wanted us to enjoy their country.

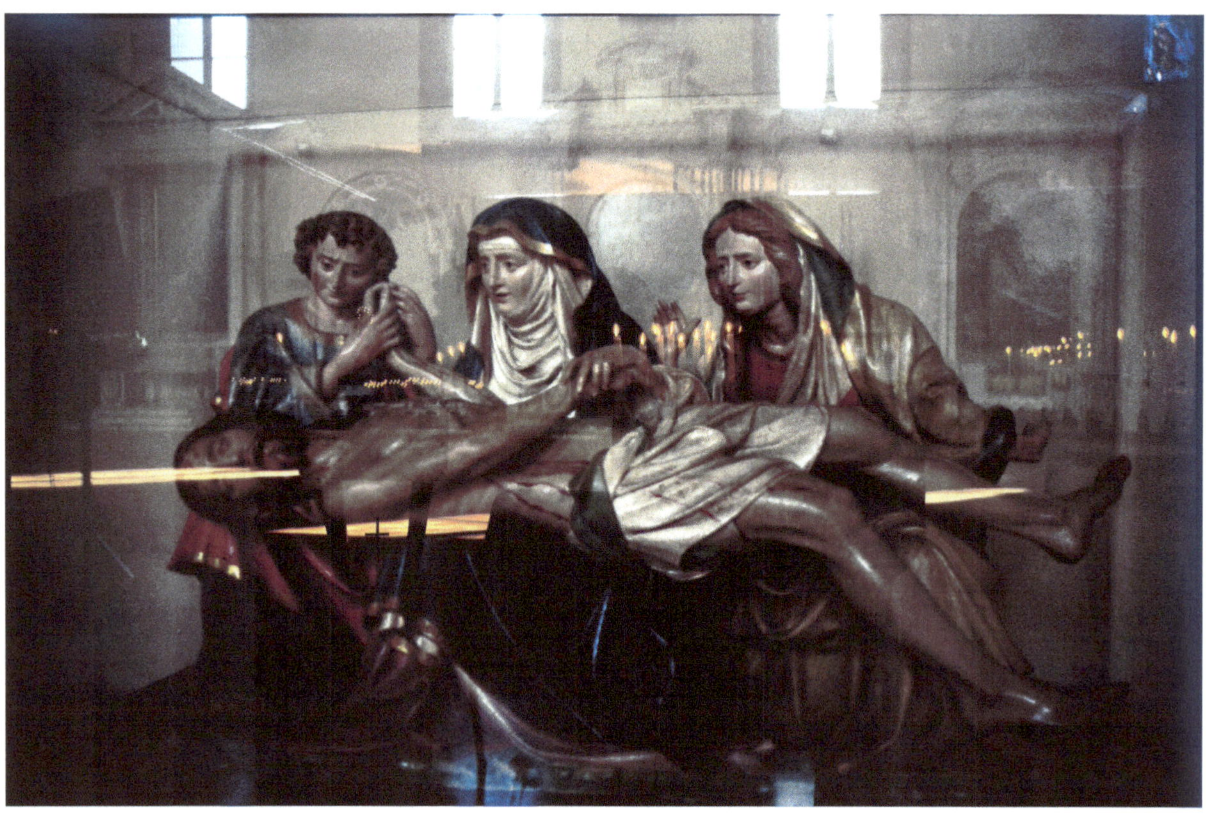

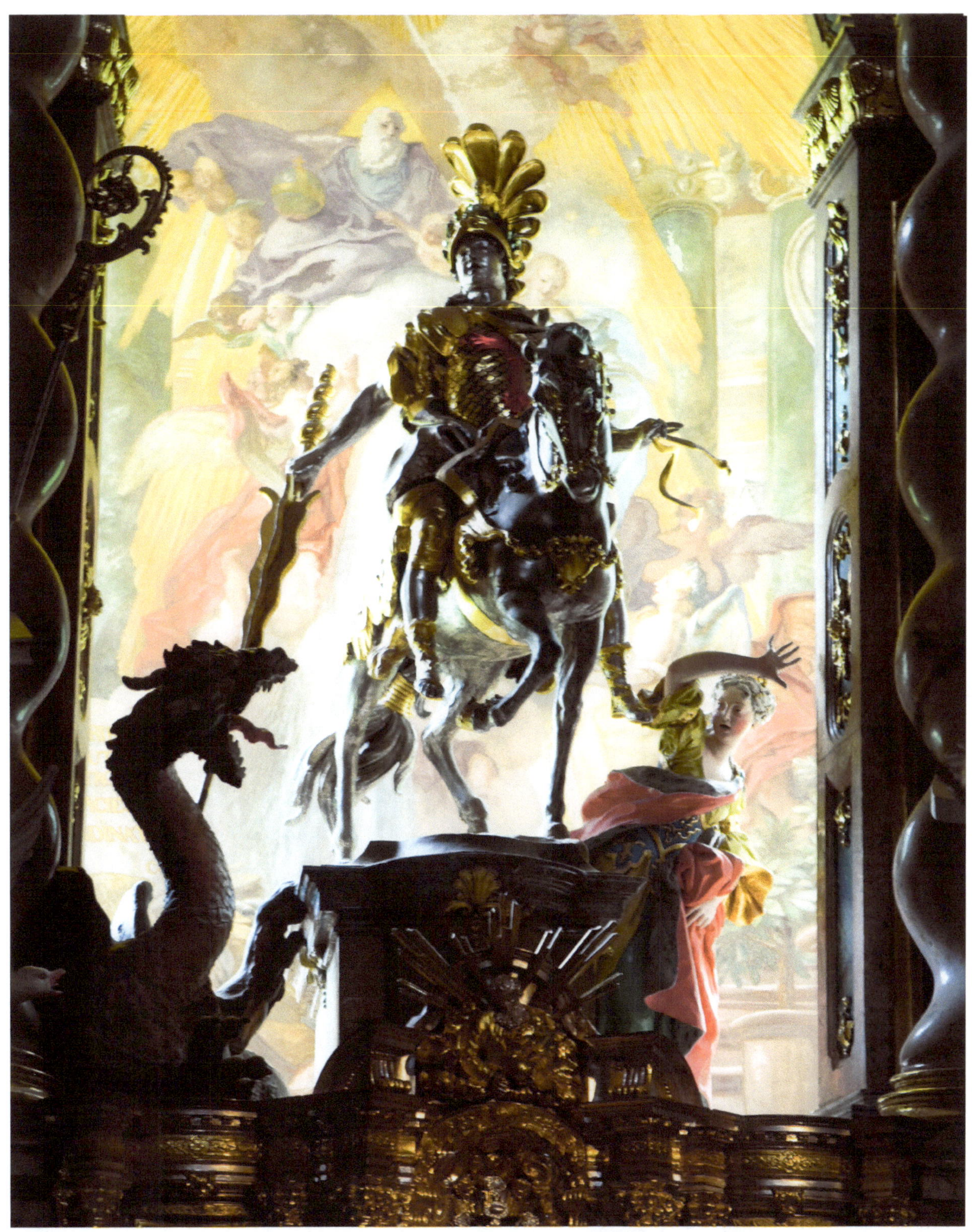

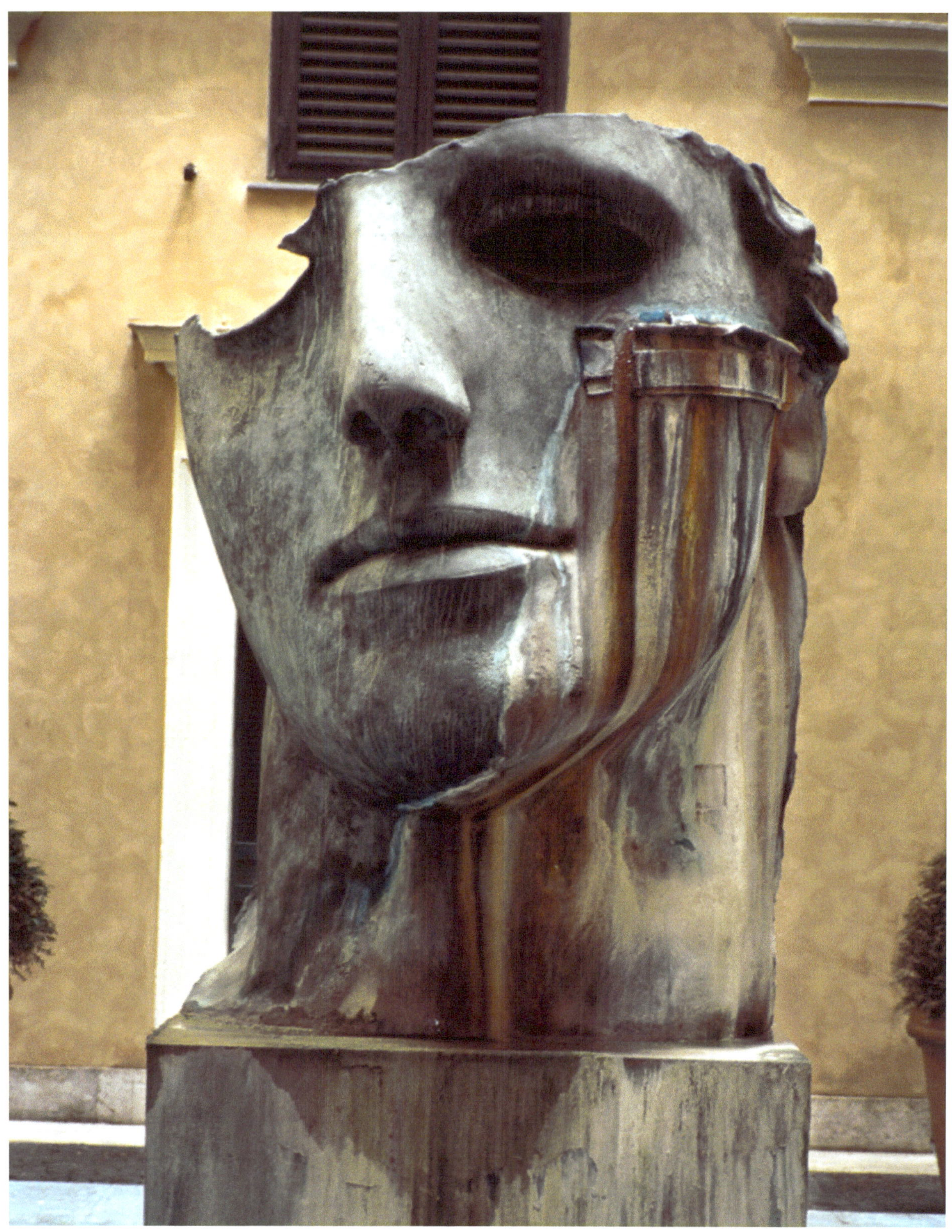

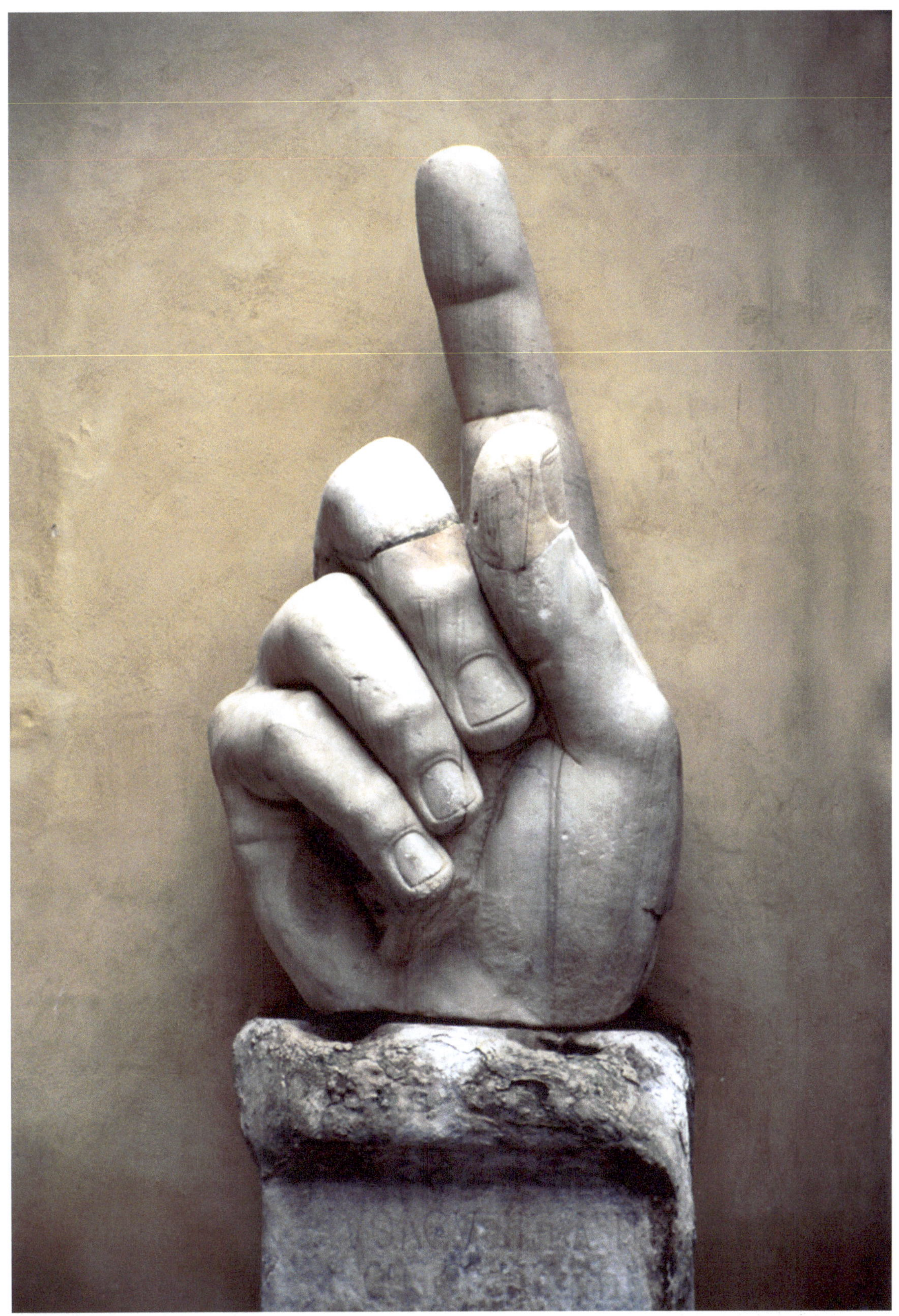

HOMESICK

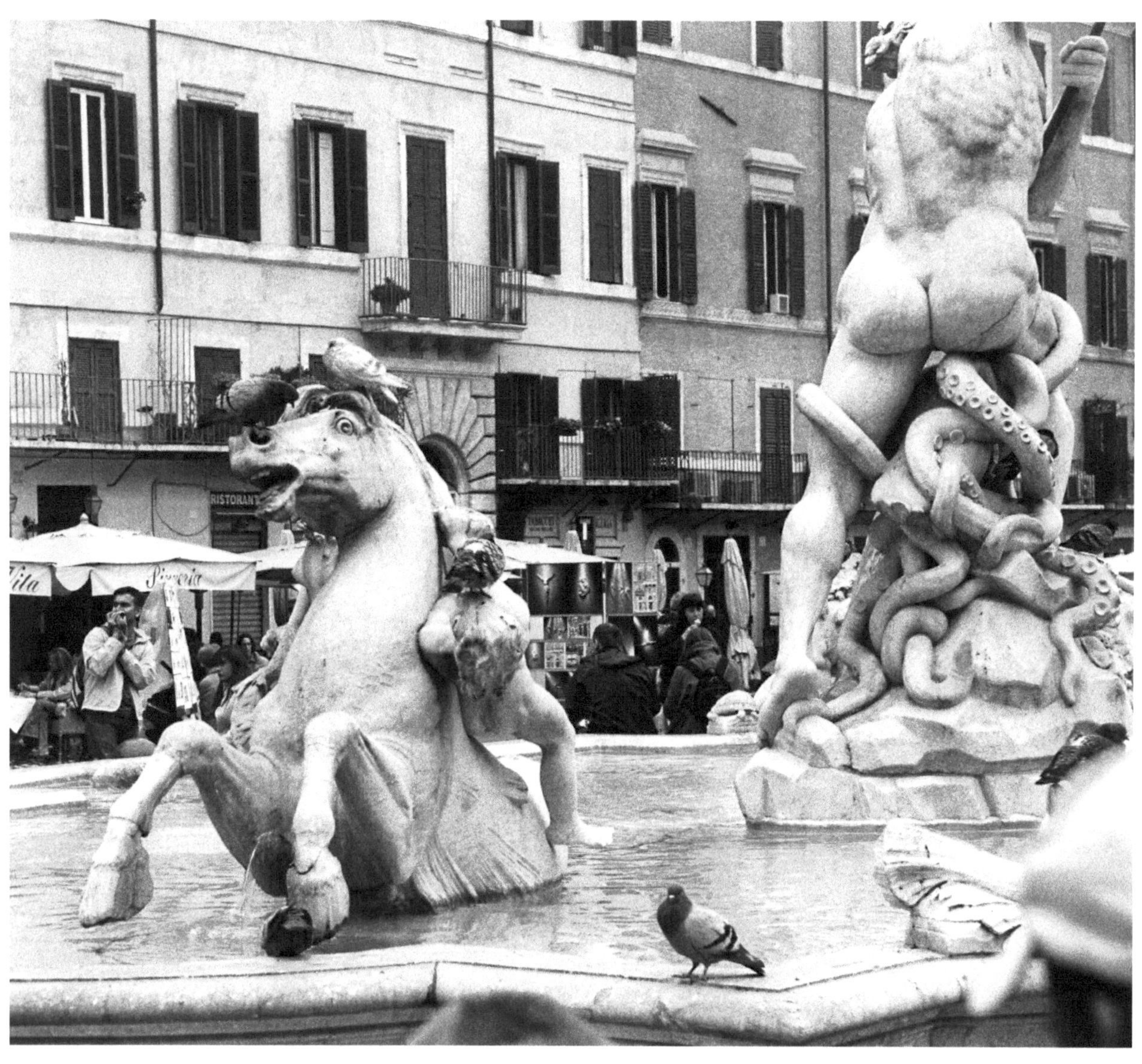

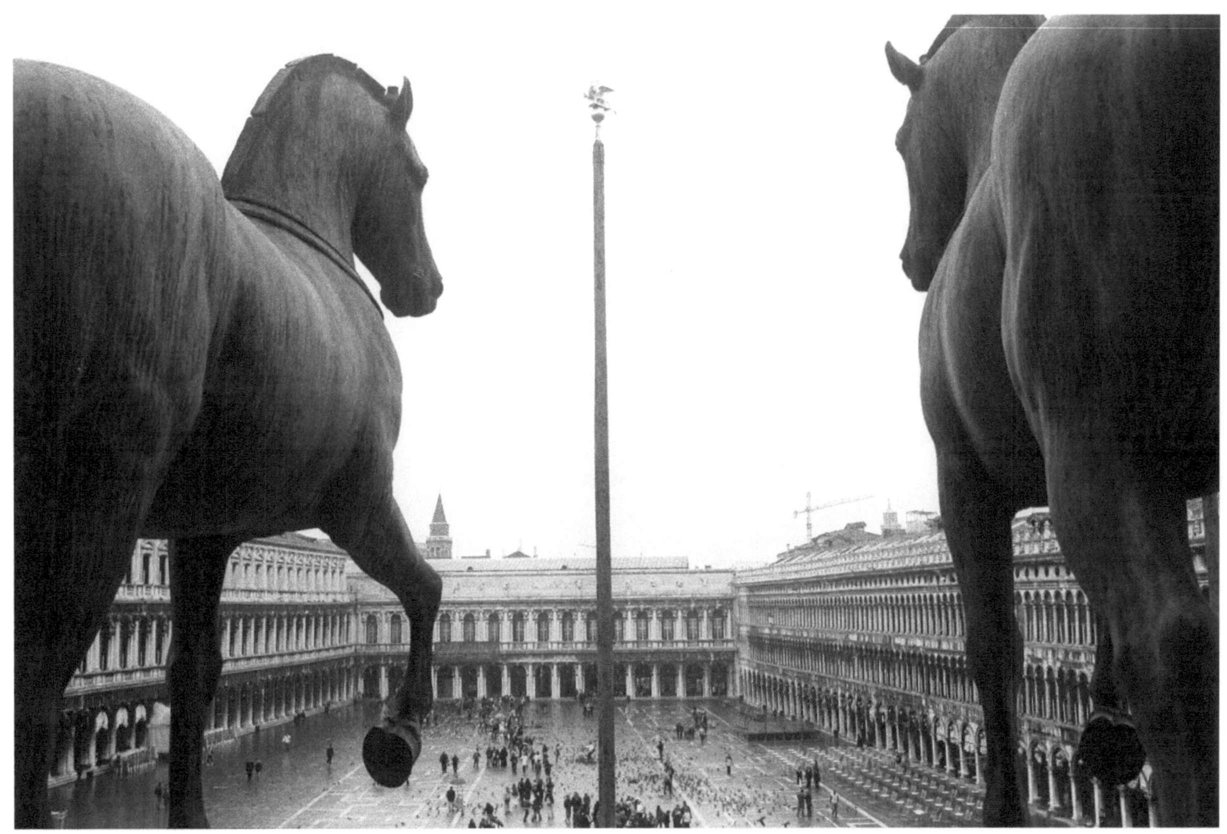

So we're at this outside café in the Piazza Navona, looking at an incredibly bizarre Bernini sculpture, and I'm thinking about when Beth and I were in Texas. What's up with that?

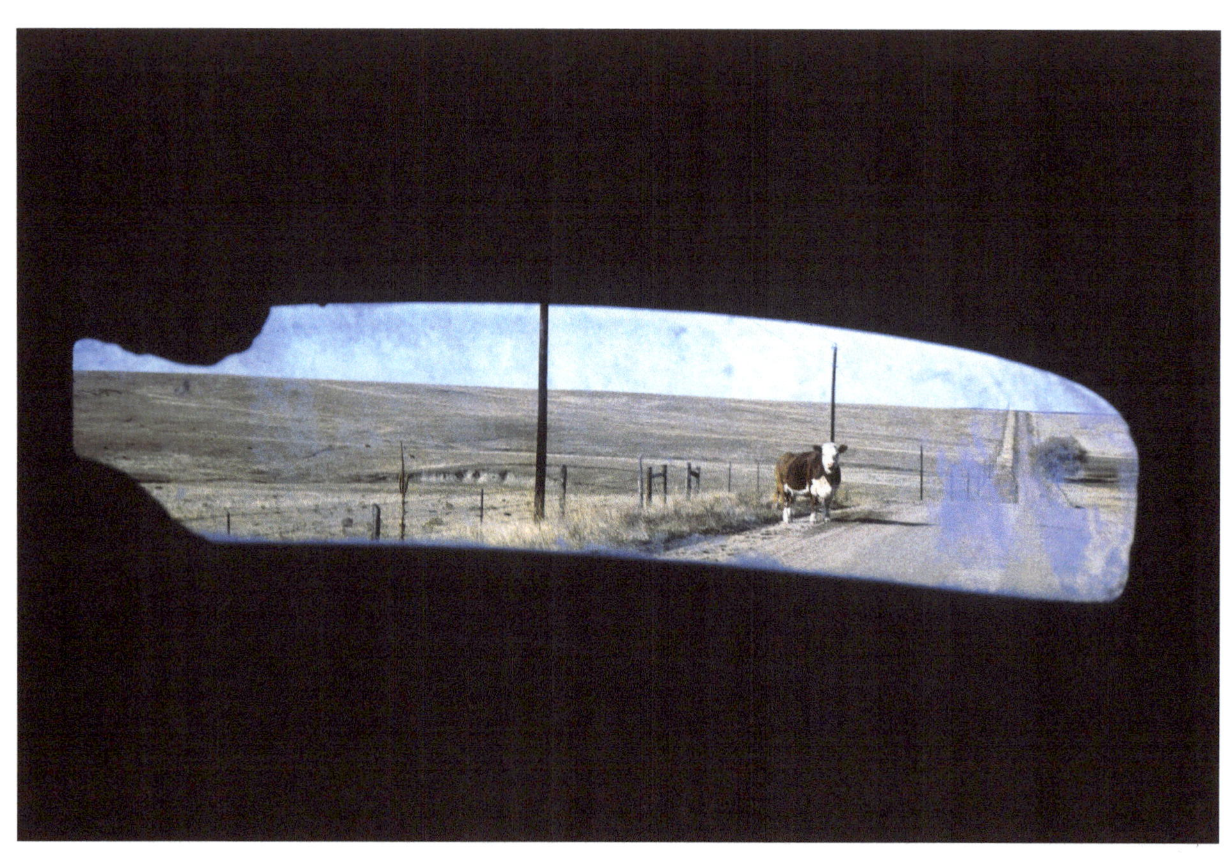

Some people are never satisfied.

—Beth McJunkin

LIST OF IMAGES

Most of the photographs depict an event that actually happened. They are listed here with a somewhat descriptive title, and the place the picture was taken. Some of the images are multiple exposures, identified below as composite. Those visual metaphors are one reason this is a work of fiction.

29. ***HACIENDA*** — Big Bend, Texas 2013
31. ***TARAHUMARA*** — Creel, Mexico 1990
32. ***CUSARARE FALLS*** — Mexico 1992
33. ***MUSHROOM ROCK*** — Mexico 1990
34. ***SITTING TARA*** — Mexico 1992
35. (top) THREE MEN — Batopilas, Mexico 1998
35. (bottom) ***#82*** — Copper Canyon 1990
36. ***COWBOYS & CACTUS*** — composite
37. ***GHOST HERD*** — composite
38. ***TRAIL RIDE*** — composite
39. ***TOY HORSE*** — composite
40. ***TEXAS SCENIC*** — composite
41. ***MARATHON RAIL*** — Texas 2014
42. ***SHEEP BLOCKAGE*** — Colorado
43. ***CLOUDS & SCHOONER*** — composite
44. ***OCTOPUS*** — Mexico
45. ***RICK*** — Palancar Reef, Mexico
46. ***INTERNATIONAL PIER*** — Cozumel, Mexico
47. ***SARDINE SWARM*** — Akumal, Mexico
48. ***GALAPAGOS TOPOGRAPHY*** — Ecuador
49. ***TORTOISE*** — Galapagos, Ecuador
51. ***HAMMERHEAD SHARKS*** — Galapagos
52. ***GALAPAGOS*** — composite — Ecuador
53. ***SEA LION*** — Galapagos, Ecuador
54. ***ARIZONA HIGHWAY*** — Arizona
55. ***RAINBOW*** — Colorado 2014
56. ***TRESTLE BRIDGE*** — central Texas
57. ***LULING CAR WASH***- Texas
58. ***BETH & JUNE*** — Cuzco, Peru
59. ***GROUP PORTRAIT*** — Big Bend, Texas
60. (top) ***TWO HEADS*** — Utah — 1979
60. (bottom) ***NEAR MOAB*** — Utah 1979
62. (top) ***FULL MOON OVER ARCHES***- Utah
62. (bottom) ***TRAVEL WARNING*** — Utah
63. (top) ***ARROWS*** — Colorado
63. (bottom) ***NAVAJO BRIDGE*** — Arizona
64. ***LAKE POWELL*** — Utah
65. ***MOKI CANYON*** — Lake Powell, Utah
66. ***COW CREEK CANYON*** — Lake Powell
67. (top) ***MARLEY & CHLOE***- Lake Powell
67. (bottom) ***CAPTAIN JUNE*** — Lake Powell
68. ***BRYCE CANYON*** — Utah
69. ***ANTELOPE CANYON*** — Utah
70. ***MACHU PICCHU*** — Peru
71. ***LLAMA & HUANA PICCHU*** — Peru

72. (top) ***PISAC*** — Peru
72. (bottom) ***GIRL & LAMB*** — Cuzco, Peru
73. ***PULLING THE CYCLE CART*** — Cuzco, Peru
74. ***LAJITAS BAR SCENE*** — Big Bend, Texas
75. ***ANTLER LAMP***- Lajitas, Texas
76. ***MOTEL EXIT*** — Longmont, Colorado
77. ***EMPTY TABLES*** — Lajitas, Texas
78. ***SPANISH STEPS*** — Rome, Italy
79. ***RED TULIPS*** — Netherlands
80. ***AMSTERDAM CANAL*** — Netherlands
81. ***CASTLE ON THE RHINE*** — Germany
82. ***PUENTE NUEVO*** — Ronda, Spain
83. ***BONES*** — Durnstein, Austria
84. ***BOAR HEAD DELI*** — Venice, Italy
85. ***THE CHAIN BRIDGE*** — Budapest, Hungary
86. ***CARROTS*** — Budapest, Hungary
87. ***TULIP FIELD*** — Bloembollenstreek, Netherlands
88. ***BEETHOVENS BOAT*** — Bratislava, Slovakia
89. ***BOAT LOCK*** — Main River
90. ***FLORENCE*** — Italy
91. ***BLUE DANUBE*** — Austria
92. ***TENDING TO JESUS*** — Italy
93. ***ST. GEORGE & THE DRAGON*** — Germany
94. ***IGORS CENTURIONE*** — Rome, Italy
95. ***CONSTANTINES FINGER*** — Rome, Italy
96. ***PIAZZA NAVONA*** — Rome, Italy
97. ***ST. MARKS SQUARE*** — Venice, Italy
98. ***COW IN THE ROAD*** — Texas
(back cover) ***ROAD TRIP*** — Arizona

www.ingramcontent.com/pod-product-compliance
Lightning Source LLC
LaVergne TN
LVHW070130110826
845147LV00002B/224
* 9 7 8 0 9 8 6 2 2 9 0 6 0 *